Mark Girolami

Self-Organising Neural Networks

Independent Component Analysis and Blind Source Separation

Springer

Mark Girolami, BSc (Hons), BA, MSc, PhD, CEng, MIMechE, MIEE
Department of Computing and Information Systems, University of Paisley,
High Street, Paisley, PA1 2BE, UK

Series Editor
J.G. Taylor, BA, BSc, MA, PhD, FlnstP
Centre for Neural Networks, Department of Mathematics, King's College,
Strand, London WC2R 2LS, UK

ISBN-13: 978-1-85233-066-8

British Library Cataloguing in Publication Data
Girolami, Mark
Self-organising neural networks : independent component analysis and blind source separation. – (Perspectives in neural computing)
1.Neural networks (Computer science) 2.Self-organizing systems
I.Title
006.3'2
ISBN-13: 978-1-85233-066-8

Library of Congress Cataloging-in-Publication Data
Girolami, Mark, 1963-
Self-organising neural networks : independent component analysis and Blind source separation / Mark Girolami.
p. cm. -- (Perspectives in neural computing)
ISBN-13: 978-1-85233-066-8 e-ISBN-13: 978-1-4471-0825-2
DOI: 10.1007/978-1-4471-0825-2
1. Neural networks (Computer science) I. Title. II. Series
QA76.87.S47 1999 99-29068
006.3'2--dc21 CIP

Typesetting: Camera ready by author

34/3830-543210 Printed on acid-free paper SPIN 10689791

Perspectives in Neural Computing

Springer
London
Berlin
Heidelberg
New York
Barcelona
Hong Kong
Milan
Paris
Santa Clara
Singapore
Tokyo

Also in this series:

Adrian Shepherd
Second -Order Methods for Neural Networks
3-540-76100-4

Dimitris C. Dracopoulos
Evolutionary Learning Algorithms for Neural Adaptive Control
3-540-76161-6

John A. Bullinaria, David W. Glasspool and George Houghton (Eds)
4th Neural Computation and Psychology Workshop, London,
9-11 April 1997: Connectionist Representations
3-540-76208-6

Maria Marinaro and Roberto Tagliaferri (Eds)
Neural Nets - WIRN VIETRI-97
3-540-76157-8

Gustavo Deco and Dragan Obradovic
An Information-Theoretic Approach to Neural Computing
0-387-94666-7

Thomas Lindblad and Jason M. Kinser
Image Processing using Pulse-Coupled Neural Networks
3-540-76264-7

L. Niklasson, M. Bodén and T. Ziemke (Eds)
ICANN 98
3-540-76263-9

Maria Marinaro and Roberto Tagliaferri (Eds)
Neural Nets - WIRN VIETRI-98
1-85233-051-1

Dietmar Heinke, Glyn W. Humphreys and Andrew Olson (Eds)
Connectionist Models in Cognitive Neuroscience
The 5th Neural Computation and Psychology Workshop, Birmingham,
8-10 September 1998
1-85233-052-X

Amanda J.C. Sharkey (Ed.)
Combining Artificial Neural Nets
1-85233-004-X

Dirk Husmeier
Neural Networks for Conditional Probability Estimation
1-85233-095-3

Achilleas Zapranis and Apostolos-Paul Refenes
Principles of Neural Model Identification, Selection and Adequacy
1-85233-139-9

Contents

Foreword

The conception of fresh ideas and the development of new techniques for Blind Source Separation and Independent Component Analysis have been rapid in recent years. It is also encouraging, from the perspective of the many scientists involved in this fascinating area of research, to witness the growing list of successful applications of these methods to a diverse range of practical everyday problems. This growth has been due, in part, to the number of promising young and enthusiastic researchers who have committed their efforts to expanding the current body of knowledge within this field of research. The author of this book is among one of their number.

I trust that the present book by Dr. Mark Girolami will provide a rapid and effective means of communicating some of these new ideas to a wide international audience and that in turn this will expand further the growth of knowledge.

In my opinion this book makes an important contribution to the theory of Independent Component Analysis and Blind Source Separation. This opens a range of exciting methods, techniques and algorithms for applied researchers and practitioner engineers, especially from the perspective of artificial neural networks and information theory. It has been interesting to see how rapidly the scientific literature in this area has grown. This present book comes at a good time, because it provides a well reasoned introduction to the basic ideas for those who are curious about the theoretical derivation of unsupervised learning algorithms for blind source separation. It also provides a self-contained analysis of algorithms with an emphasis on recent research results that include the well-balanced research works of the author.

Due to the many promising applications the subject of independent component analysis will continue to be a fruitful area of research.

Dr. Andrzej Cichocki
Head of Laboratory for Open Information Systems,
Brain Science Institute, Riken, Japan
and Warsaw University of Technology, Poland
E-mail: cia@brain.riken.go.jp
April 1999

1. Introduction

This book charts the process and reports on the product of a systematic program of enquiry that subsequently led to the award of a doctorate in computer science. The subsequent investigation into self-organising artificial neural networks and the problem of blind separation of sources is laid out in this volume. The algorithms developed and perspectives taken in the writing of this book, by the nature of the doctoral process, are unique and personal to the author.

1.1 Self-Organisation and Blind Signal Processing

The purpose of this book is to investigate the emergent properties of certain self-organising neural network models. The pioneering work of Oja (1982) demonstrated that a self-organising neuron based on constrained linear Hebbian learning was capable of extracting the maximal amount of information, in a least squares sense, from the observed data. The weights connected to the neuron would then converge to the eigenvector associated with the largest eigenvalue of the observed data covariance matrix. Subsequent algorithms for self-organisation were able to perform complete eigenvalue decomposition on the data presented to the network of neurons, e.g. (Sanger, 1989). The form of constrained Hebbian learning utilised within these networks allowed the neuron weights to seek and converge to the principal directions of the data.

A large body of literature is now available on the properties of forms of self-organising networks which perform a Principal Component Analysis (PCA) on the data observations. The least squares nature of the PCA transformation indicates that the variance of the data from each neuron within the network is maximised in directions which are orthogonal to each other. For normally distributed data the maximisation of the transformed data variance indicates that the entropy or average information content of the data is maximised. If, on the other hand, the observed data is generated by a naturally occurring signal source such as speech or music as would be the case for auditory input, the data will be distinctly non-Gaussian. In the case of visual input such as natural images the observed data, a range of pixel values, will also be non-Gaussian. PCA networks will only focus on the Gaussian statistics of the data and ignore the higher order structure of the data. Non-linear self-organising networks have been shown to respond to higher order structure within non-Gaussian data. This book examines the emergent properties of various non-linear self-organising neural networks within the context of a parallel area of research from the statistical signal processing community, Blind Signal Processing.

The fact that humans can segment mixtures of sound and focus on one in particular has given rise to a phenomenon popularly known as the 'Cocktail Party Problem'. Sensorimotor signals from the brain are transmitted via nerves that are also simultaneously used for other forms of signal transmissions, yet the intrinsic information of each signal is neither lost nor degraded. The ability of the Olfactory bulb, an organ common to many mammals, to discriminate between individual scents and odours is yet another example of blind signal processing (Herrault and Jutten, 1986). On receiving data or signals that are degraded by mixing, whose form is unknown, with other unknown signals the mammalian neural processing is somehow able to extract the original signals and make sense of the observed cacophony. The aim of blind signal processing is to design structures that can separate mixtures of signals in a blind manner or identify unknown mixing channels with only the observed mixed data. Classical statistical signal processing and adaptive filter theory has been applied to this problem with varying degrees of success.

Self-organising neural networks naturally lend themselves to the problem of blind signal processing in that there is no teacher or no desired response for the observed data. The network responds to the information contained in the statistics of the observed data, which is all that is available in blind signal processing. Within this book there is no claim to develop neural models which can be regarded as biologically plausible. However, locality of update and simplicity of learning are among the main motivations throughout the following chapters.

The particular problem of blind signal processing which is under investigation is Blind Source Separation (BSS), the ability to separate unknown sources from a received mixture whose method of mixing is unknown. BSS in the broadest sense includes separation of mixtures which may be linear, non-linear, memoryless or convolved (with memory). A linear data transformation termed Independent Component Analysis (ICA) can be considered as performing linear memoryless BSS (Jutten & Herrault, 1991). The study of this transformation will form a significant part of the book.

1.2 Outline of Book Chapters

The study of blind signal processing, by its very nature, relies heavily on information theory and advanced statistics. Chapter 2 introduces elements of information theory and statistics, required for the analysis introduced in subsequent chapters. Chapter 3 presents the early batch and adaptive algorithms developed for BSS. Self-organising neural networks are introduced in Chapter 4. Both linear and non-linear models based on Hebbian and anti-Hebbian learning are introduced. The focus of the chapter is on network models, which lend themselves directly to the BSS problem. Chapter 5 introduces the non-linear PCA algorithm and it is studied in the light of the ICA transformation. A direct link with non-linear PCA learning and ICA is made and compound activation functions are presented which provide a more general ICA. Variants of the Exploratory Projection Pursuit (EPP) network, originally proposed by Fyfe and Baddeley (1995), are applied to the BSS problem in Chapter 6.

Chapter 7 considers information theoretic indices for exploratory projection pursuit. The duality of EPP and ICA based on negentropy maximisation is presented. A negentropy maximisation algorithm is developed and it is shown that this algorithm is capable of performing ICA on mixtures of either sub- or super-Gaussian sources. This is shown to be a generalised extension of the 'infomax' algorithm originally proposed by Bell and Sejnowski (1995).

Chapter 8 considers the cocktail party problem where natural speech is transmitted via acoustic transfer functions to receivers such as microphones. A form of temporal anti-Hebbian learning is proposed and extended to the Maximum Likelihood Estimation (MLE) framework. This model of self-organisation is applied to the 'Cocktail Party Problem' and is compared with earlier reported work on BSS applied to convolutive mixtures. Chapter 9 considers a number of applications and outlines possible areas of further research and application.

2. *Background to Blind Source Separation*

This chapter presents the fundamental concepts relating to Blind Source Separation in general and the linear transformation Independent Component Analysis specifically.

2.1 Problem Formulation

Assume that at time t, an observation of an N dimensional data vector $\mathbf{x}(t) \in \Re^N$ is made, i.e.

$$\mathbf{x}(t) = [x_1(t) \dots x_N(t)]^T. \qquad (2.1)$$

We define the statistical model which generates the vector observation $\mathbf{x}(t)$ as

$$\mathbf{x}(t) = \mathbf{A}\mathbf{s}(t) + \mathbf{n}(t). \qquad (2.2)$$

In the strictly linear and real case, the matrix $\mathbf{A} \in \Re^{N \times N}$ is termed the mixing matrix. The underlying and unobservable data vector or source vector $\mathbf{s}(t) \in \Re^N$

$$\mathbf{s}(t) = [s_1(t) \dots s_N(t)]^T$$

will be considered here as having zero mean and finite covariance, that is

$$E\{\mathbf{s}(t)\} = \mathbf{0} \text{ and } E\{\mathbf{s}(t)\mathbf{s}^T(t)\} \neq [\mathbf{0}],$$

where $\mathbf{0}$ denotes the $N \times 1$ zero vector and $[\mathbf{0}]$ denotes the $N \times N$ zero matrix. The noise term within the model (2.2) is not restricted to any specific distribution and the additive vector $\mathbf{n}(t)$ is non-deterministic. The aim of source separation is to recover the unobserved sources $\mathbf{s}(t)$ from the observations $\mathbf{x}(t)$ when there is no knowledge of the mixing term **A**. This book will consider the case where the dimensionality of both the observed and source vectors are equal and as such, the mixing matrix in the linear case will be square and full rank. Chapter 8, will consider the specific situation where the matrix $\mathbf{A} \in \Re^{N \times NL}$ is a polynomial matrix representing impulse responses of finite length filters (Lambert, 1996). The transformation presented in (2.2) is not strictly deterministic and as such cannot be fully considered here.

We will investigate the strictly deterministic transformation in this book:

$$\mathbf{x}(t) = \mathbf{A}\mathbf{s}(t) \tag{2.3}$$

The fundamental assumption made on the source vector is that it has individual components that are mutually independent and have, at most, one Gaussian distribution. This is the basis of all research into Blind Signal Separation (BSS) and Independent Component Analysis (ICA). Denote the multivariate non-Gaussian probability density function (pdf) of the vector $\mathbf{s}(t)$ by $p_{\mathbf{s}}(\mathbf{s})$, where the bold subscript indicates distribution over the vector **s**. Then, irrespective of the natural form of distribution the marginal densities possess, the assumption of mutual independence implies that the multivariate density can be written as the product of the individual marginal densities

$$p_{\mathbf{s}}(\mathbf{s}) = \prod_{i=1}^{N} p_i(s_i) \tag{2.4}$$

Intuitively, it appears that after the transformation (2.3) the observation vector will no longer obey the pdf factorisation equality and so

$$p_{\mathbf{x}}(\mathbf{x}) \neq \prod_{i=1}^{N} p_i(x_i) \tag{2.5}$$

The following sections explore this by considering the differential Shannon entropy of the multivariate distributions (Cover and Thomas, 1991) to give a measure of the mixing effect of the matrix transform. The first step is to introduce the concepts of entropy and information.2.2 Entropy and Information

The concept of entropy as a measure of uncertainty or degree of disorder of a random variable has been used in physical sciences such as statistical thermodynamics. Within the context of BSS we consider entropy from an information theoretic perspective, that is, as a measure of the information content of a variable (Shannon, 1948).

2.2 Entropy and Information

2.2.1 Entropy

Consider a probability density function $p(x)$of a single random variable x. We can approximate the pdf of the variable by a discrete histogram where the range of the variable x is broken up into a set of discrete bins. We will recover $p(x)$ when we take the limit as the size of these bins tends to zero. If N objects distributed within the series of bins constitute the histogram and the ith bin has N_i objects then the number of ways the objects can be arranged is called the multiplicity of the histogram.

$$M = \frac{N!}{\prod_i N_i!} \tag{2.6}$$

The entropy is then defined as a constant term multiplied by the negative logarithm of the multiplicity.

$$H = -\frac{1}{N}\log(M) \tag{2.7}$$

Using the definition of M from (2.6) this gives

$$H = \frac{1}{N}\left(\sum_i \log(N_i!) - \log(N!)\right) \tag{2.8}$$

Noting that Stirling's approximation gives $\log(N!) \cong N\log(N) - N$ we see that in the limit as N tends to infinity the entropy can be written as

$$H = -\sum_i p_i \log(p_i) \tag{2.9}$$

where $p_i = N_i/N \quad : N \rightarrow \infty$ is a representation of the probability associated with the ith bin. If the probability of a particular event happening is very small (that is the event is very rare) then N_i will be small. The measure of entropy (2.9) for a rare event will be large and so a large amount of information has been conveyed due to this event. The occurrence of a rare event conveys more information regarding the state of a system than the occurrence of an event which is highly probable. We now take the limit where the size of each bin tends to zero. Denoting the width of each bin as Δ, and the number of bins as N_B, the amount of probability mass in each bin will be $p_i = N_i / N = p(x_i)\Delta$ and the entropy can then be written as

$$H = -\lim_{N_B \rightarrow \infty} \sum_{i=1}^{N_B} p(x_i)\Delta \log(p(x_i)\Delta) \tag{2.10}$$

Noting for a continuous pdf that $\int p(x)\,dx = 1$ then the entropy is

$$H = -\int p(x)\log(p(x))\,dx + \lim_{N_BS \rightarrow \infty} \log(\Delta) \tag{2.11}$$

The rightmost term in (2.11) will diverge in the limit, however if we take the difference of two entropies then this term will cancel out. Because of this differential cancellation and noting that $\lim(N_B \rightarrow \infty)\log(\Delta)$is independent of the pdf, then this term can be discarded.

$$H(x) = -\int p(x)\log(p(x))\,dx \tag{2.12}$$

The form of (2.12) is termed the differential entropy of a continuous distribution and, taken as an information measure on its own, it may not necessarily be bounded. The notation $H(x)$ is now introduced to denote the measure of entropy of the variable x.

Recall that for a general function of the variable x the expected value of the function is given as

$$E\{f(x)\} = \int f(x)p(x)\,dx \tag{2.13}$$

The identity function would give

$$E\{x\} = \int x\, p(x)\, dx \tag{2.14}$$

This is simply the mean value or first moment of the random variable distributed as $p(x)$. Similarly

$$E\{x^2\} = \int x^2\, p(x)\, dx \tag{2.15}$$

is the variance of the distribution or the expected value of the second moment. Higher order moments of a distribution are computed using (2.13) when $f(x) = x^n, n = 3, 4, \ldots,$. These have particular significance for Blind Source Separation and will be considered in detail further on in this chapter.

Consider a zero mean variable which is normally distributed according to

$$p(x) = \frac{1}{\sigma\sqrt{2\pi}}\, e^{\frac{-x^2}{2\sigma^2}} \tag{2.16}$$

where the variance is denoted as $\sigma^2 = E\{x^2\}$.

We now calculate the entropy associated with a normally distributed variable. Substituting (2.16) into (2.12) gives the following expression

$$H = -\int p(x)\left(\frac{-x^2}{2\sigma^2} - \frac{1}{2}\log\left(2\pi\sigma^2\right)\right) dx = \frac{1}{2}\log\left(2\pi e\sigma^2\right) \tag{2.17}$$

From (2.17) it appears that the entropy of a normally distributed variable increases in proportion to the logarithm of the variance of the distribution. If the variance of the distribution is low, then the majority of values will be generated from a small region of probability space. A high variance distribution would suggest that values of the variable were drawn from a wider distribution and so would convey more information than a low variance distribution.

From (2.12) it follows that the entropy of a vector $\mathbf{x}(t) = [x_1(t) \; \ldots \; x_N(t)]^T$ distributed as $p_\mathbf{x}(\mathbf{x})$ will be given by

$$H(\mathbf{x}) = -\int p_\mathbf{x}(\mathbf{x})\log(p_\mathbf{x}(\mathbf{x}))\, d\mathbf{x}. \tag{2.18}$$

We now consider some of the properties of entropy, which will be referred to and utilised within this book. For clarity we shall consider the simple case of two variables and then generalise to the case of an *N* dimensional vector.

2.2.2 Kullback-Leibler Entropy and Mutual Information

Within a statistical context, it is often important to define a measure of the efficiency of the estimation of a true probability $p(x)$ where the estimate is given by $q(x)$. The Kullback-Leibler entropy (sometimes referred to as the Kullback-Leibler divergence), also termed the relative or cross entropy, is a measure of the distortion between the two distributions.

$$D(p\|q) = \int p(x)\log\frac{p(x)}{q(x)}\, dx \tag{2.19}$$

as $\int p(x)\log p(x) dx \geq \int p(x)\log q(x) dx$ (Cover and Thomas, 1991)

then $D(p\|q) \geq 0$ with equality existing when $q(x) = p(x)$. Note also that $D(p\|q) \neq D(q\|p)$ and therefore the Kullback-Leibler entropy is not a symmetric measure between distributions.

The multivariate equivalent of this divergence measure is simply

$$D(p\|q) = \int p_\mathbf{x}(\mathbf{x})\log\frac{p_\mathbf{x}(\mathbf{x})}{q_\mathbf{x}(\mathbf{x})}\, d\mathbf{x}. \tag{2.20}$$

The mutual information between variables gives a measure of their statistical independence and is of fundamental importance to the study of blind source separation and independent component analysis. For two variables the mutual information is defined as the Kullback-Leibler divergence between the joint probability density of the variables and the factorised marginals.

$$I(x;y) = D\left(p(x,y) \| p(x)p(y)\right)$$
$$= \int p(x,y)\log\frac{p(x,y)}{p(x)p(y)}\,dx\,dy \tag{2.21}$$

Mutual information is a measure of the amount of information that each variable conveys about the other. This can be considered as a measure of the statistical correlation between the variables. With the probability equality, where $p(x|y)$ denotes the probability of x conditioned on y (Ripley, 1996)

$$p(x,y) = p(x|y)p(y) \tag{2.22}$$

and then using (2.21) we find that

$$\int p(x,y)\log\frac{p(x,y)}{p(x)p(y)}\,dx\,dy = \int p(x,y)\log\frac{p(x|y)}{p(x)}\,dx\,dy$$

$$= -\int p(x,y)\log(p(x))\,dx\,dy + \int p(x,y)\log(p(x|y))\,dx\,dy$$

$$\Rightarrow I(x;y) = H(x) - H(x|y) \tag{2.23}$$

Employing the joint and conditional distribution equality (2.22) the conditional entropy can be written as (Cover and Thomas, 1991)

$$H(x|y) = H(x,y) - H(y) \tag{2.24}$$

where $H(x, y)$ denotes the joint entropy of the variables. This gives the more general definition for the mutual information between two random variables as

$$I(x;y) = H(x) + H(y) - H(x,y) \tag{2.25}$$

It is a straightforward matter (Cover and Thomas, 1991) to extend this measure of mutual information to the multivariate case and consider the mutual information of a vector **x**.

$$I(\mathbf{x}) = D\left(p_{\mathbf{x}}(\mathbf{x}) \middle\| \prod_{i=1}^{N} p_i(x_i) \right)$$

$$= \int p_{\mathbf{x}}(\mathbf{x}) \log \frac{p_{\mathbf{x}}(\mathbf{x})}{\prod_{i=1}^{N} p_i(x_i)} d\mathbf{x}$$

This is equivalent to the following,

$$= -\int p_{\mathbf{x}}(\mathbf{x}) \log \prod_{i=1}^{N} p_i(x_i) + \int p_{\mathbf{x}}(\mathbf{x}) \log p_{\mathbf{x}}(\mathbf{x}) d\mathbf{x}$$

$$\Rightarrow I(\mathbf{x}) = \sum_{i=1}^{N} H_i(x_i) - H_{\mathbf{x}}(\mathbf{x}) \tag{2.26}$$

Note that from the definition of Kullback-Leibler entropy $D(p\|q) \geq 0$ and so $I(\mathbf{x}) \geq 0$ (Cover and Thomas, 1991). Re-arranging (2.26) we find that the entropy of a vector distributed with multivariate pdf is equal to the sum of the marginal entropies minus the mutual information between the marginal components.

$$H(\mathbf{x}) = \sum_{i=1}^{N} H(x_i) - I(\mathbf{x}) \tag{2.27}$$

From (2.27) and noting that $I(\mathbf{x}) \geq 0$ we see that the inequality (2.28) holds

$$H(\mathbf{x}) \leq \sum_{i=1}^{N} H(x_i) \tag{2.28}$$

with equality existing if and only if the mutual information equals zero, $I(\mathbf{x}) = 0$, i.e. when the multivariate density is fully factorable $p_{\mathbf{x}}(\mathbf{x}) = \prod_{i=1}^{N} p_i(x_i)$.

$$I(\mathbf{x}) = \int p_{\mathbf{x}}(\mathbf{x}) \log \frac{p_{\mathbf{x}}(\mathbf{x})}{\prod_{i=1}^{N} p_i(x_i)} d\mathbf{x} = \int p_{\mathbf{x}}(\mathbf{x}) \log(1) d\mathbf{x} = 0$$

This following inequality for the mutual information is of particular significance to blind source separation

$$I(\mathbf{x}) \geq 0 \tag{2.29}$$

An important inequality we shall require is that among all distributions with the same mean and covariance matrix a multivariate Gaussian distribution has maximal entropy. Consider again the *N* dimensional zero mean vector **x**, which has a Gaussian multivariate distribution with covariance matrix $\mathbf{C} = E\{\mathbf{x}\mathbf{x}^T\}$,

$$p_{G\mathbf{x}}(\mathbf{x}) = \frac{1}{(2\pi)^{\frac{N}{2}} (\det(\mathbf{C}))} e^{-\frac{\mathbf{x}^T \mathbf{C}^{-1} \mathbf{x}}{2}} \tag{2.30}$$

where det (..) is the determinant of the associated matrix term and $p_{G\mathbf{x}}(\mathbf{x})$ denotes the multivariate Gaussian distribution of the vector **x**. It can be shown (Cover and Thomas, 1991) that the entropy associated with the multivariate Gaussian distribution is

$$H_G(\mathbf{x}) = \frac{1}{2} \log\left((2\pi e)^N \det(\mathbf{C})\right) \tag{2.31}$$

By considering an arbitrary non-Gaussian pdf with identical mean and covariance as the Gaussian distribution, $p_{G\mathbf{x}}(\mathbf{x})$, using (2.20) we can see that

$$0 \leq D\left(p \| p_G\right) = \int p_{\mathbf{x}}(\mathbf{x}) \log \frac{p_{\mathbf{x}}(\mathbf{x})}{p_{G\mathbf{x}}(\mathbf{x})} d\mathbf{x} \tag{2.32}$$

Since both distributions have the same covariance and $\log\left(p_{G\mathbf{x}}(\mathbf{x})\right)$ is a polynomial of order two then from (Comon, 1994)

$$\int p_{\mathbf{x}}(\mathbf{x}) \log\left(p_{G\mathbf{x}}(\mathbf{x})\right) d\mathbf{x} = \int p_{G\mathbf{x}}(\mathbf{x}) \log\left(p_{G\mathbf{x}}(\mathbf{x})\right) d\mathbf{x} \tag{2.33}$$

Utilising (2.33) in (2.32) and using the entropy of a multivariate Gaussian (2.31) we then have that

$$0 \leq D\left(p \| p_G\right) = -H(\mathbf{x}) + \frac{1}{2}\log\left((2\pi e)^N \det(\mathbf{C})\right) \tag{2.34}$$

This inequality shows that the normal distribution maximises the entropy over all distributions with the same covariance matrix. The term given to (2.32) is negentropy and it has been shown that it is always greater than zero and vanishes if and only if $p_{\mathbf{x}}(\mathbf{x})$ is Gaussian. By denoting negentropy as $J(\mathbf{x})$ we can write the mutual information (2.26) of a distribution in terms of negentropy. From (2.31) and (2.34) the multivariate negentropy is given as

$$J(\mathbf{x}) = H_G(\mathbf{x}) - H(\mathbf{x}) \tag{2.35}$$

Now, using (2.26) and denoting the marginal negentropy as $J_i(x_i)$

$$J(\mathbf{x}) - \sum_{i=1}^{N} J_i(x_i) = H_{\mathbf{G}}(\mathbf{x}) - H(\mathbf{x}) - \sum_{i=1}^{N} H_{Gi}(x_i) + \sum_{i=1}^{N} H_i(x_i)$$

$$\Rightarrow J(\mathbf{x}) - \sum_{i=1}^{N} J_i(x_i) = I(\mathbf{x}) + H_{\mathbf{G}}(\mathbf{x}) - \sum_{i=1}^{N} H_{Gi}(x_i)$$

The univariate and multivariate forms of Gaussian entropy (2.17) and (2.31) are used here

$$\Rightarrow J(\mathbf{x}) - \sum_{i=1}^{N} J_i(x_i)$$

$$= I(\mathbf{x}) + \frac{1}{2}\log\left((2\pi e)^N \det(\mathbf{C})\right) - \sum_{i=1}^{N} \frac{1}{2}\log\left(2\pi e\sigma^2\right)$$

$$\Rightarrow I(\mathbf{x}) = J(\mathbf{x}) - \sum_{i=1}^{N} J_i(x_i) + \frac{1}{2}\log\frac{\prod_{i=1}^{N} 2\pi e\sigma^2}{(2\pi e)^N \det(\mathbf{C})}$$

$$\Rightarrow I(\mathbf{x}) = J(\mathbf{x}) - \sum_{i=1}^{N} J_i(x_i) + \frac{1}{2}\log\frac{\prod_{i=1}^{N} \mathbf{C}_{ii}}{\det(\mathbf{C})} \qquad (2.36)$$

The mutual information in the form of (2.36) shows that the redundancy of information within the multivariate pdf is attributed, in part, to the second order information within the pdf which is embodied in the covariance matrix terms. The additional terms within (2.36) take account of non-Gaussian information terms.

2.2.3 Invertible Probability Density Transformations

For an invertible non-linear transformation of vector-valued random variables $\mathbf{y} = f(\mathbf{u}) = f(\mathbf{M}\mathbf{x})$ where $\mathbf{M}$ is a square non-singular matrix and f is an invertible function acting component-wise on $\mathbf{u}$, both variables are distributed as $p_{\mathbf{x}}(\mathbf{x})$ and $p_{\mathbf{y}}(\mathbf{y})$, then (Papoulis, 1984)

$$p_{\mathbf{y}}(\mathbf{y}) = \frac{p_{\mathbf{x}}(\mathbf{x})}{|J_f|} \qquad (2.37)$$

The term $|J_f|$ is the absolute value of the determinant of the Jacobian of the transformation and is given as

$$J_f = \det\begin{bmatrix} \frac{\partial \mathbf{y}_1}{\partial \mathbf{x}_1} & \cdots & \frac{\partial \mathbf{y}_1}{\partial \mathbf{x}_N} \\ \vdots & \ddots \frac{\partial \mathbf{y}_i}{\partial \mathbf{x}_j} \ddots & \vdots \\ \frac{\partial \mathbf{y}_N}{\partial \mathbf{x}_1} & \cdots & \frac{\partial \mathbf{y}_N}{\partial \mathbf{x}_N} \end{bmatrix} \tag{2.38}$$

$$J_f = \det\begin{bmatrix} \frac{\partial \mathbf{y}_1}{\partial \mathbf{u}_1}\frac{\partial \mathbf{u}_1}{\partial \mathbf{x}_1} & \cdots & \frac{\partial \mathbf{y}_1}{\partial \mathbf{u}_1}\frac{\partial \mathbf{u}_1}{\partial \mathbf{x}_N} \\ \vdots & \ddots \frac{\partial \mathbf{y}_i}{\partial \mathbf{u}_i}\frac{\partial \mathbf{u}_i}{\partial \mathbf{x}_j} \ddots & \vdots \\ \frac{\partial \mathbf{y}_N}{\partial \mathbf{u}_N}\frac{\partial \mathbf{u}_N}{\partial \mathbf{x}_1} & \cdots & \frac{\partial \mathbf{y}_N}{\partial \mathbf{u}_N}\frac{\partial \mathbf{u}_N}{\partial \mathbf{x}_N} \end{bmatrix}$$

$$= \det(\mathbf{M})\det\begin{bmatrix} \frac{\partial \mathbf{y}_1}{\partial \mathbf{u}_1} & \cdots 0 & 0 \\ \vdots & & \\ 0 & \frac{\partial \mathbf{y}_i}{\partial \mathbf{u}_i} & 0 \\ & & \vdots \\ 0 & 0 \cdots & \frac{\partial \mathbf{y}_N}{\partial \mathbf{u}_N} \end{bmatrix}$$

$$\Rightarrow J_f = (\det(\mathbf{M}))\prod_{i=1}^{N}\frac{dy}{du_i} \tag{2.39}$$

In the strictly linear case where $f(\ldots)$ is the identity, (2.39) indicates that the Jacobian of the transformation is simply the determinant of the linear transformation matrix. For a strictly linear transformation then (2.37) can be written as

$$p_{\mathbf{y}}(\mathbf{y}) = \frac{p_{\mathbf{x}}(\mathbf{x})}{|\det(\mathbf{M})|} \tag{2.40}$$

The differential entropy of the input and output variables is given as (2.18) so taking logarithms and integrating both sides of (2.40) in density gives

$$\int p_{\mathbf{y}}(\mathbf{y})\log\left(p_{\mathbf{y}}(\mathbf{y})\right)d\mathbf{y} = \int p_{\mathbf{x}}(\mathbf{x})\log\left(\frac{p_{\mathbf{x}}(\mathbf{x})}{|\det(\mathbf{M})|}\right)d\mathbf{x}$$

$$\Rightarrow -H(\mathbf{y}) = -H(\mathbf{x}) - \log\left(|\det(\mathbf{M})|\right)$$

$$\Rightarrow H(\mathbf{y}) = H(\mathbf{x}) + \log\left(|\det(\mathbf{M})|\right) \tag{2.41}$$

The above expression indicates the effect a linear transformation has on the entropy value of a multivariate distribution. An important form of transformation to be considered is the rotation. A rotation matrix satisfies the conditions of orthonormality

$$\mathbf{M}^T\mathbf{M} = \mathbf{I} \tag{2.42}$$

Noting that the inverse of a matrix is given as $\mathbf{M}^{-1} = \left(\mathbf{M}_{jk}\right)^T / \det(\mathbf{M})$ where $\left(\mathbf{M}_{jk}\right)$ is the matrix of cofactors, then from (2.42)

$$\mathbf{M}^T\mathbf{M} = \mathbf{I} \Rightarrow \mathbf{M}^{-1} = \mathbf{M}^T \Leftrightarrow \det(\mathbf{M}) = 1.$$

By transforming the variable vector $\mathbf{x}$ to $\mathbf{y}$ using a rotation, we see that $H(\mathbf{y}) = H(\mathbf{x}) + \log(1) = H(\mathbf{x})$ and so differential entropy is invariant under an orthogonal change of co-ordinates. It is a straightforward matter to see that this invariance will also hold for negentropy (2.32), (2.35). Within this section the concepts of entropy and information have been considered. These concepts are of the utmost importance in the study of blind source separation and independent component analysis. They underpin all algorithms and methods which will be considered within this book. The important definition of a contrast function as defined by Comon (1994) is now set forth. As with the fundamentals of information theory the concept of contrast functions will occur frequently during the exposition of this book.

The fundamental problem of identifying the underlying source vector when only a deterministically transformed observation is available was discussed in Section 2.1. We can now see that the unknown transformation (2.3) has caused an increase in the mutual information of the observed data vector such that

$$H_{\mathbf{x}}(\mathbf{x}) = \sum_{i=1}^{N} H_i(x_i) - I(\mathbf{x})$$

and

$$H(\mathbf{x}) = H(\mathbf{s}) + \log(|\det(\mathbf{A})|).$$

From (2.29) the vector **x** will have mutually independent components if and only if $I(\mathbf{x}) = 0$ i.e.

$$I(\mathbf{x}) = \int p_{\mathbf{x}}(\mathbf{x}) \log \frac{p_{\mathbf{x}}(\mathbf{x})}{\prod_{i=1}^{N} p_i(x_i)} d\mathbf{x} = 0$$

$$\Leftrightarrow \; p_{\mathbf{x}}(\mathbf{x}) = \prod_{i=1}^{N} p_i(x_i)$$

2.3 A Contrast Function for ICA

At first glance it would appear that a measure of the mutual information would indicate whether **x** has independent components but we first have to consider the definition of a contrast function, (Comon, 1994), (Cardoso, 1996). Contrast functions are employed extensively within the field of statistical inference (Ripley, 1996). Effectively we seek a mapping ψ from the set of probability densities

$$\left\{ p_{\mathbf{x}}\left(\mathbf{x}, \hat{\theta}\right), \mathbf{x} \in \Re^N, \hat{\theta} \in \Theta \right\}$$

that are modelled by the parameter variables $\hat{\theta} \in \Theta$, to the set of real numbers $\Re$ such that the function ψ is minimised for the best values of the parameters θ. The concept of maximum likelihood estimation (Ripley, 1996) can be considered as the minimisation of a contrast function in that, at each parameter update, then

$$\hat{\theta}_1 \neq \hat{\theta}_2 \Rightarrow \psi\left(\hat{\theta}_2\right) < \psi\left(\hat{\theta}_1\right).$$

The minimum value of contrast being reached when the parameter estimate takes the true value $\hat{\theta}_i = \theta \Rightarrow \psi(\theta) < \psi\left(\hat{\theta}_i\right) \forall i$. When the concept of contrasts is applied to source separation. Comon (1994) sets forth three requirements for a valid contrast.

These are

$$\psi(p_{\mathbf{Px}}) = \psi(p_{\mathbf{x}}) \; \forall \mathbf{P} \quad \text{Where } \mathbf{P} \text{ is Permutation Matrix} \tag{2.43}$$

$$\psi(p_{\Lambda\mathbf{x}}) = \psi(p_{\mathbf{x}}) \; \forall \Lambda \quad \Lambda \text{ is a Invertible Diagonal Matrix} \tag{2.44}$$

$$\psi(p_{\mathbf{Ax}}) \geq \psi(p_{\mathbf{x}}) \; \forall \mathbf{A} \quad \mathbf{A} \text{ is any Invertible Matrix} \tag{2.45}$$

The equality (2.43) indicates that the contrast is invariant if the components of **x** are permuted. The equality (2.44) states that the contrast is required to be invariant by a change in the scaling of the individual components of **x**. Finally, (2.45) states that the contrast must take its minimal value when the components of **x** are mutually independent. The notion of an absolute contrast function is proposed by Cardoso (1996). If it holds that $\psi(\mathbf{WAs}) = \psi(\mathbf{s})$ where **x** = **As**, (2.3) and **W** is a further transformation of **x**, implying that **WA** = **I**, then ψ can be considered as an absolute contrast function. This requires that no two sources have identical distributions, otherwise there is an inherent permutation indeterminacy. If any of the sources have a symmetric distribution then positive and negative terms of the same absolute value will have the same value of probability. If the power of each component is unknown then this cannot be blindly identified because the power term simply gives a scaling of the corresponding column of the mixing matrix **A**. These give rise to the sign and scaling indeterminacy inherent in blind source separation. The conditions (2.43, 2.44, 2.45) can be satisfied by the mutual information measure (2.26) (Comon, 1994).

By taking the mutual information as a contrast to be minimised a search can be made for a transformation which will minimise the defined contrast and so yield transformed data which have mutually independent components. This is the basis of independent component analysis where we seek to separate N underlying sources from an observation of N instantaneous mixtures. We shall consider this further in subsequent chapters, however, a point of practical interest must be raised at present. As the mutual information is a function of marginal and multivariate densities whose parametric form is unknown, we now consider moment and cumulant based expansions of probability densities.

2.4 Cumulant Expansions of Probability Densities and Higher Order Statistics

As we are considering data drawn from probability densities whose parametric form is unknown, we now consider descriptive statistics that can be computed from data samples. These statistics can in many ways provide valuable indicators of the densities characteristics. We introduce the concepts of moments and cumulants of a distribution within the context of probability density estimation via series expansions of distributions. When dealing with non-Gaussian distributions, which are characterised by higher order moments, we are required to consider Higher Order Statistics (HOS), i.e. moments and cumulants higher than second order. Higher Order Statistics have been exploited considerably in recent years within the signal processing discipline (Nikias and Mendel, 1993) for applications such as higher-order spectral analysis of deterministic signals (Nikias and Petropulu, 1993), identification of non-minimum phase systems (Lii and Rosenblatt, 1982), and of course blind separation of sources (Cardoso, 1989; Cardoso, 1990; Cardoso, 1991; Comon, 1989; Lacoume and Ruiz, 1989).

The exploitation of sample cumulants of distributions of stochastic processes is fundamental to the study of blind source separation and independent component analysis. We now introduce the principles of characteristic functions along with moments and cumulants of distributions.

2.4.1 Moment Generating and Cumulant Generating Functions

The univariate probability density function for a zero mean scalar variable is given as $p(x)$. The first characteristic function or moment generating function is given as the Fourier transform of the pdf. (Stuart *et al*, 1987; Papoulis, 1984).

$$\varphi(w) = \int p(x)\, e^{i(wx)}\, dx \tag{2.46}$$

For clarity, we shall consider the univariate case.

$$\varphi(w) = \int p(x)\, e^{i(wx)}\, dx$$

$$\varphi(w) = E\left\{ e^{i(wx)} \right\} \tag{2.47}$$

where in this case $E\{\dots\}$ denotes expectation over the density *p(x)*. Now considering the derivatives of (2.47)

$$\frac{d^l \varphi(w)}{dw^l}\Big|_{w=0} = (i)^l\, E\left\{x^l\right\} \forall l = 1,2,3,\dots \tag{2.48}$$

and so the Taylor expanded series representation of the characteristic function (2.47) is then

$$\varphi(w) = \sum_{l=0}^{n} \frac{(w)^l}{l!} \frac{d^l \varphi(w)}{dw^l}\Big|_{w=0} + o_n(w) = \sum_{l=0}^{n} \frac{(iw)^l}{l!} E\left\{x^l\right\} + o_n(w)$$

The remainder term $o_n(w)$ will tend to zero in the limit as w approaches zero. The expansion of the moment generating function is exactly represented by the summation term of all the considered moments of the distribution which exist.

$$\varphi(w) = \sum_{l=0}^{\infty} \frac{(iw)^l}{l!} E\left\{x^l\right\} \tag{2.49}$$

The coefficient terms in the expansion are termed the moments of the distribution. As we are considering a zero mean distribution this definition suffices, however, if the mean takes a finite value then the moments are usually centred about the mean value. Let us consider some specific examples

$$l = 1 : m_1 = \int x \, p(x) dx = E\{x\} \tag{2.50}$$

The expression (2.53) is the first moment and is termed the mean of the distribution.

$$l = 2 : m_2 = \int x^2 \, p(x) dx = E\{x^2\} \tag{2.51}$$

The expression (2.54) is the second moment about the mean and is termed the variance of the distribution. The expression (2.52) is usually termed the l'th order moments.

$$l > 2 : m_l = \int x^l \, p(x) dx = E\{x^l\} \tag{2.52}$$

It is important to note that we have been considering zero mean distributions. The more general form of (2.52) centred about a non-zero mean μ is simply

$$m_l = \int (x - \mu)^l \, p(x) dx = E\{(x - \mu)^l\} \tag{2.53}$$

The form of (2.53) can be expanded to compute moments of any order about the mean and we shall return to this expression in later chapters of this book. What we have here is a moment generating function which will exhibit the same characteristics as the probability density function. So by utilising the coefficients of the characteristic function expansion, that is the order moments, information regarding the pdf can be conveyed.

The multivariate probability density function of the N dimensional zero mean vector $\mathbf{x}$ is given as $p_{\mathbf{x}}(\mathbf{x})$ and the related characteristic function is

$$\varphi_{\mathbf{x}}(\mathbf{w}) = \int p_{\mathbf{x}}(\mathbf{x}) e^{i(\mathbf{w}.\mathbf{x})} d\mathbf{x} \tag{2.54}$$

where $i = \sqrt{-1}$.

The joint characteristic function (2.54) of the vector **x** can be written as

$$\varphi_{\mathbf{x}}(\mathbf{w})=\sum_{l_1,\ldots,l_N=0}^{\infty}\frac{i^{(l_1+l_2+\ldots+l_N)}}{l_1!l_2!\ldots l_N!}M_{\mathbf{x}}^{(l_1,\ldots,l_N)}w_1^{l_1}w_2^{l_2}\ldots w_N^{l_N} \tag{2.55}$$

Where the coefficients $M_{\mathbf{x}}^{(l_1,\ldots,l_N)}$ of order $l=l_1+l_2+\ldots+l_N$ in the Taylor expanded series of the first characteristic function are called the joint moments. From Taylor's theorem these are

$$M_{\mathbf{x}}^{(l_1,\ldots,l_N)}=(-i)^l\frac{\partial^l\varphi_{\mathbf{x}}(\mathbf{w})}{\partial w_1^{l_1}\partial w_2^{l_2}\ldots\partial w_N^{l_N}}\bigg|_{w_1=\ldots=w_N=0} \tag{2.56}$$

The second characteristic function, or the cumulant generating function, is defined as the natural logarithm of the first characteristic function (2.46)

$$\phi(\mathbf{w})=\log(\varphi_{\mathbf{x}}(\mathbf{w}))=\log\left(E\left\{e^{i(\mathbf{w}.\mathbf{x})}\right\}\right) \tag{2.57}$$

writing

$$\log(\varphi_{\mathbf{x}}(\mathbf{w}))=\sum_{l_1,\ldots,l_N=0}^{\infty}\frac{i^{(l_1+l_2+\ldots+l_N)}}{l_1!l_2!\ldots l_N!}\kappa_{\mathbf{x}}^{(l_1,\ldots,l_N)}w_1^{l_1}w_2^{l_2}\ldots w_N^{l_N} \tag{2.58}$$

Taylor's theorem gives

$$\kappa_{\mathbf{x}}^{(l_1,\ldots,l_N)}=(-i)^l\frac{\partial^l\log(\varphi_{\mathbf{x}}(\mathbf{w}))}{\partial w_1^{l_1}\partial w_2^{l_2}\ldots\partial w_N^{l_N}}\bigg|_{w_1=\ldots=w_N=0} \tag{2.59}$$

We shall consider the univariate case again to give examples of the cumulants of a distribution.

$$\phi(w)=\log(\varphi(w))=\log\left(E\left\{e^{i(wx)}\right\}\right) \tag{2.60}$$

As with the definition of moments, the cumulants are defined as the coefficients of the Taylor series terms

$$\phi(w)=\sum_{l=0}^{n}\frac{(-i)^l}{l!}(iw)^l\frac{d^l\phi(w)}{dw^l}\Big|_{w=0} \tag{2.61}$$

explicitly

$$\kappa^{(l)}=(-i)^l\frac{d^l\phi(w)}{dw^l}\Big|_{w=0} \tag{2.62}$$

Cumulants can be evaluated explicitly by taking into account (2.60) and (2.61). Consider the first and second derivatives of (2.60)

$$\frac{d\phi(w)}{dw}=\frac{d\varphi(w)}{dw}\frac{1}{\phi(w)} \tag{2.63}$$

and

$$\frac{d^2\phi(w)}{dw^2}=\frac{d^2\varphi(w)}{dw^2}\frac{1}{\phi(w)}-\left(\frac{d\varphi(w)}{dw}\frac{1}{\phi(w)}\right)^2 \tag{2.64}$$

Employing (2.63) and (2.64) within (2.62) expressions for the first and second order cumulants can be derived as

$$\kappa^{(1)}=m_1 \text{ and } \kappa^{(2)}=m_2-(m_1)^2 \tag{2.65}$$

What is clear from (2.65) is that the cumulants of a distribution (if they exist) are related to the moments of the particular distribution. Further tedious manipulation of the second characteristic function will yield expressions for higher order cumulants. We list the third and fourth order cumulants here.

$$\kappa^{(3)}=m_3-3m_2m_1+2(m_1)^3$$

$$\kappa^{(4)}=m_4-3(m_2)^2-4m_3m_1+12m_2(m_1)^2-6(m_1)^4$$

Expressions for cumulants of order higher than fourth become increasingly complex and derivation of further expressions are left for the adventurous and ambitious reader. We now provide an example of computing cumulants for a distribution by way of example. The distribution to be considered is the Gausian pdf defined in (2.13) and the characteristic function will be

$$\varphi(w)=\int \frac{1}{\sqrt{2\pi\sigma^2}} e^{\frac{-(x-\mu)^2}{2\sigma^2}} e^{i(wx)} dx \tag{2.66}$$

where $\sigma^2 = m_2 - (m_1)^2$ is the usual definition of variance. Note that this is also equal to the value of the second order cumulant.

$$\Rightarrow \varphi(w)=\frac{1}{\sqrt{2\pi\sigma^2}} \int e^{\frac{iwx-(x-\mu)^2}{2\sigma^2}} dx \tag{2.67}$$

$$\Rightarrow \varphi(w)= e^{iw\mu-\frac{\sigma^2 w^2}{2}} \tag{2.68}$$

The cumulant generating function will then be

$$\phi(w)=\log(\varphi(w))= iw\mu - \frac{\sigma^2 w^2}{2} \tag{2.69}$$

Employing the form of (2.69) the cumulants can be evaluated by using (2.62)

$$\kappa^{(1)}=(-i)\frac{d\phi(w)}{dw}\Big|_{w=0} = (-i)(i\mu - \sigma^2 w)\Big|_{w=0} = \mu \tag{2.70}$$

$$\kappa^{(2)}=(-i)^2\frac{d^2\phi(w)}{dw^2}\Big|_{w=0} = (-i)^2(-\sigma^2)\Big|_{w=0} = \sigma^2 \tag{2.71}$$

$$\kappa^{(n)}=(-i)^n\frac{d^n\phi(w)}{dw^n}\Big|_{w=0} = 0 \; : n>2 \tag{2.72}$$

We learn that the first and second order cumulants of a Gaussian distribution are the mean and variance of the distribution. For a Gaussian distribution we also note that all higher order cumulants (2.72) equal zero and this indicates that a Gaussian distribution can be fully defined by the mean and variance.

Although this has been a simple illustrative example, the result embodied in (2.70), (2.71), (2.72) is of fundamental importance to blind source separation and independent component analysis. We shall make important inferences from this result in the light of the Central Limit Theorem (Stuart *et al*, 1987). Distributions which exhibit normality will have zero higher order cumulants, however, distributions which exhibit forms of anormality may possess higher order cumulants of significant value. This is an important property in that higher order cumulants can be used to distinguish observed data, which is normally and anormally distributed.

The examples which have been given are for univariate distributions (2.65); the case for multivariate distributions is a little more complicated in terms of notation. Two notations for multivariate cumulants will be introduced here. From (2.59) it can be shown (Rosenblatt, 1985) that the Nth order cumulant of the components of the vector **x** can be defined as

$$cum(x_1, x_2, \ldots, x_N) = \sum_p (-1)^{p-1}(p-1)!\,E\left\{\prod_{j\in v_1} x_j\right\}E\left\{\prod_{j\in v_2} x_j\right\}\ldots E\left\{\prod_{j\in v_p} x_j\right\} \quad (2.72)$$

where $v_1, v_2, \ldots, v_p$ is a partition of the index set $\{1, 2, \ldots, N\}$ and one sums over all of these partitions. Using this notation, we can write the second, third and fourth order cumulants for zero-mean **x**

$$cum(x_1, x_2) = E\{x_1 x_2\} \quad (2.73)$$

$$cum(x_1, x_2, x_3) = E\{x_1 x_2 x_3\} \quad (2.74)$$

$$\begin{aligned} cum(x_1, x_2, x_3, x_4) &= E\{x_1 x_2 x_3 x_4\} - E\{x_1 x_2\}E\{x_3 x_4\} \\ &\quad - E\{x_1 x_3\}E\{x_2 x_4\} - E\{x_1 x_4\}E\{x_2 x_3\} \end{aligned} \quad (2.75)$$

An alternate notation is the subscript notation (Stuart and Ord, 1987) i.e.

$$\kappa_{11} = cum(x_1, x_2),\ \kappa_{111} = cum(x_1, x_2, x_3),\ \kappa_{1111} = cum(x_1, x_2, x_3, x_4)$$

Computation of higher order cumulants of data with high dimensionality becomes a very complex operation. As an illustrative example of the use of subscript notation we list all fourth order cumulants of a zero-mean two-dimensional vector $\mathbf{x} = [x_1, x_2]^T$

$$\kappa_{04} = m_{04} - 3(m_{02})^2 = E\{x_2^4\} - 3E\{x_2^2\} \tag{2.76}$$

$$\kappa_{13} = m_{13} - 3m_{20}m_{11} = E\{x_1 x_2^3\} - 3E\{x_1^2\}E\{x_1 x_2\} \tag{2.77}$$

$$\kappa_{22} = m_{22} - m_{20}m_{02} - 2m_{11}^2 = E\{x_1^2 x_2^2\} - E\{x_1^2\}E\{x_2^2\} - 2E\{x_1 x_2\}^2 \tag{2.78}$$

$$\kappa_{31} = m_{31} - 3m_{02}m_{11} = E\{x_1^3 x_2\} - 3E\{x_2^2\}E\{x_1 x_2\} \tag{2.79}$$

$$\kappa_{40} = m_{40} - 3(m_{20})^2 = E\{x_1^4\} - 3E\{x_1^2\} \tag{2.80}$$

The subscript notation is used throughout this book.

2.4.2 Properties of Moments and Cumulants

The moment and cumulant generating functions of a distribution possess some interesting and significant properties which are now considered. Random independent variables x, x_1 and x_2 have first characteristic functions (moment generating) $\varphi_x(w)$, $\varphi_{x_1}(w)$ and $\varphi_{x_2}(w)$. If a is a scalar then the following hold

$$y = x + a \Leftrightarrow \varphi_y(w) = e^{iwa}\varphi_x(w) \tag{2.81}$$

$$y = ax \Leftrightarrow \varphi_y(w) = \varphi_x(aw) \tag{2.82}$$

$$y = x_1 + x_2 \Leftrightarrow \varphi_y(w) = \varphi_{x_1}(w)\varphi_{x_2}(w) \tag{2.83}$$

Property (2.81) indicates that an additive constant to a random variable influences only the phase behaviour of the function and the magnitude is not affected. Property (2.82) shows that a scale change in the random variable is mirrored by a scale change in the w variable. Finally the sum of two random independent variables has a moment generating function that is the product of the moment generating functions of the individual random variables being summed. Similar properties hold for the cumulant generating function.

$$y = x + a \Leftrightarrow \phi_y(w) = iwa + \phi_x(w) \tag{2.84}$$

$$y = ax \Leftrightarrow \phi_y(w) = \phi_x(aw) \tag{2.85}$$

$$y = x_1 + x_2 \Leftrightarrow \phi_y(w) = \phi_{x_1}(w) + \phi_{x_2}(w) \tag{2.86}$$

The properties (2.84) and (2.85) follow on from (2.81) and (2.82), however (2.86) is of particular significance. Remember that the random variables x_1 and x_2 are independent. (2.86) can be generalised by the use of (2.58) and (2.60) to an N dimensional vector of independent components.

$$\phi_{\mathbf{x}}(\mathbf{w}) = \sum_{p=1}^{N} \phi_{x_p}(w_p) \tag{2.87}$$

$$\Rightarrow \phi_{\mathbf{x}}(\mathbf{w}) = \sum_{l_1,\ldots,l_N=0}^{\infty} \frac{i^{(l_1+l_2+\ldots+l_N)}}{l_1!l_2!\ldots l_N!} \kappa_{\mathbf{x}}^{(l_1,\ldots,l_N)} w_1^{l_1} w_2^{l_2} \ldots w_N^{l_N} = \sum_p \sum_{l=0}^{n} \frac{(iw)^l}{l!} \kappa_{x_p}^{l} \tag{2.88}$$

The generalised independence property (2.88) indicates that the multivariate cumulant of order l is equal to the sum of the marginal cumulants of order l for all l. For clarity let us consider the fourth order cumulant of a two-dimensional data vector. From (2.88)

$$\kappa_4 = \kappa_{04} + \kappa_{13} + \kappa_{22} + \kappa_{31} + \kappa_{40} = \sum_{p=1}^{N=2} \kappa_4(p) \tag{2.89}$$

$$\Rightarrow \kappa_4 = \kappa_{04} + \kappa_{40} \Leftrightarrow \kappa_{13}, \kappa_{31}, \kappa_{22} = 0 \tag{2.90}$$

This will of course be the case for cumulants of all orders. What we have in (2.88) and (2.89) in particular is that for multivariate data with independent marginal distributions all cross-cumulant terms will be zero. If the vector **x** has two normally distributed marginals from the results of (2.70), (2.71) and (2.72) statistical independence would be satisfied when

$$\kappa_2 = \kappa_{02} + \kappa_{11} + \kappa_{20} = \sum_{p=1}^{N=2} \kappa_2(p) \Leftrightarrow \kappa_{11} = E\{x_1 x_2\} = 0 \tag{2.91}$$

As cumulants of higher order than two are zero in normally distributed data, then elimination of all cross-covariance suffices for independence. Of course, if cumulants of all orders are non-zero within the data distributions then from (2.88) all cross-cumulants of all orders require to be zero for strict independence. We have now considered some of the properties of moment and cumulant generating functions and have found that these properties are of fundamental importance to the study of blind source separation and independent component analysis. One further important property is introduced here.

The sum of squared elements of an rth order cumulant of a zero-mean variable is invariant under orthogonal transformation.

$$S_r = \sum_{l_1,l_2,\ldots,l_r}^{N} \kappa_{l_1,l_2,\ldots,l_r}^2 \tag{2.92}$$

Before considering the proof for this theorem, reconsider the major point from section (2.2.3): the entropy of an N dimensional variable is invariant under an orthogonal transformation (2.41). As the cumulants of the distribution are characteristic of the form of the distribution then intuitively (2.92) sits well from an information theoretic perspective. The proof of theorem 2.2 is that presented in (Comon, 1994) reproduced here for completeness of presentation.

Proof :

The input variable $\mathbf{x}$ is transformed by the linear rotation $\mathbf{W}$ such that $\mathbf{W}\,\mathbf{W}^T=\mathbf{I}$, to $\mathbf{y}$, and $\mathbf{y}=\mathbf{W}\mathbf{x}$. The rth order cumulant of $\mathbf{x}$ is defined as $\Gamma_{j_1,j_2,\ldots,j_r}$ and so the following holds due to the multilinearity of cumulants (Brilinger, 1981)

$$\kappa_{ijk} = \sum_{pqr} \mathbf{W}_{ip}\mathbf{W}_{jq}\mathbf{W}_{kr}\Gamma_{pqr} \tag{2.93}$$

$$S_r = \sum_{i_1\ldots i_r}\sum_{p_1\ldots p_r}\sum_{q_1\ldots q_r} \mathbf{W}_{i_1p_1}\ldots\mathbf{W}_{i_rp_r}\mathbf{W}_{i_1q_1}\ldots\mathbf{W}_{i_rq_r}\Gamma_{p_1\ldots p_r}\Gamma_{q_1\ldots q_r} \tag{2.94}$$

As $\mathbf{W}$ is orthogonal then

$$\sum_i \mathbf{W}_{ip}\mathbf{W}_{iq} = \delta_{pq} = \begin{cases} 1 : p = q \\ 0 : p \neq q \end{cases} \tag{2.95}$$

using (2.95) then (2.94) can be rewritten as

$$S_r = \sum_{p_1\ldots p_r}\sum_{q_1\ldots q_r} \delta_{p_1q_1}\ldots\delta_{p_rq_r}\Gamma_{p_1\ldots p_r}\Gamma_{q_1\ldots q_r} = \sum_{p_1\ldots p_r}\Gamma_{p_1\ldots p_r}^2 \tag{2.96}$$

This theorem has been the basis of many of the batch-based algorithms and techniques which will be considered in Chapter 3. It also implicitly underlies many of the self-organising neural networks which can be applied to blind separation of sources and independent component analysis.

2.5 Gradient Based Function Optimisation

The concept of stochastic gradient based adaptive or learning algorithms for general nonlinear optimisation is well known, especially within the artificial neural network research community (Haykin, 1995). In this section the gradient based optimisation of a function is considered along with the associated application to the BSS problem and ICA transformation.

Consider a sequence of independent random vector variables $\{\mathbf{x}\}$ i.e. $\mathbf{x}_1, \mathbf{x}_2, \mathbf{x}_3, \cdots \mathbf{x}_t, \cdots$ where $\mathbf{x} \in \Re^N$ which is then transformed by some matrix variable defined as $\mathbf{W} \in \Re^{M \times N}$ into the sequence $\{\mathbf{y} = \mathbf{Wx}\}$ where $\mathbf{y} \in \Re^M$. We can then attach some loss or cost to this transformation defined as $\phi(\mathbf{y}; \mathbf{W})$. The average loss or cost of the transformation over a sequence of observations is then given as

$$\Phi(\mathbf{W}) = E\{\phi(\mathbf{y}; \mathbf{W})\} \tag{2.97}$$

where E denotes expectation with respect to $\mathbf{y}$. The optimisation of the cost function requires a search for the optimum value of the transformation matrix, denoted as $\mathbf{W}^{\mathrm{O}}$. Stochastic gradient techniques have been proposed and developed for the optimisation of objective functions (Haykin, 1995). In this particular case the minimisation of a loss function is desired, the standard stochastic gradient method modifies the variable parameters based on each of individual sequence of observations $\mathbf{y}_1, \mathbf{y}_2, \mathbf{y}_3, \cdots \mathbf{y}_t, \cdots$.

The standard stochastic gradient method modifies $\mathbf{W}_t$ into $\mathbf{W}_{t+1}$ after observing the variable $\mathbf{y}_t$ at time instant t using the following

$$\mathbf{W}_{t+1} = \mathbf{W}_t + \mu_t \frac{\partial \phi(\mathbf{y}_t; \mathbf{W}_t)}{\partial \mathbf{W}} = \mathbf{W}_t + \mu_t \nabla \phi(\mathbf{W}_t) \tag{2.98}$$

The learning rate or step size is defined as μ_t which should be decreased to zero as $t \to \infty$ (Amari, 1967). Many gradient based learning algorithms for neural learning have been developed based on (2.98) . There is however, a fundamental shortcoming with (2.98) when this is applied to artificial neural networks.

2.5.1 The Natural Gradient and Covariant Algorithms

When considering the stochastic online optimisation of an objective function the nature of the parameter space has to be taken into account. In the case of ICA then the space of matrices $\{\mathbf{W}\}$ has to be examined.

It has been shown (Amari, 1967; 1998) that the space of separating matrices has a Riemannian metric structure (Aris, 1962) as opposed to the more familiar Euclidean structure. As this is the case then the gradient given in (2.98) will not give the steepest descent direction, what is required is the gradient natural to the Riemannian space of matrices (Amari, 1985, 1996, 1998). We now follow (Amari, 1998) in elucidating the natural gradient for the ICA and instantaneous BSS problem.

Consider the parameter space $S=\{\mathbf{w}\}$, where the vector of parameters is defined by $\mathbf{w} \in \Re^N$. This is the space on which the objective function $\phi(\mathbf{w})$ is defined. If $\mathbf{w}$ defines an orthonormal co-ordinate system that is the parameter space S is Euclidean then the squared length of an infinitesimally small perturbation vector $\delta\mathbf{w}$ of $\mathbf{w}$ is given by

$$|\delta\mathbf{w}|^2 = \delta\mathbf{w}^T\delta\mathbf{w} = \sum_{i=1}^{N} \delta\mathbf{w}_i^2 \tag{2.99}$$

However, if the parameter space S is Riemannian, and so no longer orthonormal, then

$$|\delta\mathbf{w}|^2 = \delta\mathbf{w}^T\mathbf{G}\delta\mathbf{w} = \sum_{i=1}^{N}\sum_{j=1}^{N} \mathbf{G}_{ij}\delta\mathbf{w}_i\delta\mathbf{w}_i \tag{2.100}$$

The matrix $\mathbf{G}$ is called the Riemannian metric tensor, detailed discussions of Riemannian spaces can be found in, for example, (Amari, 1985; Aris, 1962). In the case of a Euclidean space the metric Tensor $\mathbf{G}$ reduces to the identity matrix and then (2.99) holds.

We wish then to identify the steepest descent direction in the Riemannian space of parameters. This is given as

$$\tilde{\nabla}\phi(\mathbf{w}) = \mathbf{G}^{-1}\nabla\phi(\mathbf{w}) \tag{2.101}$$

Where $\tilde{\nabla}\phi(\mathbf{w})$ denotes the natural gradient in the Riemannian parameter space and

$$\nabla\phi(\mathbf{w}) = \left[\frac{\partial\phi(\mathbf{w})}{\partial\mathbf{w}_1} \quad \cdots \quad \frac{\partial\phi(\mathbf{w})}{\partial\mathbf{w}_i} \quad \frac{\partial\phi(\mathbf{w})}{\partial\mathbf{w}_N}\right]^T \tag{2.102}$$

which is the standard vector gradient term. The term $\mathbf{G}^{-1}$ is the inverse of the metric defined in (2.100). We follow (Amari, 1998) in providing the proof for (2.101).

Proof:

Let $\delta\mathbf{w} = \varepsilon\,\mathbf{a}$, we require the gradient vector $\mathbf{a}$ which minimises $\phi(\mathbf{w} + \delta\mathbf{w})$ subject to the constraint that $|\mathbf{a}|^2 = \mathbf{a}^T\mathbf{G}\ \mathbf{a} = 1$.

Now note that for a small perturbation then

$$\phi(\mathbf{w} + \delta\mathbf{w}) = \phi(\mathbf{w}) + \varepsilon\,\nabla\phi(\mathbf{w})^T\mathbf{a} \tag{2.103}$$

Using Lagrangean multipliers to enforce the above constraint we then have

$$\frac{\partial}{\partial\mathbf{a}}\phi(\mathbf{w} + \delta\mathbf{w}) - \frac{\partial}{\partial\mathbf{a}}\lambda\mathbf{a}^T\mathbf{G}\,\mathbf{a} = 0 \tag{2.104}$$

$$= \frac{\partial}{\partial\mathbf{a}}\nabla\phi(\mathbf{w})^T\mathbf{a} - \frac{\partial}{\partial\mathbf{a}}\lambda\mathbf{a}^T\mathbf{G}\,\mathbf{a}$$

This then equals

$$\nabla\phi(\mathbf{w}) - 2\lambda\mathbf{G}\,\mathbf{a} = 0 \tag{2.105}$$

Rearranging (2.105) gives the steepest descent direction $\mathbf{a}$ which is

$$\mathbf{a} = \tfrac{1}{2\lambda}\mathbf{G}^{-1}\nabla\phi(\mathbf{w}) \tag{2.106}$$

As the vector $\mathbf{a}$ is the steepest descent direction we can see that the natural gradient in the parameter space is then given by (2.101).

The next question, which has to be considered, is the form which (2.101) will have for the ICA transformation. Amari has elegantly expounded this, (Amari *et al*, 1996; Amari, 1998) and we now investigate the natural gradient for instantaneous BSS and ICA.

Consider the matrix $\mathbf{W}$ and extend this by an infinitesimally small deviation ε such that $\mathbf{W} \rightarrow \mathbf{W} + \varepsilon\ \mathbf{W}$. We denote the tangent vector at $\mathbf{W}$ as $\mathbf{X}$ and define the inner product at $\mathbf{W}$ as

$$trace\left(\mathbf{X}^T\mathbf{X}\right)_{\mathbf{W}} \tag{2.107}$$

The matrix **W** can now be mapped to the unit matrix **I** by applying the inverse of the matrix **W**. Note that for BSS we seek the inverse of the transformation $\mathbf{x} = \mathbf{A}\mathbf{s}$ that is $\mathbf{W} = \mathbf{A}^{-1}$. The following mappings exist

$$\mathbf{W}\mathbf{A} = \mathbf{W}\mathbf{W}^{-1} = \mathbf{I} \tag{2.108}$$

$$(\mathbf{W} + \varepsilon\,\mathbf{X})\mathbf{W}^{-1} = \mathbf{I} + \varepsilon\,\mathbf{X}\,\mathbf{W}^{-1} \tag{2.109}$$

What we can see from (2.108) and (2.109) is that the tangent vector **X** of **W** corresponds to the tangent vector $\mathbf{X}\,\mathbf{W}^{-1}$ of **I**. This being the case they must both have the same length (Aris, 1962; Amari, 1998) which can be expressed by the respective inner products i.e.

$$trace\left(\mathbf{X}^T\mathbf{X}\right)_{\mathbf{W}} = trace\left(\left(\mathbf{X}\,\mathbf{W}^{-1}\right)^T\mathbf{X}\,\mathbf{W}^{-1}\right)_{\mathbf{I}}$$

$$= trace\left(\mathbf{W}^{-T}\,\mathbf{X}^T\mathbf{X}\,\mathbf{W}^{-1}\right)_{\mathbf{I}} \tag{2.110}$$

Now the gradient operator is defined as (2.103) and so for square matrices

$$\phi(\mathbf{W} + \delta\mathbf{W}) = \phi(\mathbf{W}) + \varepsilon\ trace\left(\nabla\phi(\mathbf{W})^T\mathbf{X}\right) \tag{2.111}$$

The natural gradient for **W** can then be defined from (2.100) using the following equality

$$trace\left(\tilde{\nabla}\phi(\mathbf{W})^T\mathbf{X}\right)_{\mathbf{W}} = trace\left(\nabla\phi(\mathbf{W})^T\mathbf{X}\right)_{\mathbf{I}} \tag{2.112}$$

and so

$$trace\left(\mathbf{W}^{-T}\,\tilde{\nabla}\phi(\mathbf{W})^T\mathbf{X}\,\mathbf{W}^{-1}\right)_{\mathbf{W}} = trace\left(\nabla\phi(\mathbf{W})^T\mathbf{X}\right)_{\mathbf{I}} \tag{2.113}$$

Noting that for any square matrices **A**, **B**, and **C** the following equality holds

$$trace(\mathbf{A}\,\mathbf{B}\,\mathbf{C}) = trace(\mathbf{C}\,\mathbf{A}\,\mathbf{B}) \tag{2.114}$$

we can now write (2.103) as

$$trace\left(\mathbf{W}^{-1}\mathbf{W}^{-T}\,\tilde{\nabla}\phi(\mathbf{W})^T\mathbf{X}\right)_{\mathbf{W}} = trace\left(\nabla\phi(\mathbf{W})^T\mathbf{X}\right)_{\mathbf{I}} \tag{2.115}$$

By equating the terms within the trace operator note that

$$\mathbf{W}^{-1}\mathbf{W}^{-T}\,\tilde{\nabla}\phi(\mathbf{W})^{T} = \nabla\phi(\mathbf{W})^{T} \tag{2.116}$$

Re-arranging (2.106) yields

$$\tilde{\nabla}\phi(\mathbf{W}) = \nabla\phi(\mathbf{W})\mathbf{W}^{T}\mathbf{W} \tag{2.117}$$

This is a particularly significant result (Amari, 1998) where we can see that the natural gradient in the Riemannian space of square matrices for BSS and ICA is the standard gradient post-multiplied by the product of the matrix transpose and the matrix itself. By examining the standard gradient based optimisation routine of (2.98) with that of (2.103) it is interesting to consider the following. Examination of the parameter update for (2.98) shows that the gradient term has dimension $1/w$, whereas the parameters for updating have dimension w. The gradient based method of (2.98) is therefore dimensionally inconsistent and will give varying results depending on the units of measurement of the variables. This is termed a non-covariant algorithm which can be transformed so that it will be dimensionally consistent and therefore covariant (Aris, 1962). This covariance will provide the uniform performance desired in an algorithm of this description and this topic is detailed extensively in (Cardoso, 1996).

Examining the natural gradient term we can see that if the inverse of the metric tensor has dimensions ww' then an update algorithm using the natural gradient will be dimensionally consistent and indeed this is the case for (2.107). It is also interesting to note that the natural gradient update of the form (2.118) is exactly the Newton algorithm (Press *et al*, 1991) when the metric tensor is taken as the Hessian matrix of the objective function. This, of course, has the benefit of removing the problem of poor convergence properties when there is significant eigenvalue disparity causing ill-conditioning of the objective function. This chapter has introduced elements of information theory such as the concepts of entropy, information, Kullback-Leibler entropy and mutual information. The concepts of moment and cumulant generating functions along with the properties of moments and cumulants of a distribution are also presented. The information theory and higher order statistics presented here will now form the basis for the methods and learning algorithms to be developed in subsequent chapters.

$$\mathbf{W}_{t+1} = \mathbf{W}_t + \mu_t\,\tilde{\nabla}\phi(\mathbf{W}_t) = \mathbf{W}_t + \mu_t\,\mathbf{G}^{-1}\nabla\phi(\mathbf{w}) \tag{2.118}$$

3. *Fourth Order Cumulant Based Blind Source Separation*

The main focus of this book is self-organising neural networks for signal separation. However, no work on blind source separation (BSS) would be complete without considering the techniques which have been developed from the classical statistical signal processing community so this chapter presents the most significant works on BSS. Chapter 4 focuses on self-organising neural networks and their emergent properties especially when considered within the bounds of the BSS problem.

3.1 Early Algorithms and Techniques

Herrault and Jutten (1986) were the first to propose Independent Component Analysis as a descriptive term for blind source separation. The term is inspired by the similarity of ICA and Principal Components Analysis (PCA). PCA (Jollife, 1986; Watanabe, 1969; Devijver & Kittler, 1982) is a linear orthogonal transformation which is optimal in the least squares sense for dimensionality reduction. In addition to optimal linear dimensionality reduction, projecting the data onto the PCA basis vectors will also maximise the variance of the data onto the given projection. As the average amount of information, or entropy, of normally distributed data is in direct proportion to the data variance (2.17, 2.31) then we can see that PCA will also maximise information transfer given the projection. We shall provide a more detailed account of the PCA transformation in Chapter 4. Herrault and Jutten (1986) considered the BSS problem and proposed a 'neuromimetic' structure for its solution. This structure and the related algorithms have been further extended by (Cichocki, Unbehauen, and Rummert, 1994) to provide robust separation of sources from ill-conditioned mixtures. The neuromimetic learning was a form of non-linear anti-Hebbian (Hebb, 1949) learning and as such implicitly introduced certain higher order statistics into the self-organisation of the network. Ruiz and Lacoume (1989) constructed a set of non-linear equations based on the solution of the system of second and fourth order cumulants being set to zero. Gaeta and Lacoume (1990) used the Maximum Likelihood Estimator (MLE) (Ripley, 1996) in performing an ICA. By employing a multi-dimensional Gram-Charlier expansion (Stuart and Ord, 1987) of the probability densities the likelihood function can be expressed in terms of fourth order cumulants and Hermite polynomials. An exhaustive search procedure is then required to maximise the approximate likelihood function. This technique was restricted to mixtures of two sources and the exhaustive search procedure made the extension to more than two sources impractical. Cardoso (1989) proposed a two step algebraic approach, which was based on fourth order statistics. This was termed Fourth Order Blind Identification (FOBI). The first step consisted of decomposing the covariance matrix of the received mixture and then orthonormalising the data. The mixture model considered is identical to that in (2.3). The first step of Cardoso's method consisted of forming the data covariance matrix $\mathbf{R}_{\mathbf{xx}} = E\{\mathbf{xx}^T\}$ and then decomposing this using a standard decomposition technique such as eigenvalue decomposition (Golub and Loan, 1989) such that $\mathbf{R}_{\mathbf{xx}} = \mathbf{C}\Lambda\mathbf{C}^{-1}$, where Λ is the diagonal matrix whose entries are the eigenvalues and $\mathbf{C}$ is the matrix whose columns are the respective eigenvectors. The orthonormalisation consists of projecting the received data onto the eigenvectors such that $\mathbf{y} = \mathbf{Cx} \Rightarrow E\{\mathbf{yy}^T\} = \mathbf{I}$. A weighted covariance matrix of the orthonormal data is then constructed such that $\mathbf{R}_{\mathbf{yy}} = E\{\mathbf{y}^2\mathbf{yy}^T\}$. Cardoso has shown that the diagonalisation of the 4th order covariance matrix $\mathbf{R}_{\mathbf{yy}}$ will then provide an ICA. At the same time as Cardoso proposed his FOBI algorithm, Comon (1989) proposed his technique which involved solving a system of equations based on fourth order cumulants. This technique has been of particular importance as it forms the basis for a seminal paper on ICA (Comon, 1994). We will present a non-linear self-organising neural network which can be considered to be performing an online adaptive equivalent to the technique proposed by Comon. We shall now focus on the cumulant based technique presented in Comon (1989).

A two step process is considered (Figure 3.1) where the received data is first of all spatially whitened and then orthogonally transformed to cancel out cross cumulants (in particular fourth order cumulants). Spatial whitening is identical to the orthonormalising technique utilised by Cardoso (1989). Spatial whitening will normalise the variance and remove all cross correlations between the components of the received data vector. Spatial whitening cancels the cross-cumulants of second order, however, statistical independence of data which is not normally distributed requires that cross-cumulants of all orders (if they exist) are cancelled. The second part of the method requires an orthogonal transform which will then cancel out the remaining orders of cumulants. We are seeking a transformation $\mathbf{y} = \mathbf{F}\mathbf{x}$ based on the mixture model of (2.3), such that $\mathbf{y}$ has independent components. As discussed in Chapter 2, Section 2.3, there is an inherent indetermination regarding the ICA transformation. If the matrix $\mathbf{F}$ is a solution to the problem then the matrix , $\tilde{\mathbf{F}} = \Lambda\mathbf{P}\mathbf{F}$ is also a solution where Λ is a diagonal matrix and $\mathbf{P}$ is a permutation matrix. By fixing the output to have an identity covariance matrix, Comon reduces the scaling indeterminacy to sign indeterminacy so that $\tilde{\mathbf{F}} = \Delta\mathbf{P}\mathbf{F}$ where Δ is a diagonal matrix with entries ± 1. The matrix transform $\mathbf{F}$ can be defined as $\mathbf{F} = \mathbf{Q}\mathbf{L}\Lambda$ where $\mathbf{L}\Lambda$ is a lower triangular matrix and $\mathbf{Q}$ is a rotation. The rotation is required to maintain the identity covariance matrix of the final output. So the first part of the algorithm computes the lower triangular matrix $\mathbf{L}\Lambda$ such that the transformed data $\mathbf{z} = \mathbf{L}\Lambda\mathbf{x}$ has an identity covariance $\mathbf{C}_{\mathbf{zz}} = E\{\mathbf{z}\mathbf{z}^T\} = \mathbf{I}$. The following transformation is constrained to a rotation to ensure that the output covariance is an identity, that is $\mathbf{C}_{\mathbf{yy}} = E\{\mathbf{y}\mathbf{y}^T\} = \mathbf{Q}\mathbf{C}_{\mathbf{zz}}\mathbf{Q}^T = \mathbf{I} \Rightarrow \mathbf{Q}\mathbf{Q}^T = \mathbf{I}$.

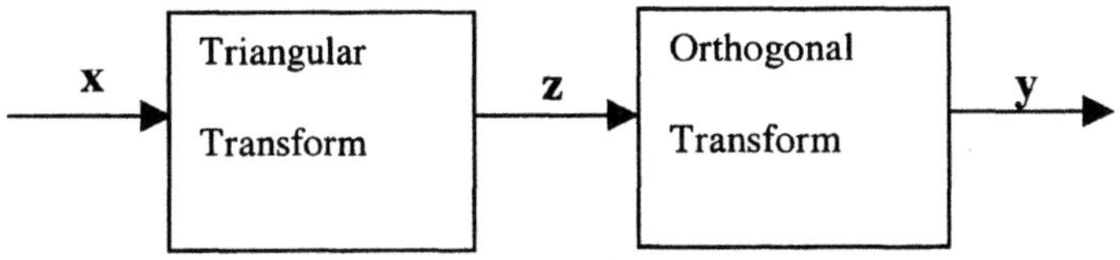

Figure 3.1: Block Diagram of Two Step ICA Process.

The second step in the process is the most significant, that is computing the rotation matrix $\mathbf{Q}$ and this shall be considered in some detail now. As has been shown in Chapter 2, (2.88) the cancellation of all cross-cumulants is required for the outputs of the transformation to be independent. Consider the output cumulants of order n as linear functions of the input cumulants of equivalent order. Comon (1989) shows that for p variables then a system of equations consisting of

$$C_{p-1}^{n+p-1} - p \tag{3.1}$$

n degree polynomial equations is generated. Where the combination term is denoted as

$$C_r^n = \frac{n!}{r!(n-r)!} \tag{3.2}$$

This suggests a combinatorial explosion of equations in the unknowns and is indicative of the impractical nature of such a technique when considering high dimensional data. However, let us consider the case where $p = 2$ and the first step of the transformation has been completed such that $\mathbf{C}_{\mathbf{zz}} = E\{\mathbf{zz}^T\} = \mathbf{I}$. It should be noted that this in itself is a computationally demanding procedure as a full data covariance matrix needs to be computed and decomposed.

The particular orthogonal matrix transformation which will be considered here is the Givens rotation. The Givens rotation is a plane rotation which is used in Jacobi transformations and also Givens and Householder reductions of matrices (Press *et al*, 1988).

$$\mathbf{Q} = \begin{bmatrix} c & c\theta \\ -c\theta & c \end{bmatrix}, \quad c = \frac{1}{\sqrt{1+\theta^2}} \tag{3.3}$$

Comon suggests the use of fourth order cumulants in generating the system of equations to be solved. He bases his argument round the observation that a symmetric probability density function will have zero third order cumulants and the majority of naturally occurring signals in the real world have symmetric pdfs. Due to the complexity explosion (3.1) when considering higher order cumulant values, the cumulant order is chosen as fourth. The rotation of the output data is then

$$\begin{bmatrix} y_1 \\ y_2 \end{bmatrix} = \begin{bmatrix} cz_1 + c\theta\, z_2 \\ -c\theta\, z_1 + cz_2 \end{bmatrix} \tag{3.4}$$

By denoting the fourth order cumulants of the whitened input data **z** as γ_{ij} and the corresponding cumulants of the output **y** as Γ_{ij} then by employing (2.77, 2.78, 2.79 and 3.4) we can derive the system of equations :

$$\Gamma_{31} = \left(-\gamma_{13}\theta^4 + (\gamma_{04} - 3\gamma_{22})\theta^3 + 3(\gamma_{13} - \gamma_{31})\theta^2 - (\gamma_{40} - 3\gamma_{22})\theta + \gamma_{31}\right)c^4 \quad (3.5)$$

$$\Gamma_{13} = \left(-\gamma_{31}\theta^4 - (\gamma_{40} - 3\gamma_{22})\theta^3 + 3(\gamma_{31} - \gamma_{13})\theta^2 + (\gamma_{04} - 3\gamma_{22})\theta + \gamma_{13}\right)c^4 \quad (3.6)$$

$$\Gamma_{22} = \left(\gamma_{22}\theta^4 + 2(\gamma_{31} - \gamma_{13})\theta^3 + (\gamma_{40} - 4\gamma_{22} + \gamma_{04})\theta^2 + 2(\gamma_{13} - \gamma_{31})\theta + \gamma_{22}\right)c^4 \quad (3.7)$$

By setting (3.5, 3.6, 3.7) to equal zero (the approximate fourth order independence criterion) and solving for θ the final rotation matrix $\mathbf{Q}$ can be identified. From the series of equations it is clear that the five fourth order cumumlants of the whitened input data need to be computed using (2.76 – 2.80). The procedure can be extended to cases where the number of sources is greater than two and this is chiefly done by considering only pairwise independence. Although focusing on only pairwise fourth order independence may be considered a weaker criterion than explicit cancellation of all possible cross-cumulants it enables a more tractable solution to the separation of mixtures consisting of more than two sources. Indeed in Comon (1994), it is shown that for a vector of arbitrary dimensionality with at most one normally distributed component, pairwise independence is equivalent to mutual independence. By then achieving pairwise independence and accumulating the identified rotations, the $N \times N$ matrix $\mathbf{Q}$ can be identified. This method is handicapped largely by the number of cumulants which have to be computed for each pair of vector components and the search and save routines for solving the systems of equations. It should also be clear that the algorithms considered here are primarily batch based for offline processing. Subsequent chapters of this book will consider online adaptive techniques embodied in self-organising neural networks.

3.2 The Method of Contrast Minimisation

A significant simplification of this procedure is presented in Comon, (1994) and is based on the concept of contrast functions (Chapter 2, 2.3). The mutual information is shown by Comon to satisfy the requirements set forth for a valid contrast function. As with the previous method a two step process is considered where second order redundancy is removed in the first step and higher order redundancy removed in the subsequent step.

Let us consider the mutual information, written in terms of negentropy (2.36), of the transformed variable **z**

$$I(\mathbf{z})=J(\mathbf{z})-\sum_{i=1}^{N}J_i(z_i)+\frac{1}{2}\log\frac{\prod_{i=1}^{N}\mathbf{C}_{\mathbf{zz}(ii)}}{\det(\mathbf{C}_{\mathbf{zz}})} \tag{3.8}$$

Noting that $\mathbf{C}_{\mathbf{zz}}=E\{\mathbf{zz}^T\}=\mathbf{I}$ due to the spatial whitening step then

$$\det(\mathbf{C}_{\mathbf{zz}})=\prod_{i=1}^{N}\mathbf{C}_{\mathbf{zz}(ii)}=\det(\mathbf{I})=1 \tag{3.9}$$

and so the rightmost term in (3.8) reduces to zero. What we see here is that the redundancy of information within the vector **z** has been reduced by the whitening or decorrelation procedure. Note also that if the data was normally distributed then the negentropy would be zero and so whitening would be sufficient to remove all redundancy within the data vector. As we are dealing with non-Gaussian data then the mutual information after whitening has a value given as

$$I(\mathbf{z})=J(\mathbf{z})-\sum_{i=1}^{N}J_i(z_i) \tag{3.10}$$

The second transformation is orthogonal, that is $\mathbf{y}=\mathbf{Qz}$. For an orthogonal transformation multivariate entropy and negentropy is invariant (2.41) in which case

$$I(\mathbf{y})=J(\mathbf{y})-\sum_{i=1}^{N}J_i(y_i)=J(\mathbf{z})-\sum_{i=1}^{N}J_i(y_i) \tag{3.11}$$

This has greatly simplified the minimisation of mutual information to the maximisation of the sums of the marginal negentropies. This in itself is a non-trivial matter as the marginal negentropies have to be evaluated. An Edgeworth series expansion (Stuart *et al*, 1987) is utilised by Comon in expressing the unknown pdf as a series expansion about a Gaussian pdf. The Edgeworth expansion of the pdf of zero mean and unit variance data is then given as a series expansion of Hermite polynomials and standardised scalar cumulants

$$
\begin{aligned}
p_y(y) = p_G(y)\Big(1 &+ \frac{1}{3!}\kappa_3 h_3(y) + \frac{1}{4!}\kappa_4 h_4(y) + \frac{10}{6!}\kappa_3^2 h_6(y) \\
&+ \frac{1}{5!}\kappa_5 h_5(y) + \frac{35}{7!}\kappa_3\kappa_4 h_7(y) + \frac{280}{9!}\kappa_3^3 h_9(y) \\
&+ \frac{1}{6!}\kappa_6 h_6(y) + \frac{56}{8!}\kappa_3\kappa_5 h_8(y) + \frac{35}{8!}\kappa_4^2 h_8(y) \\
&+ \frac{2100}{10!}\kappa_3^2\kappa_4 h_{10}(y) + \frac{15400}{12!}\kappa_3^4 h_{12}(y) + \ldots\Big)
\end{aligned}
\tag{3.12}
$$

By substituting (3.12) into the definition of negentropy (2.32) it can be shown (Comon, 1994) that the univariate negentropy can be approximated by

$$
J_i(y_i) \cong \frac{1}{12}\kappa_3^2 + \frac{1}{48}\kappa_4^2 + \frac{7}{48}\kappa_3^4 - \frac{1}{8}\kappa_3^2\kappa_4 \tag{3.13}
$$

The assumption that the underlying probability density functions are symmetric gives us the following simplification, due to the third order cumulants being zero:

$$
J_i(y_i) \cong \frac{1}{48}\kappa_4^2 \tag{3.14}
$$

Substituting (3.14) into (3.11) finally gives

$$
I(\mathbf{y}) = J(\mathbf{z}) - \sum_{i=1}^{N} \frac{1}{48}\kappa_4^2(i) \tag{3.15}
$$

The term $\kappa_4^2(i)$ is the square of the fourth order marginal cumulant of the ith component of the vector $\mathbf{y}$. Now in the minimisation of the mutual information under an orthogonal transformation the multivariate negentropy is invariant, so all that is required is to maximise the rightmost term. We have then arrived at a contrast function which can be maximised and whose maximum will yield transformed vector components which are approximately mutually independent.

An important point to note is that the independence criterion indicates that the multivariate characteristic function is equal to the sum of marginal characteristic functions (2.88). This then indicates that all cross-cumulants of all orders are zero. The sum of the squared elements of an rth order cumulant of a zero-mean variable is invariant under orthogonal transformation (2.92) so by maximising the sum of marginal terms we are effectively minimising the cross terms.

For example, considering a two dimensional vector the sum of squares of fourth order cumumlants

$$\left(\kappa_{04}^{2}+\kappa_{40}^{2}\right)+\left(\kappa_{13}^{2}+\kappa_{31}^{2}+\kappa_{22}^{2}\right)=\text{constant} \qquad (3.16)$$

which is a constant term under a rotation. Therefore maximising the sum of the squared marginal terms indicates that the sum of squares of all cross terms is minimised.

This signifies a major simplification in identifying the orthogonal transformation required to approximate independence of the transformed components. For N dimensional data N marginal fourth order cumulants need to be computed. This is an improvement on computing of the order $O(N^4)$ cross cumulants. However although the contrast has been significantly reduced in complexity from that given in Section 3.1, the process presented in (Comon, 1994) for maximisation of the contrast is complex, involving computing polynomial roots. In Chapter 5, we shall present a self organising neural network learning algorithm based on non-linear principal component analysis which will be seen to be an approximate stochastic equivalent to the algorithm and process discussed here and presented originally in Comon, (1994).

3.3 Adaptive Source Separation Methods

The approaches to source separation considered in the previous section have been batch based algorithms. (Cardoso and Laheld, 1997; Delfosse and Loubaton, 1995) have both presented adaptive algorithms for source separation. These algorithms can be considered very similar to the effective self-organising neural methods which will be considered in Chapter 4. The notion of equivariance was originally proposed by Cardoso and Laheld[1] (1997) when using the relative gradient for the adaptive algorithm. Independent of this work, Cichocki, Unbehauen, and Rummert (1994) proposed a new neural learning algorithm, which also exhibited equivariant properties. More recently Amari, Cichocki and Yang (1995) presented a neural network algorithm for source separation which utilised the natural gradient (Amari, 1967; Amari, 1997); this will be considered in detail in Chapter 7. The relative

[1] It should be noted that this paper was originally submitted in 1994 and the citation date does not indicate the true vintage of the ideas presented in the paper.

gradient and natural gradient, for blind source separation, are identical. We shall further explore the equivariant property of the relative or natural gradient.

The important point about the equivariant properties of source separation algorithms which utilise the relative or natural gradient, is that the algorithm performance does not depend on the mixing matrix. This is of great significance in the case of linear memory-less mixing where the mixing matrix may be ill-conditioned. An ill-conditioned matrix is one where its determinant approaches zero and so may be rank deficient (Cichocki and Unbehauen, 1994). In the limiting case where the rank of the square mixing matrix is less than the number of rows or columns, the matrix will be singular and has determinant zero (Golub and Loan, 1989).The EASI algorithm as developed in Cardoso & Laheld (1997) is a two step process (Figure 3.2) consisting of pre-whitening and non-linear orthogonal distortion. The pre-whitening is incorporated in an elegant way into the main adaptation procedure thus providing a one-stage parameter update. The derivation and analysis of the algorithm are presented in detail within the paper (Cardoso & Laheld, 1997). The final separating matrix update is given as

$$\mathbf{B}_{t+1} = \mathbf{B}_t - \lambda_t \left[\mathbf{y}_t \mathbf{y}_t^T - \mathbf{I} + g(\mathbf{y}_t)\mathbf{y}_t^T - \mathbf{y}_t g(\mathbf{y}_t)\right]\mathbf{B}_t \tag{3.17}$$

The function $g(\ldots)$ is chosen depending on the sign of the normalised fourth order cumulant of the original source signals. The normalised fourth order cumulant is also referred to as kurtosis (Stuart and Ord, 1987). Delfosse & Loubaton (1995) propose an extraction and deflation technique where the N dimensional, pre-whitened mixture is projected onto a unit norm vector. The objective function of the form of

$$H(\mathbf{g}) = \frac{E\{(\mathbf{g}^T\mathbf{x})^4\}}{4} \tag{3.18}$$

where $\mathbf{g} = [g_1 \quad g_2 \quad g_3 \quad \ldots \quad g_N]^T$ is the unit norm vector $\|\mathbf{g}\| = \mathbf{g}^T\mathbf{g} = 1$, is maximised. They prove that the extremal points $\mathbf{g}$ of (3.18) are the independent basis vectors. A deflation algorithm is developed and its performance is evaluated. The algorithm is somewhat complex and simpler, yet as effective, extraction and deflation approaches based on self organising neurons have been proposed and studied by several authors, Hyvarinen & Oja (1996), Cichocki, Amari, & Thawonmas (1996), Cichocki, Thawonmas & Amari (1997).

3.4 Conclusions

In this chapter we have considered the early work on source separation from the statistical signal processing community. The work has focused on batch type algorithms which seek to explicitly cancel out fourth order cross cumulants (Comon, 1989). This was then simplified by exploiting the invariance of cumulants when undergoing orthogonal transformations which allowed a relatively simple contrast function to be considered. This contrast, the sum of squares of fourth order marginal

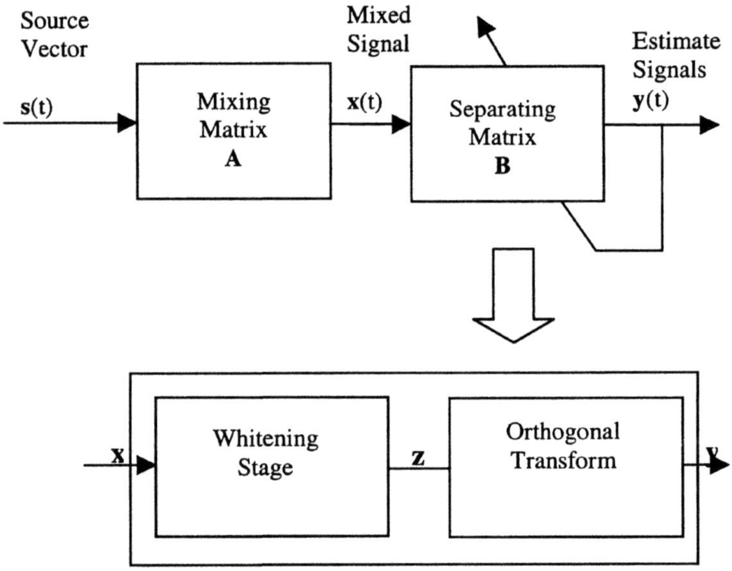

Figure 3.2: Serial Adaptation of Separating Matrix.

cumulants, allowed a significant step forward in identifying computationally tractable algorithms for source separation of large linear mixtures. The maximisation of the simplified contrast function was nevertheless still a complex operation.

The equivariant adaptive approach was a significant step forward in moving away from batch based algorithms to online adaptive algorithms. In many ways this technique has been the pre-cursor of a number of the neural network approaches to source separation. The work of Delfosse and Loubaton, (1995)[2] is of crucial importance as the maximisation of a simple criterion such as kurtosis will have extremal points which are each extracting solutions. In the following chapter various forms of self-organising neural networks will be considered along with their emergent properties. We shall see that non-linear extensions of previously studied linear neural networks have interesting and significant properties in terms of blind source separation and independent component analysis.

[2] As with the work of Cardoso and Laheld, this work was originally presented in 1993.

4. *Self-Organising Neural Networks*

This chapter focuses on self-organising neural networks with linear and non-linear activation functions. Many researchers have studied the properties of linear networks and their ability to extract or transfer information regarding the statistics of the observed data. The natural progression to non-linear networks requires alternative analysis tools due to their additional complexity. The emergent behaviour of non-linear networks is much richer than their linear counterparts. A brief review of linear and non-linear self-organising networks within the context of source separation is presented here.

4.1 Linear Self-Organising Neural Networks

This particular section introduces linear self-organising models based primarily on Hebbian style learning.

4.1.1 Linear Hebbian Learning

The aim of unsupervised learning is that when presented with raw data a neural network can make its own representation of the data. Learning in an unsupervised manner is often realised by some form of Hebbian learning. Donald Hebb (1949) postulated that:

> *'When an axon of a cell A is near enough to excite a cell B and repeatedly or persistently takes part in firing it, some growth process or metabolic change takes place in one or both cells such that A's efficiency, as one of the cells firing B, is increased.'*

Artificial neural networks which use the form of Hebbian learning are characterised by making the activation of a unit dependent on the sum of the weighted activations which feed into the unit. The network weights are adapted by a learning rule, which is dependent on the strength of the simultaneous activation of the sending and receiving neuron. Figure 4.1 shows the network model employed here. The activation of the output is then given as

$$y_i = \sum_j w_{ij} x_j \tag{4.1}$$

and in vector notation $y_i = \mathbf{w}_i^T \mathbf{x}$ where the vector representing the network input is given as $\mathbf{x} = [x_1 \ \dots \ x_N]^T$, the weight vector corresponding to the particular neuron is $\mathbf{w} = [w_{i1} \ \dots \ w_{iN}]^T$. The Hebbian weight adaptation rule for each weight in the model is then simply

$$\Delta w_{ij} = \eta \ x_j y_i \tag{4.2}$$

The term η is referred to as the learning rate and is usually a small non-negative scalar value which often varies with time. By expanding (4.2) using the expression for the activation (4.1) we start to gain an insight into the statistical nature of Hebbian learning

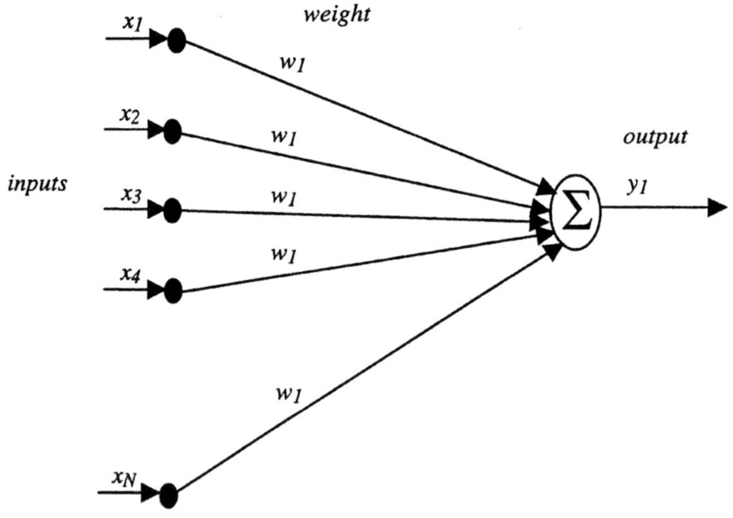

Figure 4.1: A Single Output Neural Network.

$$\Delta w_{ij} = \eta \; x_j \sum_k w_{ik} x_k = \eta \; \sum_k w_{ik} x_k x_j \tag{4.3}$$

By taking the time average of the weight adaptation we then have

$$E\{\Delta w_{ij}\} = \eta \sum_k w_{ik} E\{x_k x_j\} = \eta \sum_k w_{ik} \mathbf{C}_{kj} \tag{4.4}$$

where $\mathbf{C}_{kj}$ is the cross covariance term of the kth and j^{th} inputs. What is clear from this is that the self-organisation of the weights within the network is dependent on the statistics of the data presented to the network. As the weights adapt according to the covariance of the incoming data, the self-organisation is then driven by second order statistics. From Chapter 2, Section 2.4, it is clear that second order statistics will fully define data which is normally distributed. The self-organisation of the linear Hebbian neuron will respond only to the inherent second order statistics of the received data which indicates that the higher order statistics which may be inherent in the data are not utilised. The Hebbian adaptation rule (4.2) as it currently stands has a major deficiency in that weights will tend to grow without bound. Consider the following argument (Hertz *et al*, 1992): a matrix **A** has an eigenvector **x** with a corresponding eigenvalue λ

$$\mathbf{A}\,\mathbf{x} = \lambda\,\mathbf{x} \tag{4.5}$$

This is the standard eigenvalue equation which indicates that multiplying the vector **x** or any of its scalar multiples by **A** is equivalent to multiplying the vector by a scalar λ. So the direction of the vector **x** is unaffected; only the magnitude of the vector is changed. Consider the Hebbian learning update rule (4.2) and assume that there is a stable weight vector $\mathbf{w}^o$ which learning rule (4.2) converges to. Then

$$0 = E\{\Delta w_{ij}\} = E\{y_i x_j\} = E\left\{\sum_k w_{ik} x_k x_i\right\} = \sum_k \mathbf{C}_{ik} w_i^o \tag{4.6}$$

where $E\{\ldots\}$ denotes expectation in distribution. **C** is the input data covariance matrix computed as $\mathbf{C} = E\{\mathbf{x}\mathbf{x}^T\}$ which is a symmetric, positive semi-definite matrix which has at least one eigenvalue greater than zero. However, (4.6) indicates that the weight vector $\mathbf{w}^o$ has a zero-valued eigenvalue. If a small perturbation is added to the weights in a direction with a positive eigenvalue then $E\{\Delta\mathbf{w}^o\} = \mathbf{C}(\mathbf{w}^o + \delta) = \mathbf{C}\delta > 0$ indicating that the weights will grow in any direction with non-zero eigenvalue and as such the fixed point is unstable. Simple Hebbian learning will cause the weights of the network to grow without bound and this will be dominated by the direction corresponding to the largest eigenvalue of the data. Many researchers have proposed constrained forms of Hebbian learning in seeking weight adaptation which will have stable stationary points. (Linsker, 1986), (McClelland *et al*, 1986), (Oja, 1982), (Fyfe, 1995). From the perspective of this book we shall now concentrate on neural adaptation rules based on linear constrained Hebbian learning which will perform Principal Component Analysis (PCA).

4.1.2 Principal Component Analysis

From a statistical perspective PCA is effectively a projection method, that is a linear combination of the original data to maximise some feature of interest. PCA (Jollife, 1986) is often referred to as the Karhunen-Loeve expansion (Watanabe, 1986) which is used extensively within signal processing for data applications such as speech recognition (Parsons, 1987). If the data is represented by the P dimensional zero-mean vectors $\mathbf{x}$ which form the rows of a $N \times P$ dimensional matrix $\mathbf{X}$, where N is the number of observations of the vector $\mathbf{x}$ the singular value decomposition (Golub & Van Loan, 1989) of the matrix $\mathbf{X}$ is such that $\mathbf{X} = \mathbf{U}\Lambda\mathbf{V}^T$. Where Λ is a diagonal matrix with decreasing non-zero entries, $\mathbf{U}$ is an $N \times P$ dimensional matrix with orthonormal columns and $\mathbf{V}$ is a $P \times P$ dimensional orthogonal matrix. The principal components are then defined as the columns of the matrix $\mathbf{XV}$. The first column of the matrix is termed the first principal component and will exhibit maximum variance, the second column will exhibit the largest variance of the remaining data which is not correlated with the first column and so on. So by projecting the data observations onto the principal component directions we are maximising the variance of the data and so variance is the feature of 'interestingness' maximised by PCA. The other point to note is that the columns of the matrix $\mathbf{XV}$ are uncorrelated as the projection directions $\mathbf{V}$ are orthogonal to each other. If the data is projected onto the PCA basis such that the dimensionality of the PCA subspace is less than the dimensionality of the data, the projection is the best lower dimensional approximation to the data in the least squares sense. From an information theoretic perspective as the variance of each dimension is maximised and the cross-correlation is minimised, then for strictly Gaussian data we can see that the information transfer is maximal (2.17), (2.13). An alternative method (Press *et al*, 1988) in numerically performing PCA is to form the data covariance matrix $\mathbf{C} = E\{\mathbf{xx}^T\}$ and perform an eigenvalue decomposition such that $\mathbf{C} = \mathbf{U}\Lambda\mathbf{U}^T$ where the orthogonal matrix $\mathbf{U}$ is the matrix of eigenvectors and the diagonal matrix Λ contains the respective eigenvalues. The columns of the matrix $\mathbf{U} = [\mathbf{u}_1 \ \ldots \ \mathbf{u}_N]$ will then be the principal directions and the following properties hold

$$E\left\{ \left(\mathbf{u}_i^T \mathbf{x}\right)^2 \right\} > E\left\{ \left(\mathbf{u}_j^T \mathbf{x}\right)^2 \right\} : i < j \in 1 \ldots N \quad (4.7)$$

$$E\left\{ \left(\mathbf{u}_i^T \mathbf{x}\right)\left(\mathbf{u}_j^T \mathbf{x}\right) \right\} = 0 : i \neq j \in 1 \ldots N \quad (4.8)$$

The variance maximisation property is indicated by (4.7) and the orthogonality of projection (or decorrelation) is given by (4.8). It must be stressed that this is a linear projection and as such is optimal, in an information theoretic sense, for normally distributed data. The PCA projection does not take into account potential higher order structure within the data, nevertheless once we have an understanding of the linear PCA projection we shall consider non-linear extensions which may be potentially useful.

It was noted in Section 4.1.1 that simple linear Hebbian learning will cause the network weights to develop without bound in the direction corresponding to the largest eigenvalue of the data. With this in mind we now consider Oja's single neuron model which acts as a principal component analyser (Oja, 1982). Oja proposed the single neuron model which was a variation on the unconstrained Hebb rule and the neuron activation is identical to that of (4.1). The weights are updated and the norm of the weight vector is normalised. To find the first principal component of a data set, a projection which maximises the variance needs to be identified. In other words a learning rule is required which will adapt a neuron's weights to maximise the variance of the neuron's output activation. This will then maximise the information transferred by the neuron, in the noise-free case, for input data which is normally distributed. The variance of the output is stochastically maximised using a constrained gradient ascent technique (Oja, 1982)

$$\Delta\mathbf{w} = \frac{d}{d\mathbf{w}} E\left\{y^2\right\} \Rightarrow \tilde{\mathbf{w}}_{n+1} = \mathbf{w}_n + \alpha_n \frac{d}{d\mathbf{w}_n}\left(\mathbf{w}_n^T \mathbf{x}\right)^2, \mathbf{w}_{n+1} = \frac{\tilde{\mathbf{w}}_{n+1}}{\left\|\tilde{\mathbf{w}}_{n+1}\right\|} \quad (4.9)$$

The second step ensures that the Euclidean norm of the weight vector is unity, which means that the weight development is constrained to the unit hyper-sphere. Oja then shows that (4.9) can be approximated by

$$\mathbf{w}_{n+1} = \mathbf{w}_n + \alpha_n\left(\mathbf{I} - \mathbf{w}_n\mathbf{w}_n^T\right)\mathbf{x}\,\mathbf{w}_n^T\,\mathbf{x} = \mathbf{w}_n + \alpha_n\left(\mathbf{x}\,y - \mathbf{w}_n y^2\right) \tag{4.10}$$

It is clear from (4.10) that the constraint on the Hebbian learning is realised by the inclusion of the $-\mathbf{w}_n y^2$ term and this can be viewed as a form of negative feedback of the activation. Fyfe (1995) further develops this viewpoint of negative feedback of activation. Oja shows that the neuron weight adaptation rule (4.10) will cause the weights to converge to the first principal component of the data. Of course, if we wish to extract a number of the principal components of the data, then a series of linear neurons adapting under Oja's single neuron rule will all extract the first principal component of the data. Oja (1989) developed the PCA subspace algorithm which would allow the weights of a multiple output neuron network to converge to an orthonormal basis of the Principal Component Space. Sanger (1990) developed the Generalised Hebbian Algorithm (GHA) which introduces a form of hierarchy or asymmetry to the learning which then allowed the weights of the network to converge to the actual principal components of the data. We shall re-consider both Oja's PCA Subspace algorithm and the GHA in the light of non-linear PCA-style learning in Chapter 5. Other PCA learning rules for multiple neurons utilise linear anti-Hebbian weights connecting the output neurons (Brause, 1993; Rubner and Tavan, 1989; Palmieri 1993). Other Hebbian PCA models are considered by (Plumbley, 1991; Fyfe, 1995; Cichocki and Unbehauen, 1994). We now consider linear anti-Hebbian learning prior to a study of non-linear Hebbian and anti-Hebbian learning. As with linear Hebbian learning, we shall see that linear anti-Hebbian learning is also a form of redundancy reduction for normally distributed data.

4.1.3 Linear Anti-Hebbian Learning

The neuron model considered in Section 4.1.2 was of the feedforward type, that is, activation was propagated in only one direction. Actual biological networks are characterised by a number of recurrent connections. Based on this a number of neural network models have been developed which have activation passing in more than one direction, for example, feedforward, lateral and feedback activation. Anti-Hebbian learning is motivated by Barlow's 'law of repulsion' (Barlow, 1990), which states that a 'repulsion constant' increases between variables which are correlated.

If two cells have pre- and post-synaptic activity y_i and y_j and the synaptic strength between them is w_{ij} then the law of repulsion is governed by the anti-Hebbian rule

$$\Delta w_{ij} = -\eta \; y_i y_j \; : i \neq j \, . \tag{4.11}$$

If the activities of the cells are positively (or negatively) correlated a negative (or positive) weight will build up between them making simultaneous firing more difficult and so eliminating the positive (or negative) correlation between them. A comprehensive study of anti-Hebbian learning is given in (Palmieri *et al*, 1993). It is clear that (4.11) will act to decorrelate the activation of the neurons, thus effectively reducing the redundancy of information being passed through the network. Unlike Hebbian learning, there is no requirement for stabilising weight decay terms as this is automatically self-limiting

$$E\{y_i y_j\} \rightarrow 0 \Rightarrow E\{\Delta w_{ij}\} \rightarrow 0 : i \neq j \, .$$

Anti-Hebbian learning has been utilised at the output of a feedfoward PCA network to decorrelate the outputs and so force them to converge to differing principal components (Rubner and Tavan, 1989; Palmieri, 1993). Foldiak (1989) developed a model to study Barlow's law of repulsion. The model (a two input / output version is discussed for clarity of presentation) is shown in Figure 4.2. At convergence the output covariance matrix $\mathbf{C_{yy}}$ will be diagonal with the off-diagonal terms all being zero, thus indicating the reduction in the output correlation. The governing equation of the neuron dynamics is given as

$$\tau \frac{dy_i}{dt} = -y_i + x_i + \sum_{j \neq i}^{N} w_{ij} y_j \tag{4.12}$$

Taking the adiabatic approximation (Foldiak, 1990), (4.12) can then be written as

$$y_i = x_i + \sum_{j \neq i}^{N} w_{ij} y_j \tag{4.13}$$

and in matrix format

$$\mathbf{y} = (\mathbf{I} - \mathbf{W})^{-1} \mathbf{x} \tag{4.14}$$

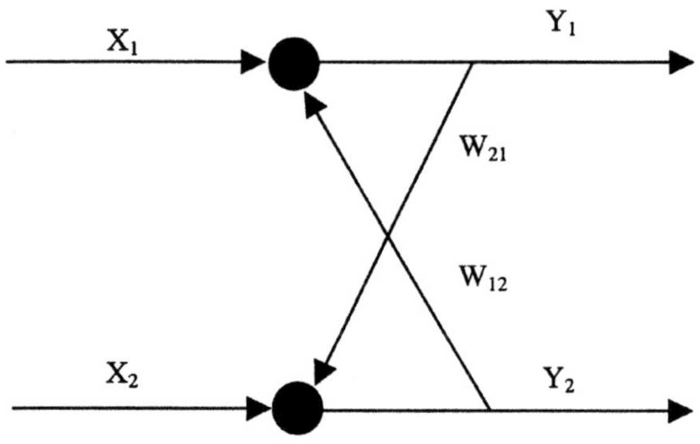

Figure 4.2: Two Neuron Version of Foldiak's Lateral Inhibition Network.

The matrix **W** has zeros on the main diagonal. Foldiak (1992) then considers an extension to the original laterally connected model by including self-connections at each neuron (Figure 4.3). Both of these linear models have special significance in the study of self-organising neural networks for blind source separation.

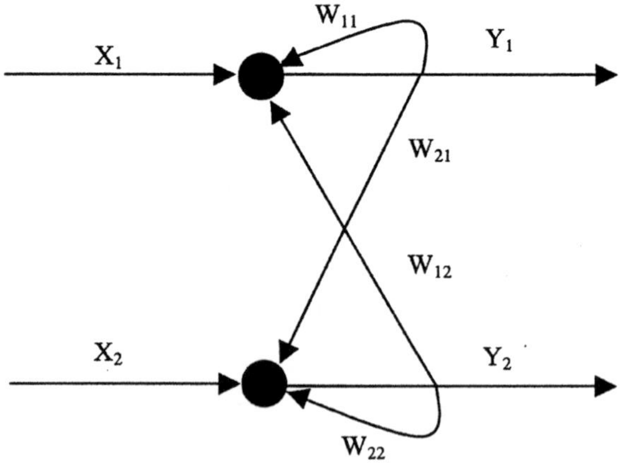

Figure 4.3: Two Neuron Version Normalised Lateral Inhibition Network.

The activation for this extended model will be as (4.14): however, the weight matrix will have non-zero entries on the main diagonal. Considering the anti-Hebbian learning of (4.11) if the covariance of the output vector is an identity matrix then

$$\mathbf{C}_{yy} = \mathbf{I} \Rightarrow \mathbf{I} - E\{\mathbf{y}\mathbf{y}^T\} \rightarrow \mathbf{0} \tag{4.15}$$

This suggests a modification to the anti-Hebbian learning of (4.11) such that

$$\Delta\mathbf{W} = \eta\left(\mathbf{I} - \mathbf{y}\mathbf{y}^T\right) \tag{4.16}$$

This will then provide decorrelated and normalised network outputs, that is, the variance of each output will be one. By considering the Kullback-Leibler divergence between two zero-mean normal distributions with covariance matrices equal to $\mathbf{C}_{yy}$ and $\mathbf{I}$, respectively, a more formal derivation of (4.16) can be given (Cardoso, 1997). Using (4.14) and (4.15) we see that the final value of the weight matrix will be related to the input data covariance matrix as

$$\mathbf{W} = \mathbf{I} - \mathbf{C}_{\mathbf{xx}}^{\frac{1}{2}} \tag{4.17}$$

The anti-Hebbian learning has required no normalisation to constrain the network weight development. What we have here is a network which will decorrelate and normalise the output data in an adaptive manner. This is sometimes termed spatial whitening or sphereing, where the mean value of the data is zero and the covariance of the data is the identity. We shall return to this when considering non-linear PCA style learning and its application to blind source separation.

In this section we have considered linear self-organising neural networks which employ both Hebbian and anti-Hebbian learning. It has been shown that constraints are required for Hebbian learning to be stable with consideration given to the single neuron rule of Oja as a principal component analyser. Mention has been made of Oja's PCA subspace rule and the GHA of Sanger. These are examples of purely feedforward networks but the point of significance is that the self-organisation of the networks considered is driven solely by the second order statistics of the data. As we have seen in Chapter 2, statistics of higher orders are required to characterise data that has non-Gaussian probability distributions. From an information theoretic or statistical perspective, linear Hebbian learning is deficient in that information regarding the data from higher order terms is not considered. Chapter 3 showed that the early approaches to blind source separation and independent component analysis required two steps. The first step removed and normalised all second order statistics within the received mixtures of signals, then utilising higher order statistics the remaining redundancy within the signals is removed. In considering linear anti-Hebbian learning, it is clear that this is stable and will provide decorrelation in a natural way, again by responding to the second order statistics within the data. We now take consideration of non-linear self-organising neural networks and consider these within the context of source separation.

4.2 Non-Linear Self-Organising Neural Networks

In this section we consider three forms of non-linear self-organising neural networks. The first network, proposed by Herrault and Jutten (1986) can be considered as a non-linear extension of Foldiak's first model of anti-Hebbian learning (Foldiak, 1989). Interestingly the classical 'neuromimetic' structure of Herrault and Jutten was proposed prior to the work of Foldiak. The 'Infomax' algorithm of Bell and Sejnowski (1995) is considered as a non-linear version of the information maximisation criterion used by Plumbley and Fallside (1988), Linsker (1992), Becker and Hinton (1992) and Atick and Redlich (1992) in developing self-organising models. The work of Bell and Sejnowski (1995) follows on from work carried out by Nadal and Parga (1994) in identifying factorial codes for maximising information transfer through neurons in the low noise limit. Although elegant, the original algorithm developed by Bell and Sejnowski has a number of shortcomings which will be discussed and considered in detail in Chapter 7. Finally non-linear extensions of Oja's PCA subspace rule are considered. We shall see that the non-linear versions possess some interesting properties which are then extended in Chapters 5 and 6. We now consider the original work of Herrault and Jutten.

4.2.1 Non-Linear Anti-Hebbian Learning: The Herrault-Jutten Network

The network structure proposed by Herrault and Jutten is identical to that shown in Figure (4.2); however the feedback weights are negative so that the output activation in matrix format is given as

$$\mathbf{y} = (\mathbf{I} + \mathbf{W})^{-1}\mathbf{x} \tag{4.17}$$

The mixing model is the noiseless version given in Chapter 2, (2.3) i.e. $\mathbf{x} = \mathbf{A}\mathbf{s}$. This structure is capable of providing estimates of the underlying source signals. Therefore the estimate of the source signals **s** is simply given as

$$\hat{\mathbf{s}} = \mathbf{y} = (\mathbf{I} + \mathbf{W})^{-1}\mathbf{x} = (\mathbf{I} + \mathbf{W})^{-1}\mathbf{A}\mathbf{s}$$

$(\mathbf{I} + \mathbf{W})^{-1}\mathbf{A} = \mathbf{I}$ provides a separating solution, however due to the permutation indetermination of source separation (Comon, 1994) then $(\mathbf{I} + \mathbf{W})^{-1}\mathbf{A} = \mathbf{P}$ is also a solution. The scaling indeterminacy will not be considered here so as to simplify the argument. The simplified two sources / two mixtures case is considered in detail in (Comon, Jutten and Herrault, 1991).

For the case where there are two sources and two observed mixtures then a separating solution exists if

$$\begin{bmatrix} 1 & w_{12} \\ w_{21} & 1 \end{bmatrix}^{-1} \begin{bmatrix} a_{11} & a_{12} \\ a_{21} & a_{22} \end{bmatrix} = \begin{bmatrix} 1 & 0 \\ 0 & 1 \end{bmatrix} \text{or} \begin{bmatrix} 0 & 1 \\ 1 & 0 \end{bmatrix}$$

$$\Rightarrow \begin{bmatrix} 1 & w_{12} \\ w_{21} & 1 \end{bmatrix} = \begin{bmatrix} 1 & a_{12}/a_{22} \\ a_{21}/a_{11} & 1 \end{bmatrix} \tag{4.18}$$

$$\text{or} \begin{bmatrix} w_{12} & 1 \\ 1 & w_{21} \end{bmatrix} = \begin{bmatrix} a_{11}/a_{21} & 1 \\ 1 & a_{22}/a_{12} \end{bmatrix} \tag{4.19}$$

As the laterally connected network can be considered as a feedback structure, then stability will require the loop gain to be less than one. This therefore makes one of the potential solutions inadmissible. Jutten and Herrault propose a weight update algorithm such that

$$\Delta w_{ij} = \alpha f(y_i) g(y_j) : i \neq j \tag{4.20}$$

where the functions f (...) and g (...) are odd and different. The term α is the adaptation rate for the algorithm. Comparing the linear anti-Hebbian learning defined by (4.11) and (4.14) with the Herrault & Jutten algorithm (4.17) and (4.20), we see that (4.20) is a non-linear anti-Hebbian learning rule, with a sign change embedded within the network weights and output activation. Now by considering (4.20) in the expectation then

$$E\{\Delta w_{ij}\}\rightarrow 0 \Rightarrow E\{f(y_i)g(y_j)\}\rightarrow 0$$

The type of functions that are considered are, for example, $f(y)=y^3$ and $g(y)=y$ which then implies that

$$E\{y_i^3 y_j\}\rightarrow 0 \text{ and } E\{y_j^3 y_i\}\rightarrow 0.$$

The learning in this case is then forcing the fourth order cross moments to zero. Remember that for pairwise fourth order independence there are three cross cumulants which require to be eliminated (2.77, 2.78, 2.79), so that this learning rule provides approximate fourth order independence. The choice of the non-linear terms in (4.20) is ad-hoc, for example the functions $f(y)=\tanh(y)$ and $g(y)=y$ may also be used.

(Comon *et al,* 1991) and (Sorouchyari, 1991) investigate the convergence properties of the algorithm and perform a stability analysis. The stability analysis for a two input, two output network (Sorouchyari, 1991) shows that there are paired equilibrium points, (4.18) and (4.19). As was shown above, these points of equilibrium are independent of the statistics of the source signals; however, the stability of the equilibrium points is dependent on the statistics of the source signals. This is a fundamental point which we shall find pervades the performance of every algorithm considered for blind source separation and independent component analysis. The stability analysis consists of introducing a small perturbation to the stationary points and considering the behaviour of the system around these points (Minorsky, 1962). By developing expressions for the time-averaged behaviour around the stationary equilibrium points, the stability can then be studied.

$$\frac{d}{dt}\delta\mathbf{W}=\mathbf{J}\,\delta\mathbf{W} \tag{4.21}$$

The terms in (4.21) correspond to the small weight perturbation $\delta\mathbf{W}$ in the converged weight $\mathbf{W}$, and $\mathbf{J}$ is the Jacobian matrix of the weight adaptation rule (4.20). It is shown (Sorouchyari, 1991) that

$$\mathbf{J} = \frac{-\alpha}{1-w_{12}w_{21}} \begin{bmatrix} 3E\{s_1^2 s_2^2\} & E\{s_1^4\} \\ E\{s_2^4\} & 3E\{s_1^2 s_2^2\} \end{bmatrix} \tag{4.22}$$

where α is the learning rate in (4.20) and $f(y) = y^3$ and $g(y) = y$. The stationary point is asymptotically stable if the eigenvalues of the matrix $\mathbf{J}$ have real parts which are negative (Minorsky, 1962). This condition ensures that any perturbations introduced to the stationary point will decay to zero.

Solving the characteristic equation of (4.22) leads to the following real valued eigenvalues

$$\lambda_1 = \frac{-\alpha}{1-w_{12}w_{21}} \left(3E\{s_1^2 s_2^2\} + \sqrt{E\{s_1^4\}\, E\{s_2^4\}} \right) \tag{4.23}$$

$$\lambda_2 = \frac{-\alpha}{1-w_{12}w_{21}} \left(3E\{s_1^2 s_2^2\} - \sqrt{E\{s_1^4\} E\{s_2^4\}} \right) \tag{4.24}$$

From these we can see that the stability conditions are

$$w_{12}w_{21} < 1 \tag{4.25}$$

$$E\{s_1^4\} E\{s_2^4\} < 9\left(E\{s_1^2 s_2^2\}\right)^2 \tag{4.26}$$

Condition (4.25) follows from the requirements that the loop gain of the network must be less than zero. Condition (4.26) is of greater significance however. Note that the fourth order cumulant for a zero-mean scalar variable is given as

$$\kappa_4 = E\{s^4\} - 3\left(E\{s^2\}\right)^2,$$

The normalised form of this measure

$$\frac{E\{s^4\}}{\left(E\{s^2\}\right)^2} - 3$$

is often termed the *kurtosis* and is used widely throughout the statistics literature as a measure of the heaviness of the tails of a distribution (Ripley, 1996). A distribution which has a negative value of kurtosis, is often referred to as sub-Gaussian as it will be flat or multi-modal. Distributions with positive values of kurtosis are termed super-Gaussian and generally tend to be heavy tailed. This will be considered further in Chapter 6.

From the measure of kurtosis, condition (4.26) indicates that the source signals require to have negative kurtosis for the separating point to be stable. (Soroucharyi, 1991) shows that only one of the stationary points will be a stable separating solution. If this condition on the source signals is not satisfied then the stable points of the learning rule are not separating solutions. What this shows is that the Herrault & Jutten network for the 2×2 case will be able to separate mixtures of sources, which have negative kurtosis, when the cubic and identity functions are used. The stability condition (4.25) shows that the stationary points are sensitive to the condition of the mixing matrix. Many other authors have attempted to extend the Herrault & Jutten network to separate large mixtures of sources and have largely failed (Bell and Sejnowski, 1995).

The stability criteria based on the condition of the mixing matrix (4.25) indicates that for poorly scaled mixtures of sources, the Herrault & Jutten network may have difficulties in converging to stable separating solutions. To make the Herrault and Jutten network more robust to badly conditioned and poorly scaled mixing, (Cichocki, Kasprzak and Amari, 1995) propose an extension to the Herrault and Jutten network. This extension introduces normalising self-connecting weights identical to those in the normalising network of Foldiak (Figure 4.3). The rationale behind the introduction of these self-connecting weights is that by normalising the scale of the network outputs the effects of ill-conditioned mixing will be counter-balanced. Simulations reported in (Cichocki, Kasprzak and Amari, 1995) suggest that the self-connections play a critical role in separating ill-conditioned mixtures. It should be noted that poor scaling of the mixtures indicates that the stability condition (4.25) becomes increasingly significant in terms of the final stability of the solution. The new update algorithm is then given as

$$\Delta \mathbf{W} = \eta\left(\mathbf{I} - f(\mathbf{y})g(\mathbf{y}^T)\right) \tag{4.27}$$

where the matrix **W** will now have variable entries on the diagonal and the functions $f(\ldots)$ and $g(\ldots)$ act component-wise on the vectors **y**, $f(\mathbf{y}) = [f(y_1) \ \ldots \ f(y_N)]^T$ and $g(\mathbf{y}^T) = [g(y_1) \ \ldots \ g(y_N)]$. This can be considered to be a non-linear extension of the whitening network algorithm (4.16). (Deville, 1996) provides a stability analysis of the Cichocki extension to the Herrault-Jutten source separation network. It is shown that for the functions $f(y) = y^3$ and $g(y) = y$, the network is capable of separating globally negatively kurtotic source signals.

Moreau and Macchi (1993[a, b]) proposed a direct, or feedforward form of the Herrault-Jutten network and learning algorithm, again the direct weights are set to one. This has the advantage that the matrix inversion required of the recurrent structure (4.13) is obviated. Cichocki, Unbehauen and Rummert (1994) and Cichocki, Unbehauen, Moszczynski, Rummert (1994), propose a fully connected feedforward (Figure 4.3) structure which has the equivariant (Cardoso, 1997) form of learning algorithm

$$\Delta \mathbf{W} = \eta\left(\mathbf{I} - f(\mathbf{y})g(\mathbf{y}^T)\right)\mathbf{W} \tag{4.26}$$

An algorithm similar in form is then developed by (Amari, Cichocki and Yang, 1995) based on the natural gradient; however the non-linear terms come from a crude approximation of the marginal entropies of the network output.

Matsuoka *et al* (1995) develop a second order learning algorithm based on the Herrault-Jutten network for separation of symmetric mixtures of non-stationary Gaussian sources. We shall re-consider this form of learning in Chapter 8 within a general Maximum Likelihood Estimation (MLE) framework. The Herrault-Jutten network and the variants proposed by Cichocki *et al* (1994) and Moreau and Macchi (1993[a]) are fundamentally seeking to explicitly cancel out the odd cross cumulants of the network output. Many non-linearities are considered and have been shown to perform well in simulations, (Cichocki, Kasprzak and Amari, 1996), and the simplest $f(y) = y^3$ and $g(y) = y$ have been analysed for stability (Sorouchyari, 1991; Deville, 1996; Macchi and Moreau, 1994). These employ a non-linear form of anti-Hebbian learning, where the non-linear activation functions explicitly introduce higher order statistics into the learning. The network in the linear case can respond only to the second order statistics within the data and so the network is insensitive to information regarding non-linear or higher order structure within the data. From an information theoretic perspective, the linear network may be transmitting information sub-optimally due to the inherent redundancy still resident within the non-Gaussian distributed data.

Prior to considering non-linear extensions of the constrained Hebbian learning algorithms for Principal Component Analysis, we shall consider a non-linear feedforward network which self-organises to maximise the amount of information passed through a non-linear neuron. The algorithm of Bell and Sejnowski (1995) will be considered as this has had a significant impact on the direction of research regarding blind source separation. Information theoretic arguments have been considered by Plumbley (1991) in designing unsupervised linear network models and algorithms to minimise information loss. Nadal and Parga (1994) investigated maximising the information transfer through non-linear neurons in the low noise limit. In the case of vanishing additive noise they concluded that maximisation of information transfer through a non-linear single layer network leads to a factorial code; Redlich, (1993) and Schuster (1992) considered maximising the information transfer through noisy non-linear neurons. This work was motivated by the hypothesis of Barlow (1961) of redundancy reduction as the first stages of sensory coding. Deco and Brauer (1994) also consider non-linear decorrelation for factorial coding and develop volume-preserving structures for higher order decorrelation. However, Bell and Sejnowski (1995) were the first to make the link between information maximisation, factorial coding and blind source separation.

4.2.2 Information Theoretic Algorithms

The fully connected single layer $N \times N$ feedforward network and neuron model (Figure 4.4) is considered by Bell and Sejnowski (1995). This is a generic structure which will also form the model of non-linear PCA style networks and algorithms. The neuron model differs from the linear one considered above in that the linear summation is followed by a non-linear function:

$$y_i = f(u_i) = f\left(\sum_j w_{ij} x_j\right) \tag{4.27}$$

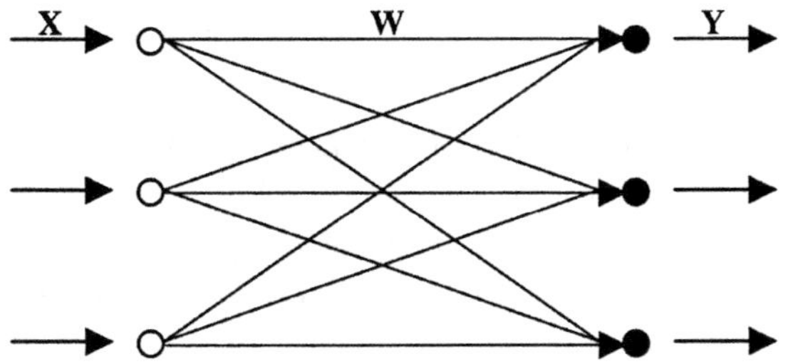

Figure 4.4: Single Layer Non-Linear Network and Non-Linear Neuron Model.

The function (4.27) for neuron models has taken the form of the McCulloch-Pitts (1943) model which is a hardlimiter or the signum function

$$signum(u) = \begin{cases} +1, & u \geq 0 \\ -1, & u < 0 \end{cases} \tag{4.28}$$

The *signum* function can be considered to be the limiting case of the hyperbolic tangent which is a saturating function. The argument presented by Bell and Sejnowski (1995) is that the choice of neuron activation function to maximise information transfer is dependent on the probability density of the data to be passed through the neuron. Based on the image processing technique of 'sampling equalisation' (Russ, 1992) a non-linearity is chosen, in the vanishing noise limit, so that the output distribution of the function is uniform. So they choose $f(u)$ such that

$$\frac{d}{du} f(u) = p_u(u) \tag{4.29}$$

the probability density of the linearly summed data is given as $p_u(u)$. The 'sampling equalisation' technique (4.29) then indicates that the optimal function is the cumulative density function (cdf) of the incoming data probability density function (Laughlin, 1981). For any normalised pdf the corresponding cdf will be bounded or saturating (Stuart and Ord, 1987). Figure 4.5 gives an example of a zero-mean, unit variance Gaussian distribution and the associated cdf defined by

$$\frac{1}{\sqrt{2\pi}} \int_{-\infty}^{u} e^{-\frac{a^2}{2}} da \tag{4.30}$$

With the cdf of the data pdf being the optimal function in terms of maximising the information transferred, the neuron function is required to be matched to the expected distribution of the signals (Laughlin, 1981). In other words the sections of high density of the pdf must be aligned with the highly sloping parts of the non-linear function (Figure 4.5).

It is clear from Figure 4.5 that a sigmoidal-type activation function will approximate the form of the cdf. Bell and Sejnowski use the logistic transfer function in the derivation of the algorithm, though other nonlinearities are also considered.

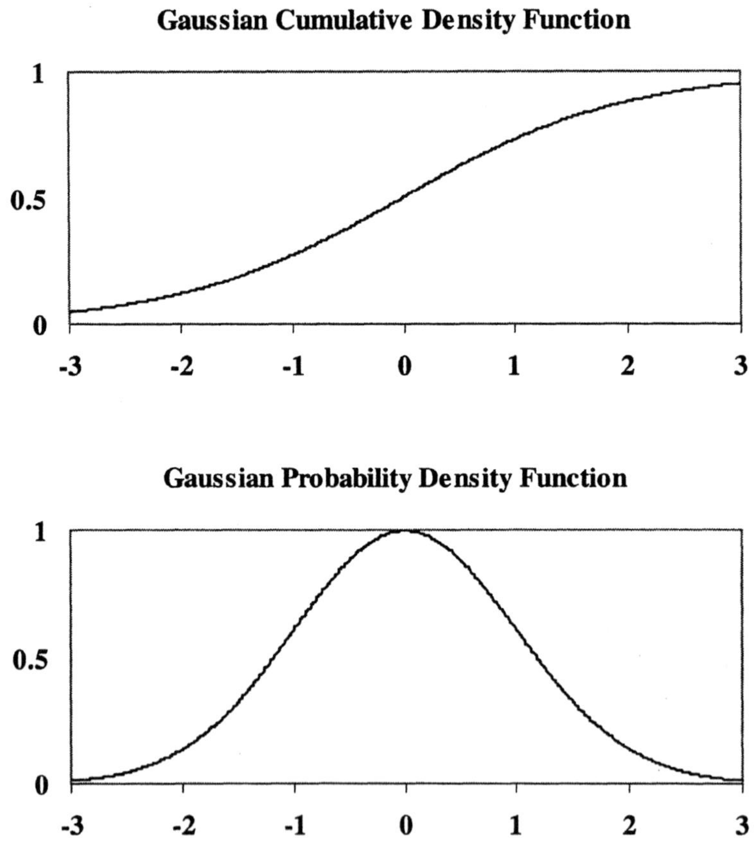

Figure 4.5: Gaussian Probability Density Function and Cumulative Density.

The multivariate probability density function of the network output is (2.37)

$$p_{\mathbf{y}}(\mathbf{y}) = \frac{p_{\mathbf{x}}(\mathbf{x})}{|J_f|}$$

providing the network is of the form $N \times N$ input / outputs i.e. the weight matrix $\mathbf{W}$ is square.

In Chapter 2 it was shown that the Jacobian of the transformation is given by (2.39)

$$J_f = (\det(\mathbf{M}))\prod_{i=1}^{N}\frac{df}{du_i}$$

if the function *f(...)* is invertible. For the network in Figure 4.4 the output of the non-linear neurons is given as

$$\mathbf{y} = f(\mathbf{u}) = f(\mathbf{W}\mathbf{x}) \tag{4.31}$$

To maximise the information transfer through the non-linear neurons we are required to consider the mutual information between the output and the input and from (2.23) we have

$$I(\mathbf{y};\mathbf{x}) = H(\mathbf{y}) - H(\mathbf{y}|\mathbf{x}).$$

As the aim of the self-organisation is to maximise the information forced through the nonlinearities of the network, Bell and Sejnowski develop a stochastic gradient ascent algorithm. The gradient of the mutual information with respect to the variable parameters, in this case the weights of the network, is given as

$$\frac{d}{d\mathbf{W}}I(\mathbf{y};\mathbf{x}) = \frac{d}{d\mathbf{W}}\left(H(\mathbf{y}) - H(\mathbf{y}|\mathbf{x})\right) = \frac{d}{d\mathbf{W}}H(\mathbf{y}) \tag{4.32}$$

The conditional entropy of the output diverges to minus infinity in the zero noise case and so we see that to maximise the information transfer through the network only the entropy at the output needs to be maximised. The derivation of the algorithm moves along the following lines. From the pdf equality (2.37)

$$\frac{d}{d\,\mathbf{W}} H(\mathbf{y}) = \frac{d}{d\,\mathbf{W}}\left(-E\left\{\log\left(p_y(\mathbf{y})\right)\right\}\right)$$

$$= \frac{d}{d\,\mathbf{W}}\left(-E\left\{\log\left(p_x(\mathbf{x})\right)\right\} + E\left\{\log\left(\left|J_f\right|\right)\right\}\right)$$

$$= \frac{d}{d\,\mathbf{W}} E\left\{\log\left(\left|J_f\right|\right)\right\}$$

The pdf of the input vector **x** is independent of **W** so the first term is removed. Utilising (2.39) gives

$$\frac{d}{d\,\mathbf{W}} H(\mathbf{y}) = \frac{d}{d\,\mathbf{W}}\left(\log\left(\det\left(\mathbf{W}\right)\right) + \log\left(\prod_{i=1}^{N} \frac{d\,y_i}{d\,u_i}\right)\right) \tag{4.33}$$

and then (Bell and Sejnowski, 1995)

$$\frac{d}{d\,\mathbf{W}} H(\mathbf{y}) = \left(\left(\mathbf{W}^T\right)^{-1} + \frac{d}{d\,\mathbf{W}}\log\left(\prod_{i=1}^{N} \frac{d\,y_i}{d\,u_i}\right)\right) \tag{4.34}$$

The rightmost term needs to be considered on an element by element basis and it is also dependent on the form of the nonlinearity chosen (4.31). In the derivation given in (Bell and Sejnowski, 1995) a bias weight is taken into consideration. By considering zero-mean input data and the hyperbolic tangent activation function, the requirement for a bias term is removed as the non-linear term and the expected value of the data will be centred about zero.

Taking

$$\mathbf{y} = \tanh\left(\mathbf{W}\,\mathbf{x}\right)$$

then

$$\frac{d}{d\,\mathbf{W}}\log\left(\prod_{i=1}^{N} \frac{d\,y_i}{d\,u_i}\right) = \frac{d}{d\,\mathbf{W}}\log\left(\prod_{i=1}^{N}\left(1 - \tanh^2\left(y_i\right)\right)\right)$$

$$\Rightarrow \frac{d}{d\mathbf{W}} \log\left(\prod_{i=1}^{N} \left(1 - \tanh^2 (y_i) \right) \right) = -2\tanh (\mathbf{y})\mathbf{x}^T$$

Which then finally gives

$$\frac{d}{d\mathbf{W}} H (\mathbf{y}) = \left(\left(\mathbf{W}^T \right)^{-1} - 2\tanh (\mathbf{y})\mathbf{x}^T \right) \tag{4.35}$$

The use of a stochastic gradient update is employed and the weight updates are finally given as

$$\mathbf{W}_{n+1} = \mathbf{W}_n + \mu_n \left(\mathbf{W}_n^{-T} - 2\tanh (\mathbf{y}_n)\mathbf{x}_n^T \right) \tag{4.36}$$

A number of comments are required concerning this algorithm. Due to the weight matrix inversion, the weight update is non-local. This means that to update a particular weight, information concerning all of the input and output neurons is required. However, in terms of the performance of the algorithm in separating mixtures of sources, the performance has been found to be good (Bell and Sejnowski, 1995) and outperforms the Herrault-Jutten algorithm in that separation of mixtures of five sources were reported in (Bell and Sejnowski, 1995).

An important point has to be made here, Bell and Sejnowski report simulations where the source signals are recordings of natural speech. The speech sources are then mixed using the linear mixing model (2.3). For demonstrative purposes this is acceptable, however, the linear mixing model for natural speech is unrealistic. Speech mixed in a natural environment (for example the 'Cocktail Party Problem') is not a linear memoryless mixture but rather a convolutional mixture of the sources. This will be studied in greater detail in Chapter 8. It is important to emphasise that a simulation which demonstrates blind source separation of linear mixtures of natural speech is at best an unrealistic 'toy' problem, in the signal processing and acoustics sense. However, this 'toy' problem will be used extensively throughout this book as it provides an effective and intuitively appealing simulation to test the various algorithms.

It is also important to consider the nature of the probability densities of the signals. We noticed in Section 4.2.1 that the Herrault–Jutten algorithm is capable of separating sources which are negatively kurtotic, in the special 2×2 case with the cubic and identity functions. Speech on the other hand, has a pdf which exhibits positive kurtosis (McDonald, 1966) and so it appears that Bell and Sejnowski's algorithm can separate sources which have the opposite sign of kurtosis from the Herrault-Jutten algorithm. Bell and Sejnowski (1995) report on the inability of their algorithm to converge to separating solutions for mixtures of sources which are negatively kurtotic. No stability analysis of the algorithm is provided, however in Chapter 7 we shall consider the issue of stability of stationary points for a different algorithm for ICA which has similar structure to that of Bell and Sejnowski. This analysis will show that the algorithm provided by Bell and Sejnowski has stable separating stationary points when the source data has positive kurtosis. Bell and Sejnowski (1995) discuss the use of a flexible sigmoid function which could be shaped to match the underlying source data pdf and thus avoid the problem of pdf mis-match. This is not developed further in their paper.

Amari, Cichocki and Yang (1995) also develop an algorithm for blind source separation of sources. They explicitly attempt to minimise the mutual information $I(\mathbf{W})$ at the output of a single layer feedforward linear network. The cost function to be minimised is given in (2.26) by using the standard Euclidean gradient and taking a Gram-Charlier expansion of the unknown probability density function to evaluate the associated marginal entropies. They arrive at a weight update equation of the form

$$\mathbf{W}_{n+1} = \mathbf{W}_n + \mu_n \left(\mathbf{W}_n^{-T} - f(\mathbf{y}_n)\mathbf{x}_n^T \right) \qquad (4.37)$$

where the function $f(\ldots)$ is given as

$$f(y) = \frac{3}{4}y^{11} + \frac{25}{4}y^9 - \frac{14}{3}y^7 + \frac{29}{4}y^3 \qquad (4.38)$$

The function (4.38) comes from the approximation of the pdf by using the Gram-Charlier expansion. However, Amari, Cichocki and Yang (1995), note that the Euclidean gradient can be replaced by the natural gradient (Amari, 1997).

$$\frac{\partial}{\partial \mathbf{W}}\Big|_{Natural} = \frac{\partial}{\partial \mathbf{W}}\Big|_{Euclidean} \mathbf{W}^{T}\mathbf{W} \tag{4.39}$$

When applied to (4.37), the above gives

$$\begin{aligned}\frac{\partial I}{\partial \mathbf{W}}\Big|_{Natural} &= \left(\mathbf{W}_n^{T}\right)^{-1}\mathbf{W}_n^{T}\mathbf{W}_n - f(\mathbf{y}_n)\mathbf{x}_n^{T}\mathbf{W}_n^{T}\mathbf{W}_n \\ &= \left(\mathbf{I} - f(\mathbf{y}_n)\mathbf{y}_n^{T}\right)\mathbf{W}_n\end{aligned} \tag{4.40}$$

The term (4.40) is then used in the discrete parameter update as in (4.35), (4.36) to finally give the learning rule of

$$\mathbf{W}_{n+1} = \mathbf{W}_n + \mu_n\left(\mathbf{I} - f(\mathbf{y}_n)\mathbf{y}_n^{T}\right)\mathbf{W}_n \tag{4.41}$$

The work of Amari, Cichocki and Yang (1995) was of particular significance in that the introduction of Information Geometric considerations (Amari, 1985) gives rise to a gradient-based learning algorithm which demonstrates the equivariant properties explored by Cardoso (1997). Bell and Sejnowski (1995b) subsequently adopt the natural gradient into their algorithm and report on improved speed of convergence during simulations. This can be attributed to the natural gradient being the optimal direction within the matrix parameter space associated with the blind source separation problem which is essentially an information theoretic problem (Amari, 1997). We also note from (4.41) that the computational problem of the matrix inversion is removed. Studying (4.41) in the context of anti-Hebbian learning it is clear that the inner term is a normalised non-linear anti-Hebbian learning rule.

Although the form of the adaptation rule (4.36) and (4.37) is similar, there is a fundamental difference between them. Bell and Sejnowski (1995) use a network of non-linear neurons in which they seek to maximise information transfer. The work of Nadal and Parga (1994), where the neuron nonlinearity for maximal information transfer is identified as the cumulative distribution of the incoming data, indicates that the neuron activation function needs to be bounded. So activation functions such as the sigmoid, hyperbolic tangent or error function are the types of admissible activation functions for the neurons considered by Bell and Sejnowski.

On the other hand the learning algorithm proposed by Amari, Cichocki and Yang (1995) can be based on linear neurons, thus giving more freedom of choice of the nonlinearity which appears in (4.41). Indeed the nonlinearity (4.38) is non-monotonic and non-saturating and so cannot be considered as a cumulative density function. In Chapter 7 we derive a similar algorithm to (4.41) from a different perspective and show the optimal form of the nonlinearity.

In this section, we have considered Bell and Sejnowski's algorithm which could be considered as a form of non-local non-linear Hebbian learning. The alternative algorithm proposed by Amari, Cichocki and Yang was reviewed and the major contribution of this work was the introduction of the equivariance property to the learning by using the natural gradient. We now consider the general form of non-linear Hebbian learning based on Oja's PCA subspace rule.

4.2.3 Non-Linear Hebbian Learning Algorithms

In Section 4.1.2 we considered principal component analysis and the neuron which acts as a principal component analyser (Oja, 1982). Although many authors have considered PCA-style neural algorithms we now concentrate on the non-linear extensions of Oja's PCA subspace rule (Oja, 1989) as developed and studied by Karhunen and Joutsensalo (1994, 1995). These non-linear extensions form an important contribution to the development of blind source separation and independent component analysis.

To recap, Oja's principal component analyser is given in (4.1). This neuron which utilises simple constrained Hebbian learning (4.10) will extract the feature best describing the incoming data in the mean square error sense. The alternative view is that it will extract the largest amount of information from the data by maximising the output entropy, with the underlying assumption that the data is normally distributed. Oja's single neuron learning algorithm can be generalised to a network with several output neurons (Oja, 1989) giving the subspace algorithm

$$\mathbf{W}_{n+1} = \mathbf{W}_n + \mu_n \left(\mathbf{I} - \mathbf{W}_n \mathbf{W}_n^T\right)\mathbf{x_n}\mathbf{x_n}^T \mathbf{W}_n \tag{4.42}$$

$$\Rightarrow \mathbf{W}_{n+1} = \mathbf{W}_n + \mu_n \left(\mathbf{x_n}\mathbf{y_n}^T - \mathbf{W}_n \mathbf{y_n}\mathbf{y_n}^T\right) \tag{4.43}$$

where the weight matrix $\mathbf{W}$ is an $N \times M$ weight matrix $\mathbf{W} = [\mathbf{w}_1 \ \ldots \ \mathbf{w}_M]$ and the weight vectors $\mathbf{w}_i$ correspond to the weights associated with the ith output neuron. The number of output neurons of the network will be either less than or equal to the number of neurons at the input, $N \geq M$. The M dimensional output of the network will then be computed as the linear projection of the input data onto the weight matrix, $\mathbf{y} = \mathbf{W}^T \mathbf{x}$. It is shown that (4.42) will learn the M dimensional subspace which spans the eigenvectors of the input data (Oja, 1992; Baldi and Hornick, 1988). If the matrix $\mathbf{W}$ has only one column then (4.42, 4.43) reduce to Oja's single neuron algorithm (4.10). Non-linear extensions of (4.42) were proposed by Oja, Ogawa and Wangviwattana (1991) replacing some of the linear terms $\mathbf{y}$ and $\mathbf{y}^T$ with nonlinearities $f(\mathbf{y})$ and $f(\mathbf{y}^T)$, where the functions acted in a component wise manner on the vectors $f(\mathbf{y}) = [f(y_1) \; \ldots \; f(y_M)]$.

However, Karhunen and Joutsensalo (1994) provide detailed derivations for the non-linear extensions of Oja's subspace algorithm (4.42). We now consider these derivations in detail.

4.2.3.1 Signal Representation Error Minimisation

The problem of representing an N dimensional vector by a non-linear projection onto a subspace of lower dimensionality M, $N \geq M$ is posed. The vector can then be represented as the approximation plus an additive error term

$$\mathbf{x} = \hat{\mathbf{x}} + \mathbf{e} = \mathbf{W} f\left(\mathbf{W}^T \mathbf{x}\right) + \mathbf{e} \tag{4.44}$$

By considering the mean square error criterion, a cost function of the weight parameters can be written as

$$J(\mathbf{W}) = \mathbf{1}^T E\left\{(\mathbf{x} - \hat{\mathbf{x}})^2\right\} = \mathbf{1}^T E\left\{\left(\mathbf{x} - \mathbf{W} f\left(\mathbf{W}^T \mathbf{x}\right)\right)^2\right\} \tag{4.45}$$

This then makes the cost (4.45) the sum of the mean square representation errors for the vector $\mathbf{x}$. By taking the instantaneous gradient of (4.45) and implementing a stochastic gradient descent, the following weight update is derived

$$\mathbf{W}_{n+1} = \mathbf{W}_n - \mu_n \frac{\partial J(\mathbf{W})}{\partial \mathbf{W}_n}$$

$$\Rightarrow \mathbf{W}_{n+1} = \mathbf{W}_n + \mu_n \left(\mathbf{x}_n \mathbf{e}_n^T \mathbf{W}_n \mathbf{f}'\left(\mathbf{x}_n^T \mathbf{W}_n\right) + \mathbf{e}_n f\left(\mathbf{x}_n^T \mathbf{W}_n\right)\right) \tag{4.46}$$

The error vector is as defined in (4.44) and the matrix $\mathbf{f}'\left(\mathbf{x}_n^T \mathbf{W}_n\right)$ is a diagonal matrix whose i^{th} entry is the derivative $f'\left(\mathbf{w}_i^T \mathbf{x}\right)$. Karhunen and Joutsensalo (1994) argue that the term $\mathbf{x}_n \mathbf{e}_n^T \mathbf{W}_n \mathbf{f}'\left(\mathbf{x}_n^T \mathbf{W}_n\right)$ appearing in (4.46) has negligible effect on the parameter development in comparison to the second term and so can be neglected.

$$\Rightarrow \mathbf{W}_{n+1} = \mathbf{W}_n + \mu_n \left(\mathbf{e}_n f\left(\mathbf{x}_n^T \mathbf{W}_n\right)\right)$$

Finally using the explicit form of the error term gives

$$\mathbf{W}_{n+1} = \mathbf{W}_n + \mu_n \left(\left(\mathbf{x}_n - \mathbf{W}_n f\left(\mathbf{W}_n{}^T \mathbf{x}_n\right)\right) f\left(\mathbf{x}_n^T \mathbf{W}_n\right)\right) \tag{4.47}$$

which is a non-linear generalisation of (4.42). This is Oja's non-linear PCA algorithm which we can see is an approximate stochastic gradient descent algorithm in minimising the mean square representation error (4.45) incurred by approximating the N dimensional vector $\mathbf{x}$ by one of lower dimensionality M.

Now consider the cost function (4.45) if the non-linear term is made an identity such that

$$J(\mathbf{W}) = \mathbf{1}^T E\left\{\left(\mathbf{x} - \mathbf{W}\mathbf{W}^T\mathbf{x}\right)^2\right\} \tag{4.48}$$

The cost function in this case is the mean square linear reconstruction error, which is minimised when the columns of the matrix $\mathbf{W}$ are the eigenvectors of the data covariance matrix (Ripley, 1996). The associated approximate stochastic gradient descent algorithm using (4.47) will then be (4.42) Oja's PCA subspace algorithm. For reasons of stability (Karhunen and Joutsensalo, 1994) the function $f(\ldots)$ needs to be a monotonically increasing function which grows approximately linearly and the hyperbolic tangent has been used extensively (Oja, Ogawa and Wangviwattana, 1991; Karhunen and Joutsensalo, 1994, 1995). We shall explore Oja's non-linear PCA algorithm and its link with blind source separation in Chapter 5. Now we examine one further form of non-linear PCA type Hebbian learning and consider the form of what has been termed Oja's Robust PCA algorithm.

4.2.3.2 Non-Linear Criterion Maximisation

Karhunen and Joutsensalo (1994) consider the specific maximisation of the objective function

$$J(\mathbf{W}) = \mathbf{1}^T E\{g(\mathbf{W}^T\mathbf{x})\} + \frac{1}{2}tr(\Lambda(\mathbf{W}^T\mathbf{W} - \mathbf{A})) \qquad (4.49)$$

where the matrix trace operator is denoted as *tr*(.). We wish to maximise the sum of the expected values of the non-linear terms under the constraint of the right hand side term which is used to bound the optimal solution of (4.49). The elements of the matrix Λ are Lagrange multipliers and the matrix $\mathbf{A}$ is the matrix whose elements are a_{ij}. The dimensionality of the weight matrix is such that the dimensionality of the outputs is less than the inputs.

Taking instantaneous derivatives with respect to the weight matrix gives

$$\frac{\partial J(\mathbf{W})}{\partial \mathbf{W}} = \mathbf{x}g'(\mathbf{W}^T\mathbf{x}) + \mathbf{W}\Lambda \qquad (4.50)$$

while instantaneous derivatives with respect to the Lagrange multipliers give

$$\frac{\partial J(\mathbf{W})}{\partial \Lambda} = \mathbf{W}^T\mathbf{W} - \mathbf{A} \qquad (4.51)$$

At the optimal value of the objective function (4.49) then

$$\frac{\partial J(\mathbf{W})}{\partial \Lambda} = \mathbf{0} = \mathbf{W}^T\mathbf{W} - \mathbf{A} \Rightarrow \mathbf{W}^T\mathbf{W} = \mathbf{A} \qquad (4.52)$$

$$\frac{\partial J(\mathbf{W})}{\partial \mathbf{W}} = \mathbf{0} = \mathbf{x}g'(\mathbf{W}^T\mathbf{x}) + \mathbf{W}\Lambda$$

$$\Rightarrow \mathbf{W}^T\mathbf{x}g'(\mathbf{W}^T\mathbf{x}) + \mathbf{A}\Lambda = \mathbf{0} \qquad (4.53)$$

Karhunen and Joutsensalo then use the optimal value of Λ in (4.50)

$$\Lambda = -\mathbf{A}^{-1}\mathbf{W}^T\mathbf{x}\,g'\left(\mathbf{W}^T\mathbf{x}\right) \tag{4.54}$$

giving for the instantaneous gradient

$$\frac{\partial J(\mathbf{W})}{\partial \mathbf{W}} = \left(\mathbf{I} - \mathbf{W}\mathbf{A}^{-1}\mathbf{W}^T\right)\mathbf{x}\,g'\left(\mathbf{W}^T\mathbf{x}\right) \tag{4.55}$$

By enforcing strict orthonormality of the weight matrices such that $\mathbf{W}^T\mathbf{W} = \mathbf{A} = \mathbf{I}$ and using the stochastic gradient ascent algorithm

$$\mathbf{W}_{n+1} = \mathbf{W}_n + \mu_n \frac{\partial J(\mathbf{W})}{\partial \mathbf{W}_n}$$

$$\Rightarrow \mathbf{W}_{n+1} = \mathbf{W}_n + \mu_n\left(\left(\mathbf{I} - \mathbf{W}_n\mathbf{W}_n^T\right)\mathbf{x}_n\,g'\left(\mathbf{x}_n^T\mathbf{W}_n\right)\right)$$

Using the function *f(...)* to denote the derivative of the function *g(...)*.

$$\mathbf{W}_{n+1} = \mathbf{W}_n + \mu_n\left(\left(\mathbf{I} - \mathbf{W}_n\mathbf{W}_n^T\right)\mathbf{x}_n f\left(\mathbf{x}_n^T\mathbf{W}_n\right)\right) \tag{4.56}$$

(4.56) is then an approximate stochastic gradient ascent algorithm to maximise a general objective function under orthonormal constraints. Fyfe (1995) discusses the effect on the algorithm convergence by the use of the optimal Lagrange values (4.54). Due to this approximation, (4.56) is not guaranteed to converge, however, in practice this has not been a major problem (Fyfe, 1995).

Both of these non-linear PCA-style algorithms (4.47) (4.56) have been found to have certain separating properties for blind source separation and their use has been reported extensively in many papers (Karhunen and Joutsensalo, 1994; Oja, 1995; Karhunen *et al*, 1997; Oja and Karhunen, 1995; Karhunen, Wang and Joutsensalo, 1995; Karhunen, 1996; Karhunen and Pajunen, 1996; Karhunen, Wang and Vigario, 1995). Both of these algorithms will be studied in detail in Chapters 5 and 6.

4.3 Conclusions

In this chapter, we have considered self-organising neural networks which utilise both Hebbian and anti-Hebbian learning and where in both cases the learning seeks to make representations of the received data in an information theoretically efficient manner. When the learning is strictly linear the representations of the data which are made by the network are also linear, for example PCA learning. However we have seen that when we move to non-linear forms of Hebbian and anti-Hebbian learning then a far richer emergent behaviour is realised. In the case of anti-Hebbian learning we find that linear learning acts to effectively decorrelate the network output and so reduces second order redundancy. Moving to the non-linear learning proposed originally by Herrault and Jutten, we find that approximate statistical independence or factorial learning can be achieved for certain types of data or signals. When considering linear Hebbian learning we find that, with suitable constraints, the learning will seek to extract the maximal amount of information from the data, in the least squares sense. Principal Component learning is seen to be the emergent property of certain Hebbian-style learning algorithms. Generalising the PCA algorithms of Oja to the non-linear extensions we shall see that the emergent behaviour is indeed richer than the linear forms. The self-organising algorithms motivated purely from information theoretic considerations have been found to perform blind source separation which is analogous to factorial learning for data generated by linear memoryless mixtures of independent sources.

5. *The Non-Linear PCA Algorithm and Blind Source Separation*

In this chapter, Oja's non-linear PCA algorithm is considered in detail. The signal separating properties exhibited by the algorithm are also studied. The non-linear PCA learning rule is an approximate stochastic gradient descent algorithm to minimise the mean square error incurred in representing a vector by a non-linear projection onto a basis of reduced dimensionality. By considering the original cost function from a differing perspective we can show that the algorithm is in fact, an approximate stochastic equivalent to the batch algorithm proposed and developed by Comon.

5.1 Introduction

The major shortcoming of applying the non-linear PCA algorithm to blind source separation is that it has been restricted, for reasons of stability, solely to the separation of sub-Gaussian sources. We present an alternative form of non-linearity which satisfies all the dynamic and asymptotic stability criteria for the algorithm. This form of nonlinearity allows a more general field of application of the non-linear PCA rule to both sub-Gaussian and super-Gaussian data. This is confirmed by extensive simulation.

5.2 Non-Linear PCA Algorithm and Source Separation

Karhunen and Joutsensalo applied the non-linear PCA algorithm to the estimation of sinusoidal frequencies within a noisy mixture as early as 1991 (Karhunen and Joutsensalo, 1991a, 1991b, 1992a, 1992b). In (Karhunen and Joutsensalo, 1994), it is shown that, for a mixture of two sinusoids in the presence of various forms of noise, Oja's non-linear PCA rule is capable of extracting the original sinusoids. They report that the standard linear PCA rule is unable to extract the underlying sinusoids. Oja (1995) considers the non-linear PCA algorithm in the case where the activation function is the hyperbolic tangent and so the algorithm is given by

$$\mathbf{W}_{n+1} = \mathbf{W}_n + \mu_n\left(\left(\mathbf{x}_n - \mathbf{W}_n \tanh\left(\mathbf{W}_n{}^T\mathbf{x}_n\right)\right)\tanh\left(\mathbf{x}_n^T\mathbf{W}_n\right)\right) \tag{5.1}$$

The algorithm is derived from the generalisation of the least squares reconstruction error (4.45). As this cost function is not directly related to an independence criterion Oja (1995) considers the fixed points of (5.1) in studying the separating ability of the algorithm. The source and mixture model we consider is that defined in Chapter 2 (2.1: 2.3). The N source signals are all zero mean and the observed mixture consists of an $N \times N$ linear memoryless mixture of the source signals. The fixed points of the averaged differential equivalent of (5.1) indicate

$$E\left\{\mathbf{x}\tanh\left(\mathbf{x}^T\mathbf{W}\right)\right\} = E\left\{\mathbf{W}\tanh\left(\mathbf{W}^T\mathbf{x}\right)\tanh\left(\mathbf{x}^T\mathbf{W}\right)\right\} \tag{5.2}$$

The linear network output is given by the vector $\mathbf{y} = \mathbf{W}^T\mathbf{x}$, which is equivalent to $\mathbf{y} = [\mathbf{w}_1^T\mathbf{x} \ \ \ldots \ \ \mathbf{w}_N^T\mathbf{x}]^T$ where each entry corresponds to the output of each neuron, and each weight vector is $\mathbf{w}_i = [\mathbf{w}_{i1} \ \ \ldots \ \ \mathbf{w}_{iN}]^T$. Using each of the expressions for the individual network outputs in (5.2) will then give the following expression for the ith column of the matrix equation (5.2).

$$E\left\{\mathbf{x}\tanh\left(\mathbf{x}^T\mathbf{w}_i\right)\right\} = E\left\{\sum_{k=1}^{N} w_{ik}\tanh\left(\mathbf{w}_k^T\mathbf{x}\right)\tanh\left(\mathbf{x}^T\mathbf{w}_i\right)\right\} \tag{5.3}$$

One solution to (5.3) is

$$E\left\{\tanh\left(\mathbf{x}^T\mathbf{w}_i\right)\tanh\left(\mathbf{w}_k^T\mathbf{x}\right)\right\} = 0 \ : \ i \neq k \tag{5.4}$$

which is satisfied if each of the network outputs are independent and each of their probability densities are symmetric. This is justified by the use of the same argument employed by Jutten and Herrault (1991). As the probability density of each zero mean signal is symmetric then the odd cumulants will be zero. The hyperbolic tangent is an odd function so (5.4) is a valid solution. This indicates that there exists a matrix **W** which makes the output of the network independent and may be an asymptotically stable limit of the averaged differential equation equivalent of (5.1), Oja (1995).

The asymptotic analysis of the non-linear PCA algorithm is developed further in (Oja, 1995). The utility of the non-linear PCA algorithm for blind source separation is reported in many papers (Karhunen *et al,* 1997; Oja and Karhunen, 1995; Karhunen, Wang and Joutsensalo, 1995; Karhunen, 1996; Karhunen and Pajunen, 1996; Karhunen, Wang and Vigario, 1995). The major shortcoming of the non-linear PCA algorithm for blind source separation is that it has been restricted to the separation of mixtures of sub-Gaussian sources. The other interesting feature of the non-linear PCA rule when applied to source separation is that the observed mixture needs to be spatially whitened. This is a fundamental point which needs to be considered.

The arguments presented (Oja and Karhunen, 1995; Karhunen *et al*, 1997) for the requirement of spatial whitening of the observed mixture prior to separation are based primarily on the observations during simulations and comparisons with the Robust PCA algorithm (4.56). The work of Cardoso (1997) and Comon (1994) indicate that the search for a separating matrix is reduced to the search for an orthogonal separating matrix if the mixture is first pre-whitened. Adaptive methods for spatial whitening of data were considered in Chapter 4 (Section 4.1.3). However, by reconsidering the cost function from which the non-linear PCA algorithm is derived we can make a more direct link with the cost function and blind source separation. This then gives further justification for the use of the non-linear PCA algorithm for the blind separation of sources.

5.3 Non-Linear PCA Algorithm Cost Function

We now re-state the assumptions which underpin the exposition of the cost function and algorithm performance. The input vectors $\mathbf{x}$ are zero mean, $E\{\mathbf{x}\} = 0$, and have identity covariance $E\{\mathbf{x}\mathbf{x}^T\} = \mathbf{I}$; the incoming data can then be referred to as spatially white. White data has common first and second moments thus allowing the learning to respond to higher order moments generated by the algorithm nonlinearities (Fyfe and Baddeley, 1995). This is an underpinning requirement for stochastic ICA as approximate independence of the network outputs is dependent on the cancellation of fourth order cross cumulants in a pair-wise manner. Returning to the cost function of (4.45) we note that the scalar valued Euclidean norm of a vector $\mathbf{z}$ is given as

$$\| \mathbf{z} \| = \left(\mathbf{z}^T \mathbf{z}\right)^{\frac{1}{2}}$$

This is the square root of the vector inner product. Applying this to the general cost function of (4.45) will then yield the following

$$J(\mathbf{W}) = \mathbf{1}^T E\left\{(\mathbf{x}-\hat{\mathbf{x}})^2\right\} = \mathbf{1}^T E\left\{\left(\mathbf{x}-\mathbf{W} f\left(\mathbf{W}^T \mathbf{x}\right)\right)^2\right\}$$

$$J(\mathbf{W}) = E\left\{\left[\mathbf{x}-\mathbf{W} f\left(\mathbf{W}^T \mathbf{x}\right)\right]^T \left[\mathbf{x}-\mathbf{W} f\left(\mathbf{W}^T \mathbf{x}\right)\right]\right\}$$

$$= E\left\{\left[\mathbf{x}^T \mathbf{x} - f\left(\mathbf{x}^T \mathbf{W}\right)\mathbf{W}^T \mathbf{x} - \mathbf{x}^T \mathbf{W} f\left(\mathbf{W}^T \mathbf{x}\right) + f\left(\mathbf{x}^T \mathbf{W}\right)\mathbf{W}^T \mathbf{W} f\left(\mathbf{W}^T \mathbf{x}\right)\right]\right\}$$

Utilising the equality $\mathbf{W}^T\mathbf{W} = \mathbf{I}$ we then have

$$= E\left\{\left[\mathbf{x}^T \mathbf{x} - f\left(\mathbf{x}^T \mathbf{W}\right)\mathbf{W}^T \mathbf{x} - \mathbf{x}^T \mathbf{W} f\left(\mathbf{W}^T \mathbf{x}\right) + f\left(\mathbf{x}^T \mathbf{W}\right) f\left(\mathbf{W}^T \mathbf{x}\right)\right]\right\}$$

Now if the linear output of the network is given as $\mathbf{u} = \mathbf{W}^T\mathbf{x}$ and the output has independent components and unit variance

$$E\{\mathbf{u}\mathbf{u}^T\} = \mathbf{I},$$

then as

$$E\{\ \mathbf{W}^T\mathbf{x}\,\mathbf{x}^T\mathbf{W}\} = \mathbf{I} \text{ and } \mathbf{W}^T E\{\mathbf{x}\mathbf{x}^T\}\mathbf{W} = \mathbf{I}$$

it is clear that the separating matrix $\mathbf{W}$ will be approximately orthogonal $\mathbf{W}^T\mathbf{W} = \mathbf{I}$. Utilising the approximate orthogonality of the weight matrix and the associative nature of matrices we can then write the cost function as

$$J(\mathbf{W}) = E\left\{\left[\mathbf{x}^T \mathbf{x} - f\left(\mathbf{u}^T\right)\mathbf{u} - \mathbf{u}^T f(\mathbf{u}) + f\left(\mathbf{u}^T\right) f(\mathbf{u})\right]\right\} \tag{5.5}$$

Consider now the form of the nonlinearity $f(\ldots)$. If we employ a polynomial or a hyperbolic function which has a cubic as the dominating element, we find an interesting form developing. We will examine the two cases of $f(\mathbf{u}) = \frac{1}{3}\mathbf{u}^3$ and $f(\mathbf{u}) = -\frac{1}{3}\mathbf{u}^3$ which are simple functions yet help to clarify the developing argument.

The positive form of the nonlinearity will be examined first giving

$$J(\mathbf{W}) = E\left\{ \left[\mathbf{x}^T\mathbf{x} - \tfrac{1}{3}\left(\mathbf{u}^3\right)^T\mathbf{u} - \tfrac{1}{3}\mathbf{u}^T\left(\mathbf{u}^3\right) + \tfrac{1}{9}\left(\mathbf{u}^3\right)^T\left(\mathbf{u}^3\right) \right] \right\}$$

Then we can write

$$J(\mathbf{W}) = E\left\{ \left[\sum_{i=1}^{N} x_i^2 - \frac{2}{3}\sum_{i=1}^{M} u_i^4 + \frac{1}{9}\sum_{i=1}^{M} u_i^6 \right] \right\} \tag{5.6}$$

We now concentrate on the case where both the input and output vectors are of the same dimension and $M = N$. Note that the observed data is spatially white and has identity covariance.

$$\mathbf{C}_{xx} = E\left\{\mathbf{x}\mathbf{x}^T\right\} = \mathbf{I}$$

This then indicates that the first term on the right hand side of (5.6) is

$$E\left\{ \sum_{i=1}^{M} x_i^2 \right\} = \sum_{i=1}^{M} E\left\{ x_i^2 \right\} = trace\left(\mathbf{C}_{xx}\right) \cong M$$

The cost function can now be written as

$$J(\mathbf{W}) = M - E\left\{ \sum_{i=1}^{M} \frac{2u_i^4}{3} \right\} + E\left\{ \sum_{i=1}^{M} \frac{u_i^6}{9} \right\} \tag{5.7}$$

We note that for a normal distribution with zero mean and unit variance, approximately 95% of the data lies within the range ± 1.93, (Fyfe, 1997). A symmetric, zero mean and unit variance super-Gaussian distribution (kurtosis value 5.0) has 93% of the data lying within the values ± 1.93. Within this range the inequality

$$\frac{2u^4}{3} > \frac{u^6}{9}$$

is valid and the quartic term dominates within (5.7). We can therefore neglect the rightmost term of (5.7) in the analysis to follow. It should also be noted that a uniform distribution (sub-Gaussian), with the zero mean and unit variance has 100% of the data lying within this particular range.

The fourth order marginal cumulant of a distribution is given as (Chapter 2, Section 2.4):

$$\kappa_4 = E\left\{u^4\right\} - 3\left(E\left\{u^2\right\}\right)^2 - 4E\left\{u^3\right\}E\left\{u\right\} + 12E\left\{u^2\right\}\left(E\left\{u\right\}\right)^2 - 6\left(E\left\{u\right\}\right)^4$$

As the data is zero mean with unit variance the first and second order moments are 0 and 1 respectively, so the expression for the fourth order marginal cumulant reduces to the much simpler form of

$$\kappa_4 = E\left\{u^4\right\} - 3$$

This being the case we can take the fourth moment as a measure of the fourth order cumulant and so the original cost function can be viewed as

$$J(\mathbf{W}) = M - \frac{2}{3}E\left\{\sum_{i=1}^{M} u_i^4\right\}$$

or $$J(\mathbf{W}) = (M - 2M) - \frac{2}{3}\sum_{i=1}^{M} \kappa_4(i) \qquad (5.8)$$

For spatially white data the cost function (4.45) can be considered as the negative sum of the marginal fourth order cumulants of the linearly transformed data. This is for the case where the activation function has a dominating positive cubic term.

When the activation function used has a negatively cubic term dominating then we have the alternative form of the cost function

$$J(\mathbf{W}) = (M + 2M) + \frac{2}{3}\sum_{i=1}^{M} \kappa_4(i) \tag{5.9}$$

Let us consider (5.8) first in attempting to interpret the recast cost function. Minimisation of $J(\mathbf{W})$ is achieved by maximisation of the term

$$\sum_{i=1}^{M} \kappa_4(i)$$

which is the sum of the fourth order marginal cumulants of the network output $\mathbf{u}$. If we impose the restriction that the sign of the normalised fourth order marginal cumulant (kurtosis) is the same throughout the original source vector $\mathbf{s}$, that is positive, then maximisation of the rightmost term will yield the same parameters as maximising the sum of the squares of fourth order marginal cumulants. The sum of squares of fourth order cumumlants is the orthogonal contrast function proposed by Comon (1994).

Considering (5.9), as above we constrain the original source vector kurtosis to be of uniform sign, in this case negative. Then minimisation of (5.9) indicates minimisation of the fourth order terms; as these are all negative we are then maximising the negative sum on the right hand side. It is clear then that minimisation of the cost function of (4.45) will minimise the contrast given in (5.8, 5.9) (depending on the sign of the source kurtosis) and so will approximately minimise the mutual information of the network outputs. This then provides an ICA or a blind separation of the mixed source signals. We now have far greater insight into how Oja's non-linear PCA algorithm can perform ICA and also the importance of the sign of the original source kurtosis when attempting to maximise the contrast. We can write (5.8) and (5.9), dropping the constant term, in the general form

$$J(\mathbf{W}) \equiv -sign(f)\sum_{i=1}^{M} \kappa_4(i) \tag{5.10}$$

Where *sign(f)* gives the sign of the nonlinearity used at each of the output neurons and

$$f(u) = \pm\frac{u^3}{3}.$$

This alternative interpretation of the minimisation of the signal representation error criterion is valid only for observed data which is zero-mean and spatially white.

If we re-consider the expression for the mutual information of a vector (3.8) and follow through the processing stages for the non-linear PCA algorithm the link with independent component analysis becomes quite explicit. The mutual information within a vector has been defined as

$$I(\mathbf{y}) = J(\mathbf{y}) - \sum_{i=1}^{M} J_i(y_i) + \frac{1}{2}\log\frac{\prod_{i=1}^{N}\mathbf{C}_{\mathbf{yy}(ii)}}{\det(\mathbf{C}_{\mathbf{yy}})}$$

Now as discussed in Chapter 3, Section 3.2, spatial whitening removes the second order correlations within the data and normalises the individual variance to unity. This then reduces the mutual information within the vector and so the remaining redundancy within the vector is the difference between the multivariate negentropy and the sum of the marginal negentropies.

$$I(\mathbf{y}) = J(\mathbf{y}) - \sum_{i=1}^{N} J_i(y_i)$$

In Chapter 2, Section 2.3, it was shown that differential entropy (and so negentropy) is invariant under orthogonal transformations and as such

$$I(\mathbf{y}) = J(\mathbf{x}) - \sum_{i=1}^{N} J_i(y_i) \text{ where } \mathbf{y} = \mathbf{W}^T\mathbf{x} : \mathbf{W}^T\mathbf{W} = \mathbf{I}.$$

This then indicates that the negative sum of the marginal negentropies is the variable component of the mutual information. Now using the Edgeworth expansion of the underlying probability distributions we can approximate the negentropy, which then leads to the simple approximation of the mutual information. The major assumption here is that the probability densities are more or less symmetric so that the third order cumulant terms within the expansion can be removed.

$$I(\mathbf{y}) = -\sum_{i=1}^{M}\frac{1}{48}(\kappa_4(i))^2 \tag{5.11}$$

Comparing (5.10) and (5.11) we can see that the cost function of (4.45) can now be interpreted as an information theoretic contrast for ICA. We also note that the requirement for white input data corresponds to the first step of Comon's algorithm, that is covariance diagonalisation. The stochastic weight update

$$\mathbf{W}_{n+1} = \mathbf{W}_n + \mu_n\left(\left(\mathbf{x}_n - \mathbf{W}_n\, f\left(\mathbf{W}_n{}^T\mathbf{x}_n\right)\right)f\left(\mathbf{x}_n^T\mathbf{W}_n\right)\right)$$

now provides the approximation to an orthogonal rotation which seeks to minimise the contrast (5.10). The parallel with the second step of Comon's algorithm, using a Givens rotation (3.3) to minimise (5.11) is now apparent. The beauty of applying Oja's non-linear PCA algorithm to source separation is the online adaptive manner in which the mutual information at the output of the network is minimised. It is worth noting that the correct minimisation of the cost function (4.45) is dependent on matching the sign of the dominating cubic nonlinearity used in the algorithm and the underlying source signal kurtosis. This indicates that (5.10) can also be written as follows

$$\begin{aligned} J(\mathbf{W}) &\equiv \sum_{i=1}^{M}\left(-sign\left(f_i\right)\kappa_4(i)\right) \\ &\equiv \sum_{i=1}^{M}\left(-sign\left(\kappa_4(i)\right)\kappa_4(i)\right) \\ &\equiv -\sum_{i=1}^{M}\left|\kappa_4(i)\right| \end{aligned}$$

So **W** as a solution of

$$\arg\min\left(-\sum_{i=1}^{M}\left|\kappa_4(i)\right|\right)$$

is also a solution of

$$\arg\min\left(-\sum_{i=1}^{M}\left(\kappa_4(i)\right)^2\right)$$

which is similar to minimisation of (5.11), the approximate mutual information. We can see that by correctly choosing the sign of the dominating cubic nonlinearity to match the sign of the kurtosis of each individual source signal makes the cost function equivalent to the sum of the absolute values of the output kurtosis. This then indicates that the cost function would be insensitive to the sign of the individual source signal kurtosis. This will be explored more fully in the next section when we seek to remove the restriction that all the sources are required to have the same type of probability density (Oja, 1995).

We have shown that Oja's non-linear PCA algorithm can be considered as approximate minimisation of an information theoretic contrast function subject to certain pre-processing of the data. This gives further justification for the use of the non-linear PCA algorithm in performing blind separation of source signals and complements the analysis in (Oja, 1995). The simulations which have been reported in (Karhunen *et al*, 1997; Oja and Karhunen, 1995; Karhunen, Wang and Joutsensalo, 1995; Karhunen, 1996; Karhunen and Pajunen, 1996; Karhunen, Wang and Vigario, 1995) have reported on separation of mixtures of sources which have sub-Gaussian probability density functions, that is, data which is negatively kurtotic. Typical data used within the simulations are simple periodic functions such as sinusoids, digital communications data and natural images. These all exhibit sub-Gaussian densities and the non-linear PCA algorithm using the hyperbolic tangent has been found to perform well in separating mixtures of such sources. It has been reported in (Karhunen, 1996) that the non-linear PCA algorithm is restricted to the separation of mixtures of solely sub-Gaussian sources for reasons of algorithmic stability. We can now see that the algorithm will maximise the sum of the absolute values of the source data kurtosis indicating that mixtures of either sub-Gaussian sources, mixtures of super-Gaussian sources, or mixtures of both types of sources may be able to be separated. We need to identify a suitable activation function which will provide both dynamic algorithmic stability during adaptation and asymptotic stability of the stationary points which are separating solutions.

5.4 Non-Linear PCA Algorithm Activation Function

In this section we wish to identify an activation function which, when taken as the nonlinearity used within Oja's non-linear PCA algorithm, will cause convergence of the algorithm during learning for general mixtures of data. We wish to extend the range of data which can be reliably separated from a mixture to include mixtures of super-Gaussian data. Mixtures which contain both super-Gaussian and sub-Gaussian sources are also desired to be accommodated. This range of data then makes the non-linear PCA algorithm a generic and therefore potentially far more attractive tool for blind source separation problems. We are required to consider the stationary points of the time averaged differential equivalent of the non-linear PCA algorithm. By studying the nature of these points and the criteria which may be required to be met for asymptotic stability of these points, we may be able to identify a generic form of activation function for the algorithm.

5.4.1 Asymptotic Stability Requirements

In considering the asymptotic stability, Oja (1995) starts from the non-linear PCA rule and performs a linear transformation of the weight matrix. Assume that the square $N \times N$ separating matrix $\mathbf{B}$ exists. Now, as has been discussed in Section 5.3, the input data is spatially white: $E\{\mathbf{xx}^T\} = \mathbf{I}$. If there exists a square separating matrix such that the linear outputs of the network are independent and retain the unit variance such that $E\{\mathbf{yy}^T\} = \mathbf{I}$ and $\mathbf{y} = \mathbf{B}^T\mathbf{x}$ then this implies that the separating matrix is orthogonal:

$$\mathbf{I} = E\left\{\mathbf{yy}^T\right\} = E\left\{\mathbf{B}^T\mathbf{xx}^T\mathbf{B}\right\} = \mathbf{B}^T\mathbf{B} \Rightarrow \mathbf{B}^{-1} = \mathbf{B}^T$$

The non-linear PCA algorithm is then transformed by multiplying both sides of the equation by the transpose of the separating matrix $\mathbf{B}$, and so

$$\mathbf{B}^T\mathbf{W}_{n+1} = \mathbf{B}^T\mathbf{W}_n + \mu_n\left(\left(\mathbf{B}^T\mathbf{x}_n - \mathbf{B}^T\mathbf{W}_n\, f\left(\mathbf{W}_n{}^T\mathbf{x}_n\right)\right)f\left(\mathbf{x}_n^T\mathbf{W}_n\right)\right)$$

$$\Rightarrow \mathbf{B}^T\mathbf{W}_{n+1} = \mathbf{B}^T\mathbf{W}_n + \mu_n\left(\left(\mathbf{B}^T\mathbf{x}_n - \mathbf{B}^T\mathbf{W}_n\, f\left(\mathbf{W}_n{}^T\mathbf{B}\mathbf{B}^T\mathbf{x}_n\right)\right)f\left(\mathbf{x}_n^T\mathbf{B}\mathbf{B}^T\mathbf{W}_n\right)\right)$$

Using the notation for the composite matrix $\mathbf{S}_n = \mathbf{B}^T\mathbf{W}_n$ the transformed non-linear PCA rule is then

$$\mathbf{S}_{n+1} = \mathbf{S}_n + \mu_n\left(\left(\mathbf{y}_n - \mathbf{S}_n f\left(\mathbf{S}_n{}^T\mathbf{y}_n\right)\right)f\left(\mathbf{y}_n^T\mathbf{S}_n\right)\right) \tag{5.12}$$

The form of (5.12) is a transformed version of the non-linear PCA rule. The limit of convergence of the difference equation (5.12) is among the asymptotically stable solutions of the averaged differential equivalent. The difference equation can then be analysed further by considering the time averaged equivalent, (Oja, 1983).

By averaging (5.12) with respect to the individual densities of $\mathbf{y}$, and using the notation $\mathbf{Z} = \mathbf{Z}(t)$ as the continuous counterpart of the transformed weights in (5.12) the following expression is given

$$\frac{d\mathbf{Z}}{dt} = E\left\{\mathbf{y}\, f\left(\mathbf{y}^T\mathbf{Z}\right)\right\} - \mathbf{Z}\, E\left\{f\left(\mathbf{Z}^T\mathbf{y}\right)f\left(\mathbf{y}^T\mathbf{Z}\right)\right\} \tag{5.13}$$

Remember that $\mathbf{S}_n = \mathbf{B}^T \mathbf{W}_n$ where **B** is a separating matrix and so the time averaged equivalent matrix **Z**, at a separating solution, will be a diagonal matrix given as

$$\mathbf{Z} = \begin{bmatrix} \alpha_1 & 0 & \cdots & 0 \\ 0 & \alpha_2 & 0 & \vdots \\ \vdots & 0 & \ddots & 0 \\ 0 & \ldots & 0 & \alpha_N \end{bmatrix}$$

Due to the inherent indeterminacy of the ICA transformation the matrix **Z** could equally well be a permutation. For simplicity and clarity of exposition the diagonal case only is considered; it should be noted that the stationary conditions are unaltered if the stationary points are permuted to **PZ** (Oja, 1995).

Oja (1995) shows that the separating matrix **Z** is indeed a stationary point of the averaged differential equation (5.13) this is done by simply considering the equilibrium point

$$\frac{d\mathbf{Z}}{dt} = 0 \Rightarrow E\{\mathbf{y}\, f\left(\mathbf{y}^T \mathbf{Z}\right)\} = \mathbf{Z}\, E\{f\left(\mathbf{Z}^T \mathbf{y}\right) f\left(\mathbf{y}^T \mathbf{Z}\right)\}$$

The i,j^{th} element is then

$$E\{y_i\, f(\alpha_j y_j)\} = \alpha_i\, E\{f(\alpha_i y_i) f(\alpha_j y_j)\} \tag{5.14}$$

By making the following assumptions

1. The zero-mean vector **y** has a symmetrical density and that $E\{\mathbf{y}\} = 0$

2. The elements of the vector **y** are statistically independent $\mathbf{y} = [\, y_1 \;\; \ldots \;\; y_N \,]^T$

3. The function $f(\ldots)$ is odd for all y, and at least twice differentiable

Oja is then able to show that (5.14) is indeed a stationary point of (5.13). Using perturbation analysis Oja examines the stability of the stationary point (Oja, 1995). The important results are as follows :-

1. The non-linear activation function $f(\ldots)$ and the probability density of the vector **y** are such that they both satisfy the following condition

$$A_i = E\left\{y_i^2 f^{'}(\alpha_i y_i)\right\} - 2\alpha_i\, E\left\{f(\alpha_i y_i) f^{'}(\alpha_i y_i) y_i\right\} - E\left\{f^2(\alpha_i y_i)\right\} < 0 \tag{5.15}$$

The scalar values α_i , $i = 1, \ldots, N$ also satisfy the stationary point condition, which is

$$E\left\{y_i f\left(\alpha_j y_j\right)\right\} = \alpha_i\, E\left\{f\left(\alpha_i y_i\right) f\left(\alpha_j y_j\right)\right\}$$

and for the case where the index $i = j$ then

$$E\left\{y_i f\left(\alpha_i y_i\right)\right\} = \alpha_i\, E\left\{f^2\left(\alpha_i y_i\right)\right\} \tag{5.16}$$

2. The eigenvalues of the following 2×2 matrix has strictly negative real parts

$$\begin{bmatrix} E\left\{y_i^2\right\}E\left\{f^{'}\left(\alpha_j y_j\right)\right\} - \alpha_i\, E\left\{f^{'}\left(\alpha_j y_j\right)\right\}E\left\{y_i\, f\left(\alpha_i y_i\right)\right\} - E\left\{f^2\left(\alpha_j u_j\right)\right\} & -\alpha_i\, E\left\{f^{'}\left(\alpha_i y_i\right)\right\}E\left\{y_j\, f\left(\alpha_j y_j\right)\right\} \\ -\alpha_j\, E\left\{f^{'}\left(\alpha_j y_j\right)\right\}E\left\{y_i f\left(\alpha_i y_i\right)\right\} & E\left\{y_j^2\right\}E\left\{f^{'}\left(\alpha_i y_i\right)\right\} - \alpha_j\, E\left\{f^{'}\left(\alpha_i y_i\right)\right\}E\left\{y_j f\left(\alpha_j y_j\right)\right\} - E\left\{f^2\left(\alpha_i u_i\right)\right\} \end{bmatrix} \tag{5.17}$$

A further simplification can be made by constraining the probability densities of each of the components of the vector **y** to have a similar form. It is then shown (Oja, 1995) that the largest eigenvalue of the above matrix is given by the following expression (for the case where the coefficients of the diagonal matrix **Z** are all positive)

$$\lambda_{Max} = E\left\{y^2\right\}E\left\{f^{'}(\alpha\, y)\right\} - E\left\{f^2(\alpha\, y)\right\} < 0$$

Oja does not consider the more general case where the probability densities of the components of the vector **y** are not identical in nature. If it is possible to identify an activation function which satisfies the stability criteria given above for super-Gaussian sources, then we will have generalised the non-linear PCA rule to mixtures of either sub-Gaussian sources or mixtures of super-Gaussian sources. It would be attractive to consider the more general situation where the observed mixtures consist of both sub- and super-Gaussian sources. To consider this situation we are required to compute the eigenvalues of the matrix (5.17). We shall first of all consider the situation where the sources all have the same form of probability distribution.

The hyperbolic tangent has been shown to satisfy the stability criteria (4) and (5) for strictly sub-Gaussian sources (Oja, 1995). This has also been corroborated through extensive simulations reported in many papers such as in (Karhunen *et al*, 1997; Oja and Karhunen, 1995; Karhunen, Wang and Joutsensalo, 1995; Karhunen, 1996; Karhunen and Pajunen, 1996; Karhunen, Wang and Vigario, 1995). If we consider the case where the sources are super-Gaussian and have kurtosis values greater than zero, it has been shown (Oja, 1995) that the polynomial $f(y) = y^3$ will satisfy the asymptotic stability criteria. Condition (3) is satisfied as the cubic function is odd and increasing and is twice differentiable. From (5.16) using the cubic term we have at a stationary point

$$E\{y^4\} = \alpha^3 E\{y^6\}$$

Substituting this into (5.15) then we see that the condition is always satisfied. Substituting this into the expression for the largest eigenvalue

$$\lambda_{Max} = E\{y^2\}E\{f'(\alpha y)\} - E\{f^2(\alpha y)\} < 0$$

then gives the condition

$$E\{y^4\} - 3E\{y^2\}^2 > 0.$$

This is the expression for the fourth order cumulant of a zero-mean variable and, as we are considering data which is spatially white, this is a measure of the kurtosis of the variable. The variable is then positively kurtotic or super-Gaussian. This indicates that if the simple cubic polynomial is used as the non-linear term within the averaged differential equation (5.12) and the independent components of the data are all super-Gaussian, then the separating matrix is an asymptotically stable point of the learning. However there is a problem with this conclusion in terms of practical implementation.

The asymptotic stationary points have been considered and we need to consider the dynamic stability of the weight update equation as well. Karhunen and Joutsensalo (1994) show that the non-linear PCA algorithm is stable if the nonlinearity is an odd function which grows at most linearly. Although the cubic polynomial is odd, its use within the non-linear PCA algorithm introduces instability to the learning. Choosing a suitably small value of the learning rate can, in some cases, counteract this instability. However, Karhunen and Joutsensalo (1994) report that a suitable choice of the learning rate for functions which are growing faster than linearly is difficult and instability is the inevitable outcome for a function such as $f(y) = y^3$. For these reasons the non-linear PCA algorithm has been restricted to separation of mixtures of sub-Gaussian sources. The hyperbolic tangent obeys the dynamic stability requirements and the asymptotic stability requirements. It is clear that for dynamic stability of learning we require almost linear growth for our activation function. Yet for separation of sources, non-linearities such as the hyperbolic tangent are required to implicitly generate higher order statistics. Consider then a function which is the summation of a series of odd polynomials

$$f(y) = \sum_{i=0}^{\infty} a_i \, y^{2i+1}$$

Amongst many others, the following odd function conforms to the above form.

$$f(y) = y + \tanh(\beta y) \tag{5.18}$$

The value of β can take values in the set of real numbers. The characteristics of a non-linearity of the form of (5.18) are governed largely by the value of the multiplicative constant embedded within the hyperbolic tangent. Let us then chart the function (5.18) for a range of values of the multiplicative constant β. Figure 5.1, shows the form of the activation function when the multiplicative constant takes positive values of +0.5, +1.0, +5.0, +100.0. It is clear that for small values of β the overall characteristic of the function is of a linear increasing nature. This is largely due to the domination of the linear term and the observation that for $0 < \beta < 0.6$ then $\tanh(\beta y) \cong \beta y$. So, as can be seen from the first two charts, for small positive values of β then the function behaves in an almost linear manner $f(y) \cong (1+\beta)y$. The next two charts show that when β is in the approximate range $0.9 < \beta < 6$ for absolute values of the variable y greater than two the function acts almost linearly.

What is more interesting is the behaviour within this range. As the value of β increases then the hyperbolic tangent tends to its limiting value, which is the signum function, $\beta \rightarrow \infty \Rightarrow \tanh(\beta y) \rightarrow signum(y)$. This has the effect of introducing a small change in gradient at small values of the variable y.

Consider now the form of the function when the multiplicative constant takes a range of negative values. Figure 5.2 shows the function behaviour for the range of values of β -0.5, -1.0, -5.0, -100. For small negative values of β the behaviour is somewhat similar to that when β takes on small positive values. However, when β takes the value -1 we can see that there is a flat region where small values are 'squashed' yet the overall function is still monotonically increasing. After this point the function takes on a non-monotonic nature within the approximate range -1 and $+1$. In the analysis, which is to follow, we shall see that this form of function has quite significant properties when applied to the non-linear PCA algorithm. Firstly, it is clear that the function increases approximately linearly for certain values of the multiplication constant. The significant exception is when the function loses its monotonic nature for $\beta < -1$ and indeed for certain small values of the variable the function is decreasing. We can expect the function to be 'well behaved' in terms of dynamic stability during weight adaptation when $-1 \leq \beta$. We now consider in more detail the effect of the form of the activation function (5.18) on the emergent properties of the non-linear PCA algorithm.

5.4.2 Stability Properties of the Compound Activation Function

We now consider the effects of the shaping parameter β on the emergent properties of the non-linear PCA algorithm. Section 5.4 considered the asymptotic stability criteria for the weight matrix to converge to a separating solution. Oja (1995) has given certain criteria which, if met, will satisfy the requirements of asymptotic stability of a separating solution (5.15, 5.16, and 5.17). Let us first of all consider the range of values for β. For small positive and negative values $\beta = \pm 0.1$ Figures 5.1 and 5.2 show the almost linear nature of the function within the limits considered.

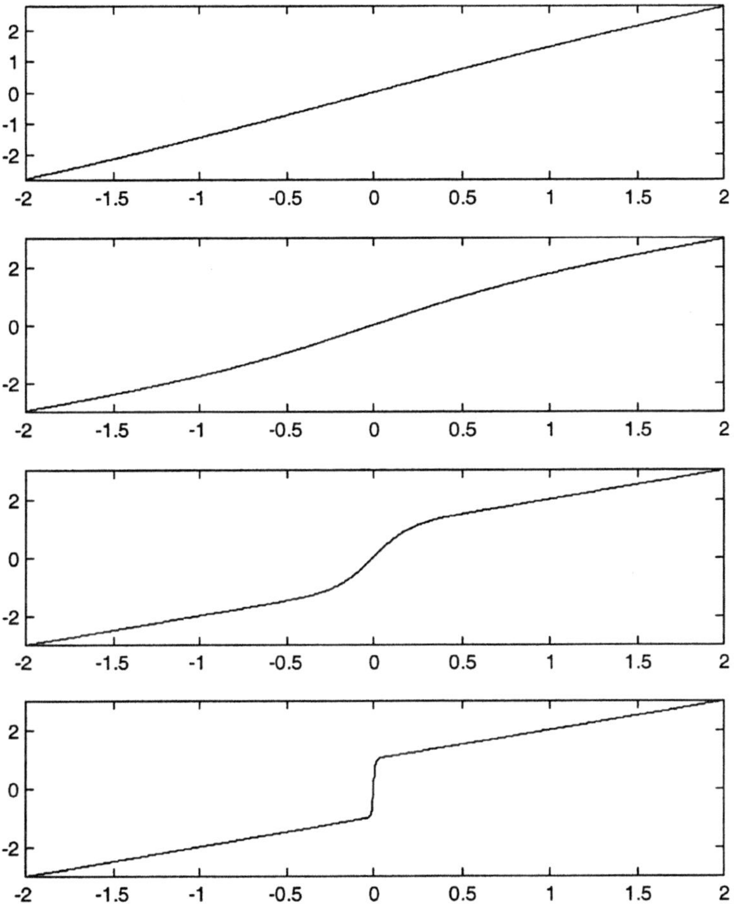

Figure 5.1: Compound Activation Function with Positive Scaling Constant.

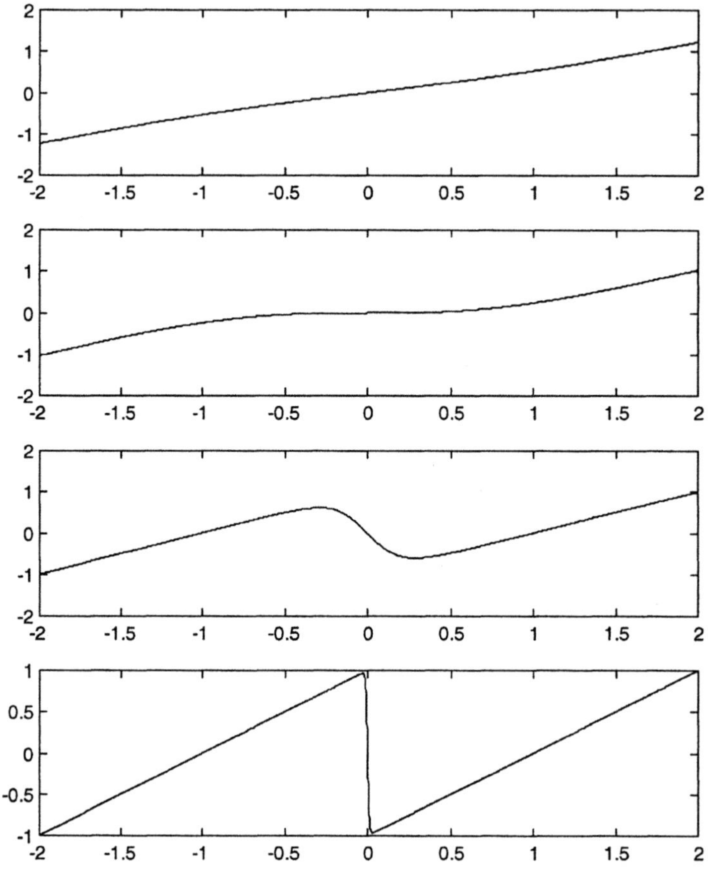

Figure 5.2: Compound Activation Function with Negative Scaling Constant.

The truncated Taylor series expansion of the hyperbolic function can be written as

$$\tanh(y) \cong y - \frac{y^3}{3} + \frac{2y^5}{15} - \dots \tag{5.19}$$

and so the overall compound function under consideration is then

$$y + \tanh(\beta y) \cong y + \beta y - \frac{\beta^3 y^3}{3} + \frac{2\beta^5 y^5}{15} - \dots \tag{5.20}$$

It is clear that for small values of β (5.20) will tend to a scalar multiple of the underlying variable that is $y + \tanh(\beta y) \cong (1 \pm \beta)y$ as the higher order terms will tend to insignificant values. This being the case we would expect the behaviour of the non-linear PCA algorithm to be identical to the linear version, which is Oja's PCA subspace algorithm (4.42). We see that from the asymptotic stability criteria outlined in Section 5.4, for sources which have similar forms of pdf then the criterion (5.17), can be reduced to

$$\lambda_{Max} = E\{y^2\}E\{f'(\alpha y)\} - E\{f^2(\alpha y)\} < 0$$

So for the case where the activation function is approximately linear we see that the largest eigenvalue of (5.17) is required to satisfy the inequality, for the case $E\{y^2\} = 1$,

$$\lambda_{Max} = E\{y^2\}(1 \pm \beta)\alpha - (1 \pm \beta)^2 \alpha^2 E\{y^2\} < 0$$

From (5.16) $\alpha = \dfrac{1}{\sqrt{1 \pm \beta}}$

$$\Rightarrow \beta \to 0 \Rightarrow \lambda_{Max} \to 0$$

This indicates that for small values of β the asymptotic stability criterion is not satisfied, and so a separating matrix will not be an asymptotically stable solution of the learning.

As the value of β increases so that the non-linear part of the function becomes active (Figures 5.1, 5.2) then we can see that the non-linear terms of the Taylor expansion will start to take on increasingly significant values. Oja (1995) has shown that the hyperbolic tangent satisfies the asymptotic stability criteria for a separating solution of the non-linear PCA rule when the underlying sources are strictly sub-Gaussian. Let us consider the case of (5.18) where the values of β takes on strictly positive values.

5.4.3 Stability of Solution with Sub-Gaussian Sources

By taking two independent sources of uniformly[1] distributed data we can then numerically test the asymptotic stability of the learning when the activation function (5.18) is utilised for positive values of β. Following Oja, (1995) we assume that the diagonal terms of the matrix **Z** have values of unity in this case. The following argument also holds for differing valid values of α in the matrix **Z**, (Oja, 1995), however the use of (5.16) allows numerical computation for the value of α for varying independent densities of data. As we have two independent, uniformly distributed signals we can use these distributed values in computing the expected terms of the matrix (5.17) and so the associated eigenvalues. By varying the values of β within the nonlinearity (5.18) we can assess the range of stability of the algorithm for differing forms of the activation function. As an indication let us consider the expression for the maximum eigenvalue when the probability distribution of both sources is either strictly sub-Gaussian or super-Gaussian

$$\lambda_{Max} = E\left\{y^2\right\}E\left\{f'(\alpha y)\right\} - E\left\{f^2(\alpha y)\right\} < 0$$

We consider the specific case where $\beta > 0$. Substituting the form of (5.18) into the above gives the following after some algebra

$$\begin{aligned}\lambda_{Max} = &\left(\alpha(1+\beta) - \alpha^2\right)E\left\{y^2\right\} - \\ &E\left\{\tanh^2(\alpha\beta y)\right\}\left(\alpha\beta E\left\{y^2\right\} + 1\right) - \\ &2\alpha E\left\{y\tanh(\alpha\beta y)\right\}\end{aligned} \tag{5.21}$$

When $\beta = 1$, and noting that the variance of the output is unity, (5.21) is given as

$$\lambda_{Max} = 1 - 2E\left\{\tanh^2(y) + y\tanh(y)\right\}$$

[1] The uniform distribution is defined herein as sub-Gaussian as it has a negative value of kurtosis and negligible skewness.

The function $\tanh^2(y) + y\tanh(y)$ is graphed in Figure 5.3. Super-Gaussian distributions such as the Laplacian or Hyperbolic-Cauchy distribution, which are symmetric and sharply peaked at the origin, exhibit decreasing values as the distribution moves from the origin. From Figure 5.3, it is clear that for a super-Gaussian density $E\{\tanh^2(y) + y\tanh(y)\}$ will tend to a small value. For a sub-Gaussian density which may be uniform or bi-modal about the origin then $E\{\tanh^2(y) + y\tanh(y)\}$ will take on a far larger value.

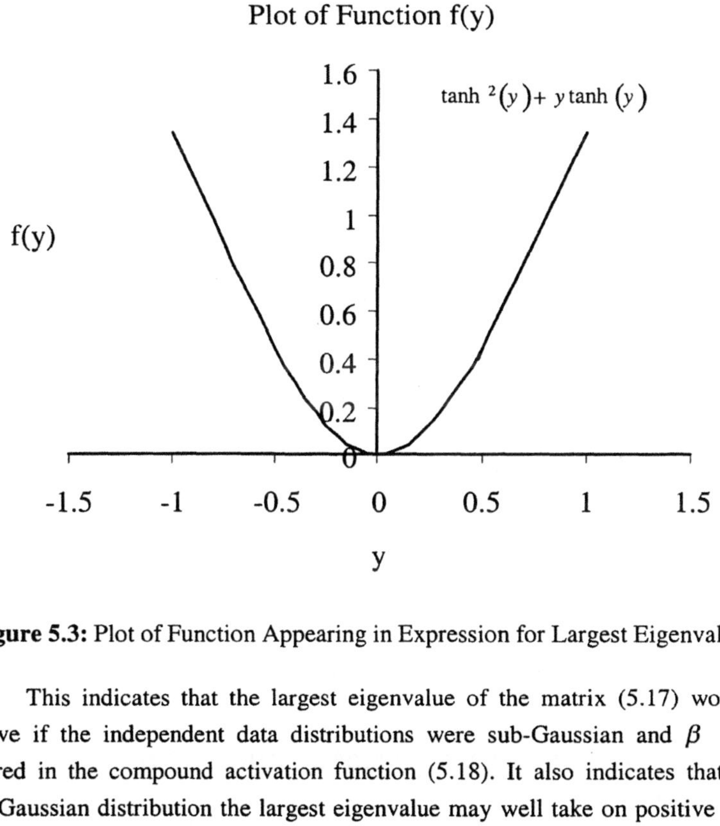

Figure 5.3: Plot of Function Appearing in Expression for Largest Eigenvalue.

This indicates that the largest eigenvalue of the matrix (5.17) would be negative if the independent data distributions were sub-Gaussian and $\beta = 1$ appeared in the compound activation function (5.18). It also indicates that for a super-Gaussian distribution the largest eigenvalue may well take on positive values and so a separating solution for super-Gaussian sources may not be stable. To further investigate this we can compute the eigenvalues of the matrix (5.17) for varying values of β, in other words differing shapes of the compound activation function (5.18). We use the values of 5000 data points drawn independently from two uniform distributions. Both distributions are zero-mean and have a kurtosis value of -1.20, indicating they are strongly sub-Gaussian. The values of each entry of the matrix (5.17) are computed numerically and the two eigenvalues of the matrix are then computed. The range of the values of β is identical to those used in generating the functions in Figure 5.1. What is clear from Figure 5.4, is that as the value of β decreases the eigenvalues tend to zero so increasing the probability of unstable solutions. As with the previous discussion small values of β do not necessarily satisfy the stability criteria as can be seen from the small eigenvalues at these points.

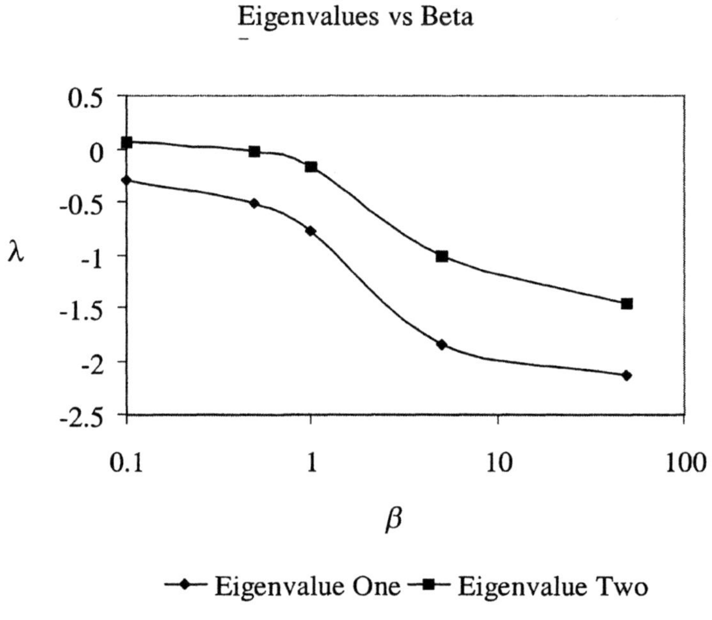

Figure 5.4: Plot of Values of Eigenvalues Vs Beta.

5.4.4 Simulation: Separation of Mixtures of Sub-Gaussian Sources

It remains now to fully test these findings for sub-Gaussian sources with a simulation. In this simulation we shall take data from five sub-Gaussian distributions. This data is in fact the pixel values of five images of dimension 202 × 202 pixels, each pixel takes a grey value between 0 and 255 and so can be coded using one byte. The images are shown in Figure 5.5.

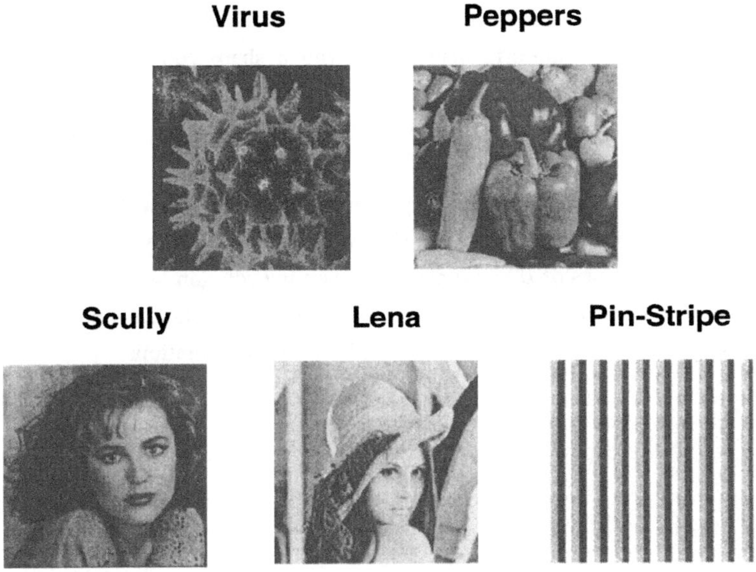

Figure 5.5: Original Unmixed Images: Virus, Peppers, Scully, Lena, Pin-Stripe.

If we compute the values for the kurtosis of each of these images we see that they are all strictly negatively kurtotic indicating that the distribution of pixel values within each image is sub-Gaussian.

IMAGE	KURTOSIS
Virus	-1.280
Peppers	-0.878
Scully	-1.140
Lena	-0.739
Pin-Stripe	-1.48

Table 5.1 : Image Title and Associated Kurtosis Values.

Although the value of kurtosis indicates that the distribution of the pixel values in each image is sub-Gaussian, the actual histograms of the distributions (Figure 5.6) give a greater indication as to the extent of the non-Gaussian nature of each distribution. In creating the histograms, the mean pixel value for each image has been subtracted from each individual pixel value. This effectively ensures that the data is now zero-mean and the associated histograms are centred. The histograms associated with the images 'Lena' and 'Peppers' have two quite distinct modes indicating almost equal areas of light and dark pixels. The histogram of the image 'Scully' shows a more uniform distribution with a sharp concentration of dark values indicating a large area of dark pixels with identical value. The histogram for the 'Pin-Stripe' image indicates that only three distinct values exist within the image.

We wish to test the separating properties of the non-linear PCA algorithm using the compound activation function (5.18). The previous analysis indicates that for small positive values of β an asymptotic separating solution will not be a stable solution. For values of β which make the effect of the hyperbolic tangent significant the analysis indicates that stable solutions will be separating solutions.

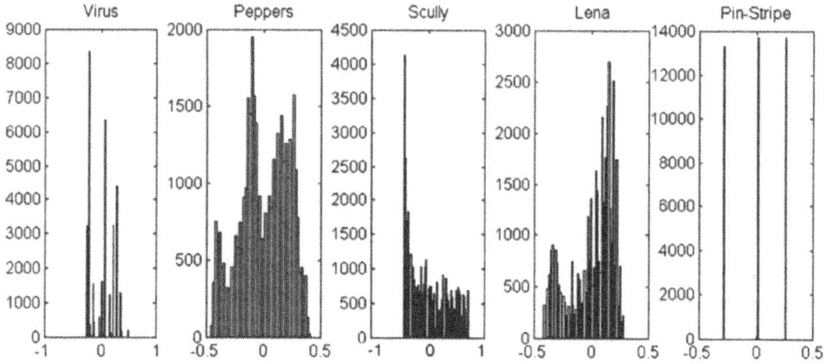

Figure 5.6: Histograms of Five Original Unmixed Images: Virus, Peppers, Scully, Lena, Pin-Stripe. The horizontal axis shows the pixel values and the vertical axis gives the relative frequency of the particular pixel values. The mean value of each image has been removed to centre the histograms about zero.

In this section we report on a simulation which corroborates the analysis in Section 5.4.3. A linear memoryless mixture of the five source images is created using a well-conditioned 5×5 matrix. The pixel values of each image are made zero-mean by subtracting the mean pixel value from each individual pixel. We then wish to run the non-linear PCA algorithm on a spatially whitened version of the mixture to test the stability of the algorithm when using the activation function $f(y) = -y + \tanh(\beta y)$ for a range of positive values of β. The arbitrary mixing matrix used was the following, which had a determinant value of –3.08 indicating no ill conditioning of the mixing.

$$\mathbf{A} = \begin{bmatrix} 1.165 & 1.696 & -1.446 & -0.360 & -0.045 \\ 0.627 & 0.059 & -0.701 & -0.135 & -0.798 \\ 0.075 & 1.797 & 1.246 & -1.349 & -0.765 \\ 0.352 & 0.264 & -0.639 & -1.270 & 0.862 \\ -0.696 & 0.871 & 0.577 & 0.985 & -0.056 \end{bmatrix}$$

The linear noiseless mixing model $\mathbf{x} = \mathbf{As}$ is employed where the source vector $\mathbf{s}$ consists of the corresponding pixel values from each of the original images. Once the images have been mixed it is instructive to view both the mixed images and their associated histograms (Figure 5.7). It is expected that due to Central Limit effects (Papoulis, 1984) the histograms will become more Gaussian in nature and so the associated kurtosis values should tend towards zero. The images themselves will become unrecognisable due to the interfering mixing of the other images. Table 5.2 lists the values of the kurtosis of each mixture. It is clear that these absolute values are significantly smaller than the original unmixed values.

MIXTURE	KURTOSIS
One	-0.476
Two	-0.520
Three	-0.417
Four	-0.376
Five	-0.327

Table 5.2 : Mixture Number and Associated Kurtosis Values.

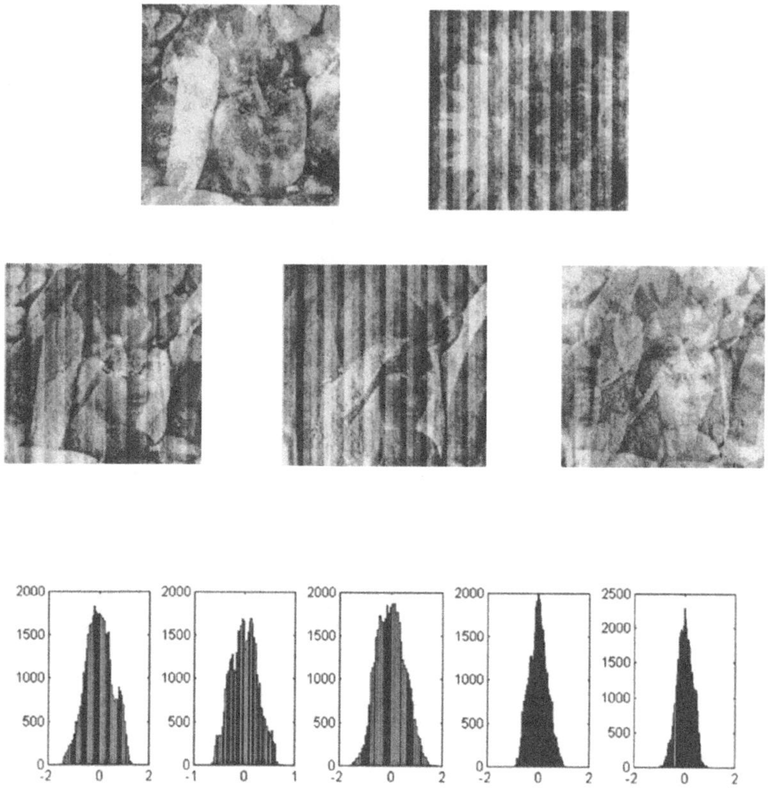

Figure 5.7: Images and Histograms of Five Mixed Images: Images in the top row are the individual mixtures of the five original images. The bottom row gives the associated histograms of the mixtures.

Prior to performing the set of simulations the mixture needs to be spatially whitened; rather than considering the adaptive techniques discussed in Chapter 4, Section 4.1.3 we simply perform a batch whitening transformation (Chapter 3, Section 3.1). Values of β were tested within the non-linear PCA algorithm by randomly setting the initial weight matrix to values between -1 and $+1$ and then presenting the data in a sequential manner to the network and updating the weights at each presentation. If a separating solution exists then

$$\hat{\mathbf{s}} = \mathbf{y} = \mathbf{W}^T \mathbf{U} \mathbf{A} \mathbf{s} = \mathbf{P} \mathbf{D} \mathbf{s}$$

To monitor the level of separation we use a performance index which gives a measure of the distance that the matrix product $\mathbf{W}^T\mathbf{U}\,\mathbf{A}$ is from a permutation and scaling. This can be computed by using the following (Amari, Cichocki and Yang, 1995)

$$E_1 = \sum_{i=1}^{N}\left(\sum_{j=1}^{N}\frac{\left|wua_{ij}\right|}{\max_k\left|wua_{ik}\right|} - 1\right) + \sum_{j=1}^{N}\left(\sum_{i=1}^{N}\frac{\left|wua_{ij}\right|}{\max_k\left|wua_{kj}\right|} - 1\right) \tag{5.22}$$

In this case the term wua_{ij} indicates the $i.j^{th}$ element of the overall transformation matrix $\mathbf{W}^T\mathbf{U}\,\mathbf{A}$. The performance index of (5.22) will reach a minimal value when the overall transformation matrix is a permutation and scaling of the original sources. Within the simulation the performance index is computed after one hundred data sample presentations. Each image is 202 × 202 pixels in size and we see that the data records are 40,804 samples in length so the permutation index is computed approximately 400 times each time the whole data record is presented to the network. A total of seven presentations of the data were made to the network during each simulation. The learning rate was experimented with and set to 0.0001. Five separate simulations were run for each distinct value of β starting at a different random set of weight vectors. Figure 5.9 shows the results of the simulations. Considering the performance curves for the simulations with $\beta = 0.1$ and as expected, due to the almost linear nature of the activation function, a separating solution was not found. As the value of β increases to 0.5 and 1.0 it is clear that the learning is causing the overall performance index to decrease towards zero. Indeed, for these particular values of β a larger learning rate ensured that a separating solution was reached in seven passes through the data. As the value of β increases from 2.0 up to 50.0 it is clear that the learning still converges to a stationary separating solution. The increasing value of β appears to accelerate the convergence to a separating solution, which is justified from the domination of the cubic term in the Taylor expansion. Figure 5.8 shows the final separated output of the network for a value of $\beta = 50.0$. The scales of the pixel values are normalised between 0 and 1, however, we can see that the outputs are permuted and there is also a sign change in the images of 'Scully', 'Virus' and 'Pin-Stripe'. As indicated by the analysis of Section 5.4.3, if β takes on a negative value a separating point may not be an asymptotically stable solution. As expected the algorithm did not converge to a separating solution with this particular data when β was negative.

Figure 5.8: Network Output For Non-Linear PCA Algorithm: Kurtosis values are respectively –1.28, -0.64, -0.87, -1.12, -1.35.

This simulation has shown that the form of activation function (5.18) with positive values of β is valid for separation of mixtures of strictly sub-Gaussian sources. It now remains to investigate the performance of the algorithm on mixtures of strictly super-Gaussian source when β takes on negative values.

5.4.5 Stability of Solution with Super-Gaussian Sources

As in Section 5.4.3, we need to consider the value which the largest eigenvalue of the matrix (5.17) will take. Let us consider the specific situation where $\beta < 0$ and the activation function takes the form of $f(y) = y - \tanh(|\beta| y)$. The expression for the largest eigenvalue of matrix (5.17) is repeated here

$$\lambda_{Max} = E\{y^2\}E\{f'(\alpha y)\} - E\{f^2(\alpha y)\} < 0$$

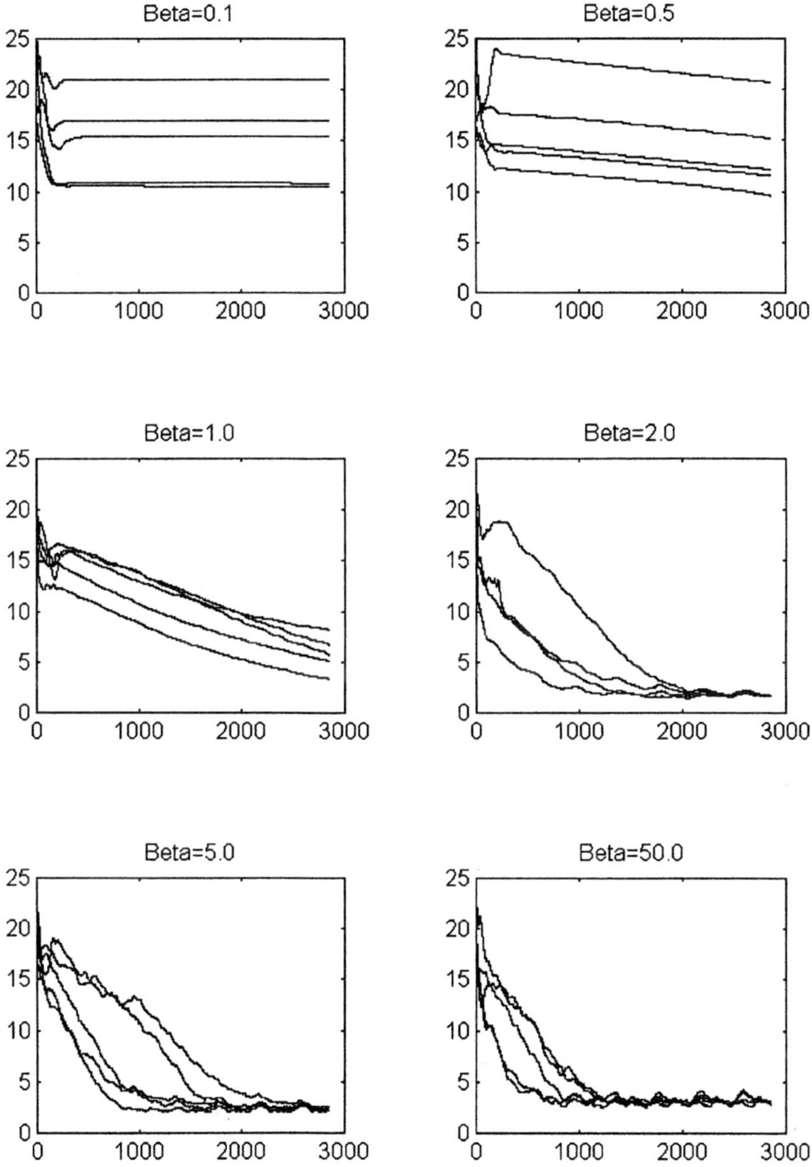

Figure 5.9: Performance Index for Various Values of β: The charts show the performance index of the product of the network weights, whitening and mixing matrices. The learning rate is set at a constant value of 0.0001 for all simulations.

Substituting the value for the activation function then gives the following, noting that the data has unit variance

$$\lambda_{Max} = \left(\alpha|\beta| - 1\right)E\left\{\tanh^2\left(|\beta|\alpha y\right)\right\} + \\ 2\alpha E\left\{y \tanh\left(|\beta|\alpha y\right)\right\} - \\ \alpha^2 + \alpha\left(1 - |\beta|\right) < 0 \tag{5.23}$$

For the particular case of $\alpha = 1$ and $|\beta| = 1$ then we have the following expression.

$$f(y) = \lambda_{Max} = 2E\{y \tanh(y)\} - 1 < 0 \tag{5.24}$$

The term $y \tanh(y)$ has an approximate quadratic nature and so for super-Gaussian distributions $E\{y \tanh(y)\}$ will tend to a small value. Numerical computation of (5.24) using a range of zero-mean super-Gaussian data confirms that

$$\lambda_{Max} = 2E\{y \tanh(y)\} - 1 < 0.$$

If we consider the more general case where α takes on a range of positive and negative values for the case where $|\beta| = 1$ we have the following simplified expression which needs to be satisfied

$$\lambda_{Max} = (\alpha - 1)E\left\{\tanh^2(\alpha y)\right\} + \\ 2\alpha E\{y \tanh(\alpha y)\} - \alpha^2 < 0 \tag{5.25}$$

Numerical computations show for a range of super-Gaussian distributions and $-10 < \alpha < +10$, $\alpha \neq 0$, show that the inequality (5.25) is always satisfied. Further computation shows that as the magnitude of β increases then the asymptotic stability is still assured (Figure 5.10).

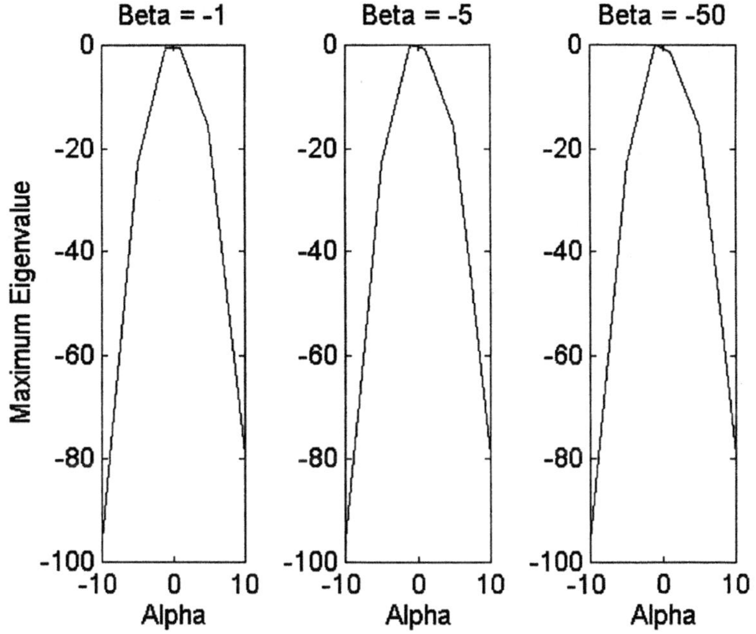

Figure 5.10: Chart of Maximum Eigenvalues Vs Values of Alpha: These values were computed from a data set which has a kurtosis value of 2.53.

This analysis does indicate that the non-linear activation function $f(y) = y - \tanh(|\beta| y)$ may separate mixtures of super-Gaussian sources for certain values of β. If we consider the shape of the activation function given in Figure 5.2, we see that the value $\beta = -1$ is a critical value. As the value of β becomes more negative then we see that the function becomes non-monotonic and indeed is a decreasing function for small values of input. This will give dynamic algorithmic stability problems (Karhunen and Joutsensalo, 1994). As the distribution of the data under consideration is super-Gaussian and as such will have a high proportion of the probability mass centred about the origin this instability problem will be exacerbated. However, it appears that we have a form of activation function which will satisfy the algorithmic dynamic stability requirements for suitably chosen values of β and provide an asymptotically stable separating solution for super-Gaussian data. We now test this finding with a series of simulations.

5.4.6 Simulation: Separation of Mixtures of Super-Gaussian Sources

In this simulation we use natural speech as our source of super-Gaussian data. We should note that speech is inherently non-stationary in terms of the statistics of short record lengths. We use five seconds of natural speech, which has been sampled at a rate of 8000hz giving a complete record length of 40,000 data points. When we quote values of statistics such as kurtosis or variance the whole record is considered. This removes the problem of the data non-stationarity as we are only considering gross statistics.

The samples of natural speech can be seen to be highly super-Gaussian (Figure 5.11), and the related histograms show the super-Gaussian symmetric nature of natural speech. The speaker giving their name and then a six-digit number generates each source. The mixing matrix is given below, as in the previous simulation the matrix is well conditioned.

$$\mathbf{A} = \begin{bmatrix} 0.65 & 0.20 & -0.43 & 0.60 & 0.467 \\ -0.3 & -0.49 & 0.7 & -0.3 & 0.57 \\ 0.68 & 1.5 & -0.8 & 0.41 & 1.34 \\ -0.234 & 0.38 & 0.35 & 0.45 & -0.76 \\ 0.85 & -0.43 & 0.6 & -0.7 & 0.4 \end{bmatrix}$$

The mixing model $\mathbf{x} = \mathbf{As}$ gives the mixed observations where the vector $\mathbf{s}$ consists of the corresponding samples of each speech trace. The mixtures and the related histograms are shown in Figure 5.12. The prime aim of this simulation is to assess whether we can achieve stable separation properties with the form of non-linearity proposed. The spatial whitening of the mixture is carried out numerically using the covariance matrix decomposition technique utilised in the previous simulation. The method employed here is identical to the simulation carried out in Section 5.4.4. Figure 5.13 shows the various performance index curves for varying values of β and initial network weight matrices.

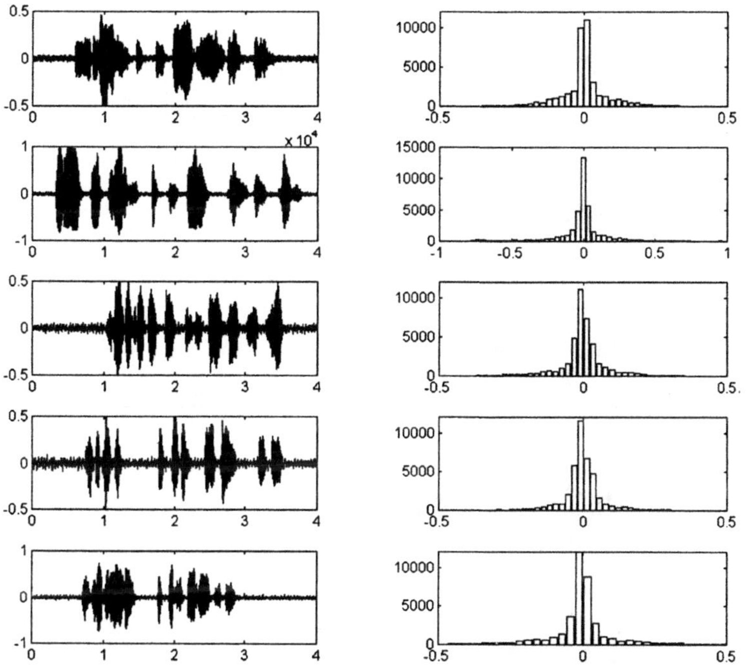

Figure 5.11: Original Source Data, Two Male and Three Female Records of Speech: The related histograms are shown alongside the time-domain amplitude traces. The amplitude traces on the left hand side graph the sample amplitude with time. The histograms show the relative frequency (vertical axis) of each amplitude value (horizontal axis). The kurtosis of each data record is 5.588, 4.829, 6.844, 6.293 and 4.709.

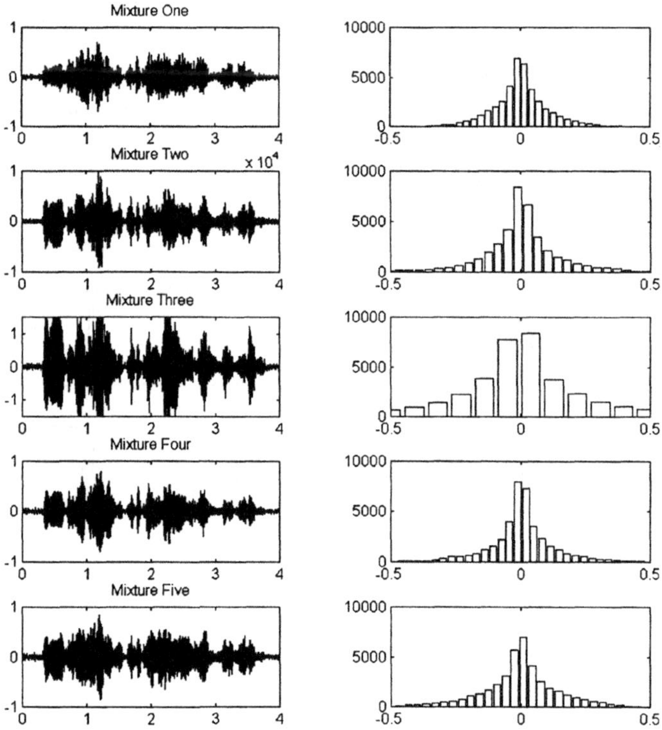

Figure 5.12: The Five Observed Mixtures of the Original Speech Records: The observed mixtures have the following respective kurtosis values, 2.588, 3.954, 3.868, 2.243, 3.754. As indicated by the time domain amplitude traces each observation is an incoherent babble.

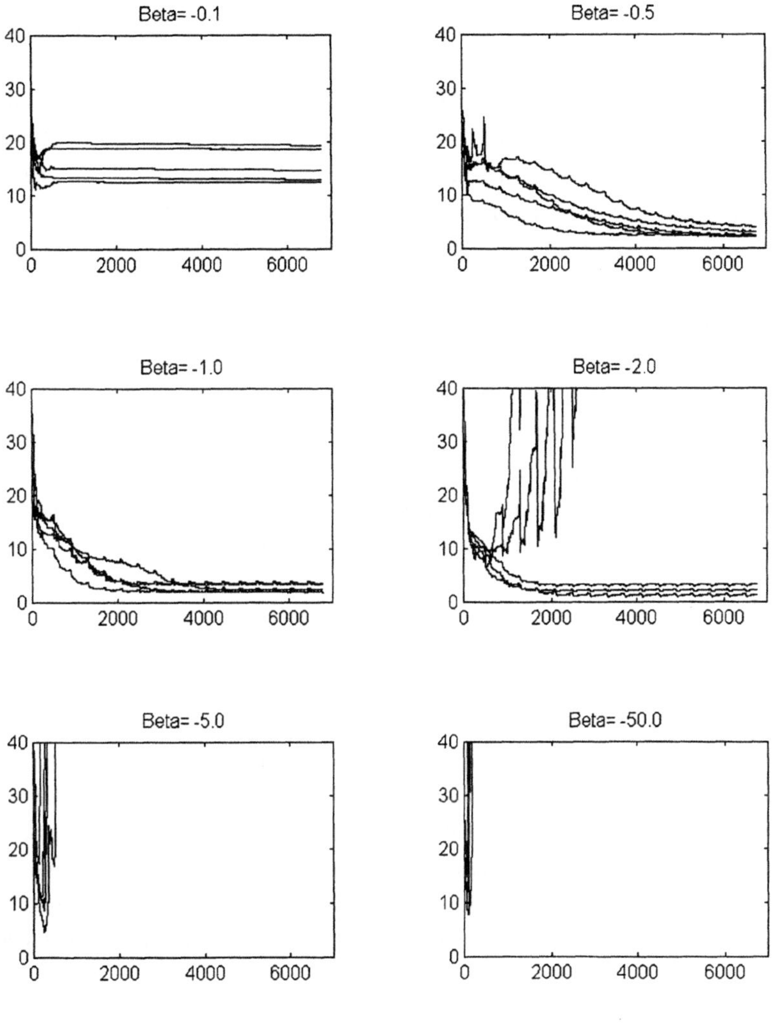

Figure 5.13: Performance Index for Various Values of β: The charts show the performance index of the product of the network weights, whitening and mixing matrices. The learning rate is set at a constant value of 0.001 for all simulations.

In considering the charts of the performance index against iteration number (Figure 5.13) we can see that for the simulation where β = -0.1, we have almost linear behaviour on the activation function and the non-linear PCA algorithm performs nothing more than a PCA subspace decomposition on the data. For the next two values of β used in the activation function, β = -0.5 and β = -1.0 we see that the performance index decreases to zero and so the algorithm successfully separates the original sources from the mixture. The larger value of β ensures that the convergence to a separating solution is more rapid. The simulations confirm the previous analysis and the form of non-linearity considered will allow mixtures of strictly super-Gaussian sources to be separated. The asymptotically stable stationary point of the learning is a separating matrix. When we consider values of β less than negative one, then we see some strange effects occurring within the learning. Consider Figure 5.2: what we see after the critical value of β = -1.0 is that the activation function begins to exhibit a non-monotonic nature. Within the range of values centred at the origin the activation function is effectively decreasing. Consider again the form of the non-linear PCA algorithm

$$\mathbf{W}_{n+1} = \mathbf{W}_n + \mu_n \left(\left(\mathbf{x}_n - \mathbf{W}_n f\left(\mathbf{W}_n{}^T \mathbf{x}_n \right) \right) f\left(\mathbf{x}_n^T \mathbf{W}_n \right) \right)$$

If the function *f(...)* is decreasing then the mean value of the weights will tend to zero. As the data we are considering has a distribution which is at its most dense about the origin, then the propensity for the weights to be nulled is high. What we see in the charts for the performance index (Figure 5.13) for β < -1 is the learning appearing to go unstable. What is actually happening is that the weights are tending to zero, due to the decreasing section of the activation function when β < -1.0. This effect is more severe as the value of β decreases. For the simulations carried out with β = -2.0 we see one or more columns of the weight matrix being nulled i.e.

$$\mathbf{W} = \begin{bmatrix} 0.122 & 0.408 & 0 & -0.154 & -0.129 \\ 0.444 & -0.348 & 0 & 0.518 & -0.298 \\ 0.383 & 0.065 & 0 & -0.066 & 0.888 \\ -0.428 & -0.025 & 0 & 0.633 & 0.412 \\ 0.109 & 0.690 & 0 & 0.3695 & -0.2285 \end{bmatrix}$$

Whereas for β = -5.0 and β = -50.0 the entire matrix is reduced to zero.

We now have a generic activation function that has been shown analytically and confirmed by simulation to separate strict mixtures of either sub-Gaussian data or also strict mixtures of super-Gaussian data. This further extends the range of data to which Oja's non-linear PCA algorithm can be applied for blind source separation. Figure 5.14 shows a sample of the separated sources compared to the original sources; the scaling of the original sources is apparent.

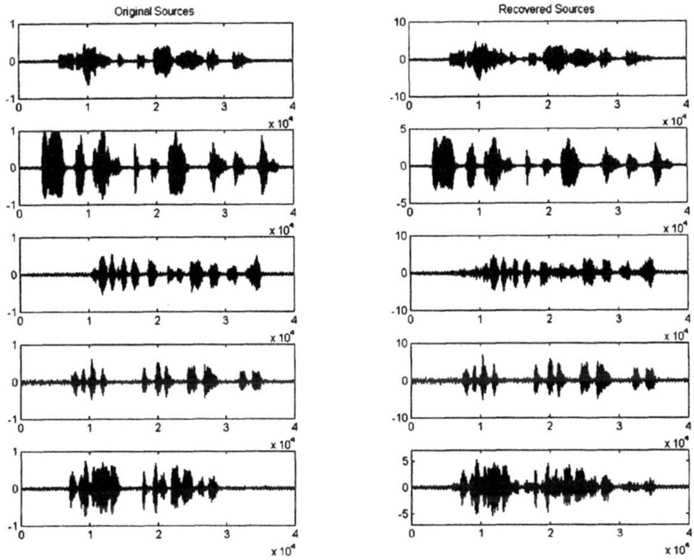

Figure 5.14: Separated Sources for β = -1: The traces show the output of the network after the weights have converged to a separating matrix. The amplitude of each source has changed due to the inherent scaling indeterminacy of the source separation problem.

5.4.7 Separation of Mixtures of Both Sub and Super-Gaussian Sources

From the previous analysis in Sections 5.4.3 and 5.4.5, we are now in the position where the non-linear PCA algorithm will separate mixtures of either strictly sub-Gaussian or strictly super-Gaussian sources. Let us remind ourselves that the non-linear PCA algorithm is a form of constrained non-linear Hebbian learning where the asymptotically stable stationary points in weight space will be separating solutions subject to certain restrictions on the data. In Section 5.3, we were able to show that the cost function which is the starting point of the derivation of the non-linear PCA algorithm can be viewed as the sum of absolute values of fourth order cumulants. This is valid if the sign of the dominating cubic non-linearity is chosen to reflect the sign of the individual source signal kurtosis (5.10). We can see that minimisation of the cost function (5.10) is dependent on the correct sign of the function appearing in the cost function.

$$\begin{aligned} J(\mathbf{W}) &\equiv \sum_{i=1}^{M}\left(-sign(f_i)\kappa_4(i)\right) \\ &\equiv \sum_{i=1}^{M}\left(-sign\left(\kappa_4(i)\right)\kappa_4(i)\right) \\ &\equiv -\sum_{i=1}^{M}\left|\kappa_4(i)\right| \end{aligned}$$

This indicates that if each source has differing signs of kurtosis then matching the sign of the non-linearity at each neuron correctly will ensure that the cost function will be minimised, at least approximately. To assess the asymptotic stability of such a scenario is more complex than the situation where the sources are drawn from the same form of distributions. This was carried out numerically where two independent sets of data were drawn from a super-Gaussian distribution and a sub-Gaussian distribution. The sub-Gaussian data was drawn from a uniformly distributed zero-mean noise source with a kurtosis value of –1.2. The super-Gaussian source was drawn from a zero-mean Hyperbolic-Cauchy distribution (Stuart and Ord, 1987); the kurtosis value of the data was +1.303. For simplicity we consider the situation where α is set to one for both sources. Using the data, each entry of the matrix (5.17) is computed and the respective eigenvalues calculated. This was carried out for varying values of β. What we find is that the eigenvalues are negative for the range of values when β takes the correct sign. As the magnitude of β tends to zero, the eigenvalues become very small as would be expected from the previous analysis. If the sign of β is positive for both sources, i.e. assuming both sources are sub-Gaussian, we find that the respective eigenvalues are negative. When β is negative, that is assuming both sources are super-Gaussian, the eigenvalues are not both negative. This suggests that a stable separating solution is possible even if β is chosen as strictly positive. The important conclusion from this is that if β is chosen to match the underlying source kurtosis, then a separating solution will be a stable stationary point of the learning.

To confirm the above we took four independent sources; two were drawn from zero-mean sub-Gaussian distributions and the other two were drawn from zero-mean super-Gaussian sources. The sources are in fact images: (Figure 5.16): an image of Alan Turing, a Fingerprint, uniformly distributed noise, and logistically distributed noise. These were then mixed using a well-conditioned matrix as in the previous simulations; Table 5.3 gives the details of the sources and mixtures.

ORIGINAL IMAGE & KURTOSIS	MIXTURE & KURTOSIS
Alan Turing +1.477	Mix 1 +0.233
Fingerprint -1.285	Mix 2 +0.621
Logistic Noise +1.303	Mix3 +0.017
Uniform Noise -1.193	Mix4 +1.296

Table 5.3: Source and Mixture Number With Associated Kurtosis Values.

We track the value of the performance index for differing configurations of β. In the first case β is set to reflect the sign of the kurtosis of each source. So two of the output activation functions will be $f(y) = y + \tanh(y)$ and the other two will be $f(y) = y - \tanh(y)$. In the second case the activation functions are all set to $f(y) = y + \tanh(y)$, and the final case the activation functions are all set to $f(y) = y - \tanh(y)$.

Figure 5.16 shows the results of the simulations. As would be expected for the case where the activation function is matched according to the source kurtosis the performance index is approximately minimised. In the second simulation where all the activation functions are set to $f(y) = y + \tanh(y)$ the minimal value of the performance index is not as low as that achieved in the first simulation. The third simulation indicates an even poorer level of separation. As the non-linearity at each neuron is $f(y) = y - \tanh(y)$ then the learning is effectively trying to maximise a positive kurtosis term at each output due to the dominating positive cubic term within the activation function (5.20). Figure 5.16 shows the original and mixed images along with the output of each simulation. As expected when the values of beta match the kurtosis sign of the original sources very good separation is seen, but when the value of beta is +1 then we can see from Figure 5.16 that the separation is poor. It is interesting to note that the image with the largest value of negative kurtosis (fingerprint) is separated well. Again this is due primarily to the dominating negative cubic term within the learning rule. For the simulations carried out when β is negative it is clear that the separation is poor, however, as with the previous simulation we can see that the source with the maximal positive kurtosis (Alan Turing) is separated well. This phenomenon is due largely to the positive cubic term tending to drive the output kurtosis as positively as possible. The simulation does confirm the previous conclusion that asymptotically stable separating solutions exist for mixtures of sub- and super-Gaussian sources when the value of β is set to match each individual source kurtosis.

5.5 Conclusions

In this chapter we have considered Oja's non-linear PCA algorithm as a form of constrained non-linear Hebbian learning. The non-linear PCA algorithm is an approximate stochastic gradient algorithm for minimising a vector reconstruction error. We have shown that by restricting the data to zero-mean, unit variance variables and considering a nonlinearity with dominating cubic terms, then the original cost function can be viewed as the sum of the absolute values of the marginal fourth order cumulants. We have shown that the non-linear PCA algorithm can then be considered as an adaptive algorithm, which seeks an approximate rotation to maximise the sum of squares of fourth order cumulants. This is the second stage of the algorithm originally proposed by Comon (1994) and so the link between the emergent properties of Oja's non-linear PCA algorithm and ICA is more direct than originally understood. This provides the most direct justification for the application of Oja's non-linear PCA algorithm for BSS. We have presented a form of activation function that can be shaped by a single parameter. The asymptotic stability of this activation function within the non-linear PCA algorithm has been studied for mixtures of sub-Gaussian sources, mixtures of super-Gaussian sources and mixtures of both. When certain constraints are imposed the asymptotic stability of separating solutions is assured. Originally the non-linear PCA algorithm was restricted to separation of mixtures of sub-Gaussian sources; we have now extended this to the more general range of mixtures, thus making the algorithm more versatile.

Extensive simulations have confirmed the analysis. However, at best the link with BSS and the algorithm derivation is indirect. The two-stage process of spatial whitening followed by approximate absolute kurtosis maximisation is cumbersome and slow in convergence. In the next chapter we consider the first problem of the indirect link of the non-linear PCA algorithm to ICA.

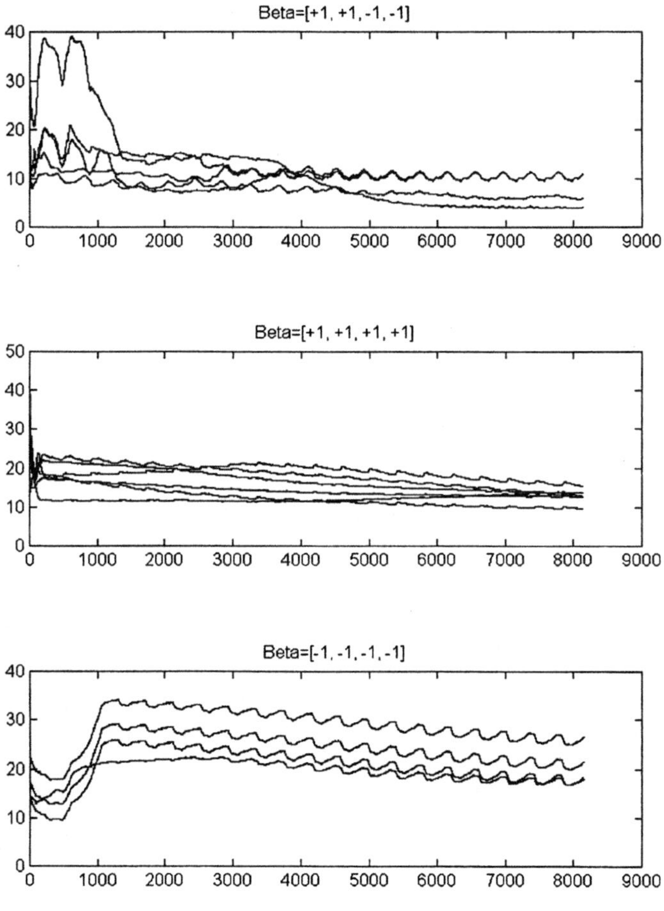

Figure 5.15: Performance Index for Various Signs of β: The charts show the performance index of the product of the network weights, whitening and mixing matrices. The learning rate was set at a constant value of 0.0001. Twenty passes through the data was used for all simulations.

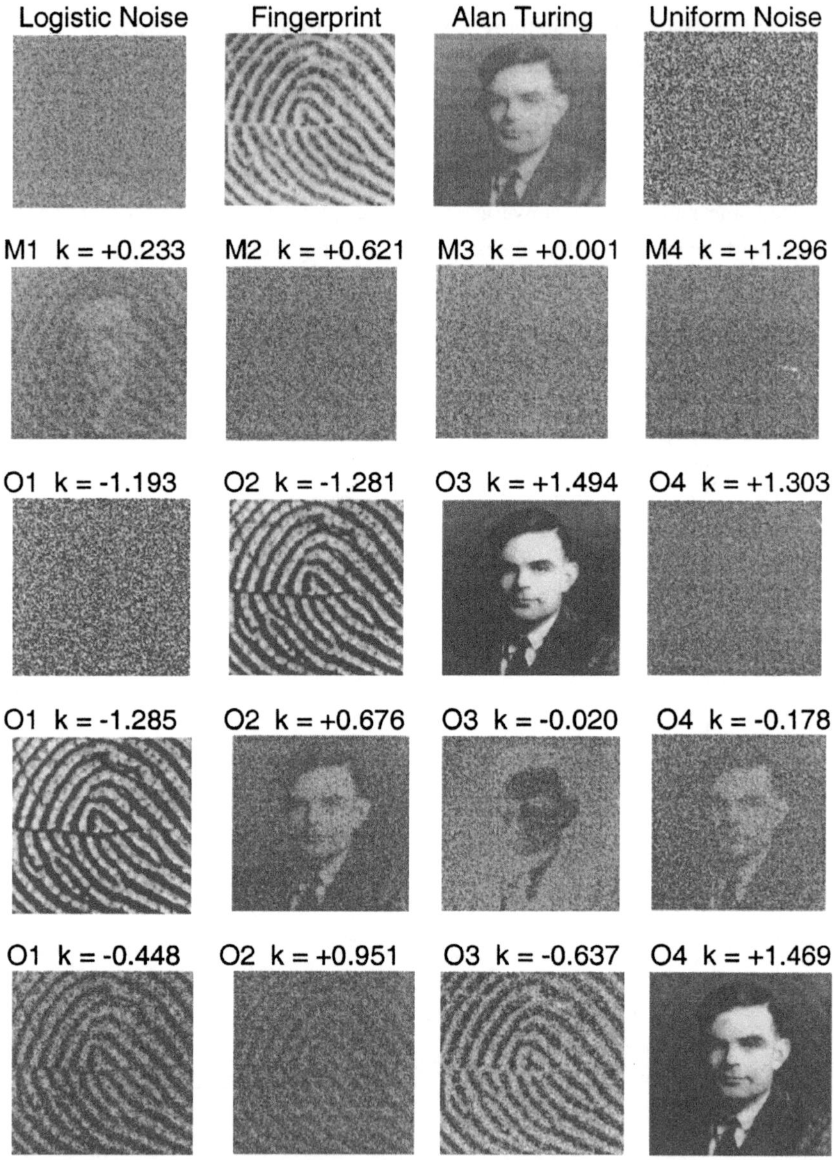

Figure 5.16: Original Images, Mixed Images and Network Output: The top row shows the original images, the values of kurtosis for each image are given. The second row shows the mixed images, prior to spatial whitening. Row three gives the network output for $\beta = [+1, +1, -1, -1]$. Row four is the output for $\beta = [+1, +1, +1, +1]$ and the final row is the output for $\beta = [-1, -1, -1, -1]$.

6. *Non-Linear Feature Extraction and Blind Source Separation*

In this chapter, non-linear Hebbian learning based on the Robust PCA algorithm is considered. We introduce the concept of Exploratory Projection Pursuit (EPP), a statistical tool for non-linear feature extraction and consider a neural network implementation of this analysis technique. For certain specific cases we show that EPP and blind source separation are equivalent.

6.1 Introduction

We present a neural network structure which employs Hebbian and anti-Hebbian learning in performing BSS on mixtures of super-Gaussian sources. The concept of asymmetry or hierarchy in parallel learning is reconsidered and a more general form of BSS is introduced.

6.2 Structure Identification in Multivariate Data

Unsupervised statistical analysis for classification or clustering of data is a subject of great interest when no classes are defined *a priori* (Gordon, 1981). The Projection Pursuit methodology as named by Friedman (1987) was developed to seek or 'pursue' N dimensional projections of the data which would maximise some measure of 'interestingness'. The dimensionality of the projection was invariably such that $N = 1$ or 2 for visualisation purposes. Diaconis and Freedman (1984) were able to show that a random projection of a high dimensional data set will appear similar to a sample from a multivariate normal distribution. This result indicates that departures from multivariate normality would be a suitable measure of interestingness. PCA can be considered as maximising an index of interestingness, in this case variance. Variance is a sufficient Gaussian statistic and departures from a Gaussian distribution will not then be identified with this index measure. Within the statistics literature a number of indices have been proposed in identifying departures from normality (Huber, 1985; Friedman, 1987). Jones and Sibson (1987) proposed indices based on higher order moments and cumulants, in particular the third order and fourth order cumulants which will identify skewness and kurtosis (Chapter 2, Section 2.4). However, moment based indices are relatively simple to compute and so are attractive from an online adaptive perspective. A normal distribution which has mean value *a* and variance *va* is no more or less interesting than a normal distribution with mean value *b* and variance *vb*. This normal structure can be removed from the data by transforming the data such that all the marginal distributions have a mean of zero and variance one. The removal of the Gaussian or second order structure from the data is referred to as 'sphereing'. The term 'sphereing' comes from creating a spherically symmetric point distribution in data space. Sphereing consists of transforming the data such that the covariance matrix is an identity. Once the data has been sphered the maximisation of the chosen index is carried out to reveal the structure of 'interest'. The statistics literature makes use of the word 'interest' to indicate structure in the data that may be informative in some well understood manner. When an interesting projection is found it will be necessary to remove the identified structure so that further interesting projections can be identified (Friedman, 1987).

Essentially Exploratory Projection Pursuit (EPP) is a two step process; the multivariate data is sphered to remove all second order structure and then index maximisation is carried out to identify projections of potential interest. Our particular interest is in unsupervised neural networks which will perform EPP. As PCA can be considered as second order EPP then we would expect that some form of non-linear PCA learning may be capable of extracting non-linear structure from multivariate data. Two methods for EPP, based on neural network models have been proposed by Intrator and Cooper, (1992) and Fyfe and Baddeley (1995). The two methods are reviewed and compared in Fyfe (1997). Essentially Intrator and Cooper use the Bienenstock, Cooper and Munro (BCM) (Bienenstock et al 1982) model of neuron selectivity to maximise Intrator's index (Intrator, 1992).

6.3 Neural Network Implementation of Exploratory Projection Pursuit

We consider further the method originally proposed by Fyfe and Baddeley (1995). Fyfe and Baddeley utilise simple non-linear Hebbian learning in a feedback network for EPP. The negative feedback network is presented and studied in detail in Fyfe (1995). Consider a vector of N dimensional zero mean input data $\mathbf{x}$, which is presented to a single layer network with N inputs and M outputs where $M \leq N$. The weights of the network will be signified by the $M \times N$ real valued matrix $\mathbf{W}$. The linear summation (6.1) of the output neurons is fed back as inhibition to the input neurons and the residual (6.2) and non-linear outputs (6.3) are used in the Hebbian learning rule (6.4).

$$r_i = \sum_{j=1}^{N} w_{ij}\, x_j\,(t) \tag{6.1}$$

$$x_j\,(t+1) \leftarrow x_j\,(t) - \sum_{k=1}^{M} w_{kj}\, r_k \tag{6.2}$$

$$y_i = f\left(\sum_{j=1}^{N} w_{ij}\, x_j\,(t)\right) = f\,(r_i) \tag{6.3}$$

$$\Delta w_{ij} = \eta_t\, y_i\, x_j(t+1) \tag{6.4}$$

$$\Delta w_{ij} = \eta_t\, f\left(\sum_{p=1}^{N} w_{ip}\, x_p(t)\right)\left\{x_j(t) - \sum_{k=1}^{M} w_{kj} \sum_{q=1}^{N} w_{kq}\, x_q(t)\right\} \tag{6.5}$$

We can write (6.5) in matrix form as

$$\Delta \mathbf{W} = \eta\left(\mathbf{I} - \mathbf{W}\mathbf{W}^T\right)\mathbf{x}\, f\left(\mathbf{x}^T\mathbf{W}\right) \tag{6.6}$$

Equation (6.6) is effectively Oja's Robust PCA algorithm (Chapter 4, Section 4.2.3.2.) This is derived from the maximisation of an objective function under orthonormal parametric constraints (4.49). The non-linear term in (6.6) is simply the derivative of the function in (4.49) that is $f(a) = g'(a)$. If we consider an EPP that seeks to identify skewness in a distribution, noting that the third order moment of a distribution is one measure of skewness, then to maximise the skewness of the output data we can choose functions such that

$$g(a) \propto a^3 \Rightarrow f(a) = g'(a) \propto a^2$$

If directions are sought which exhibit sparseness or multi-modality then kurtosis is one moment based index which will identify these departures from Gaussian. A sparse distribution (one which has heavy tails) has kurtosis values in the range $]0 \ \ldots \ +\infty[$; that is, a positive real value and a multi-modal distribution will have kurtosis values in the range $]-2 \ \ldots \ 0[$. Note that this is the lower limit for kurtosis values which are negative. Note that the statistics literature refers to distributions which have positive kurtosis as platykurtic and the signal processing community describe such distributions as super-Gaussian. Negatively kurtotic distributions are described as leptokurtic and sub-Gaussian respectively.

As discussed in Section 6.2 the first step in performing EPP is the sphereing of the data. Throughout this book we assume that the data is zero-mean, however, it is a trivial matter to centre the data by subtracting the sample mean value from each data point. The sphereing requires that the data is transformed such that it has an identity covariance. In seeking to develop an online adaptive method for EPP, Fyfe and Baddeley (1995) use a PCA network to provide the sphereing transformation. It should be noted, however, that sphereing using PCA also requires a normalisation step, where the transformed data is divided by the square root of the eigenvalues of the original data covariance matrix. Without this step the transformed data will have a diagonal covariance matrix which may not be an identity. The normalisation ensures that the transformed data has an identity covariance. The local eigenvalue information then needs to be computed and stored which is not suitable for a full online adaptive sphereing process. From Chapter 4, Section 4.1.2 the PCA decomposition of the covariance matrix is

$$\mathbf{C}_{xx} = \mathbf{U} \Lambda \mathbf{U}^T$$

and the complete sphereing operation is then

$$\mathbf{z} = \Lambda^{-\frac{1}{2}} \mathbf{U} \mathbf{x}.$$

The transformation **U** is the matrix whose columns are the eigenvectors of the covariance matrix of the data series **x** and Λ is the diagonal matrix whose entries are the associated eigenvalues. In the following sections we shall consider a computationally simpler adaptive method for sphereing.

Once the data is sphered the higher order or non-linear structure within the data can be identified using (6.5) to maximise the specific projection pursuit index. As has been noted, if further structure within the data needs to be identified then the current projection needs to be removed from the data. However, consider the matrix form of the non-linear Hebbian rule (6.6) which is derived from maximisation of the objective function (4.49) under orthonormal constraints. As the matrix **W** is strictly orthonormal then each column of the matrix is linearly independent. This ensures that each output neuron will respond to different features within the data due to the linear independence of each column, which is enforced explicitly in the objective function. This is a key point which will be returned to in subsequent sections. So, a multi-output neural network with two layers will be capable of performing an EPP on multivariate data. Our motivation in considering this unsupervised projection technique is Blind Source Separation or Independent Component Analysis.

6.4 Neural Exploratory Projection Pursuit and Blind Source Separation

Fyfe and Baddeley (1995) maximise the kurtosis in identifying non-linear structure within data generated from natural images. If we choose to seek a direction which identifies kurtotic structure within the data, then we have a particularly significant equivalence with blind source separation techniques.

Generative statistical models describe the probability distribution of observed data in terms of a mixture of hidden or latent variables which possess simple distributions (Everitt, 1984). In many cases the latent variables have a simple factorable distribution, i.e. they are independent. In our blind source separation model the mixture of several independent latent variables can model the observed data which may well have a complex multivariate pdf. We of course restrict the dimensionality of the latent variables to be less than or equal to that of the observables. Delfosse and Loubaton (1995) prove that the local maxima (or minima) encountered when maximising the kurtosis of a pre-whitened noiseless mixture on the unit sphere will be separating solutions. Performing an EPP which identifies kurtotic structure in data which can be modelled by the restricted noiseless latent variable model which is the BSS / ICA model will in fact extract the latent variables.

By using a single output neuron and performing kurtosis-seeking EPP on observed data which is an $N \times N$ mixture of independent sources, we are in effect extracting one of the independent sources. The theme of adaptive sequential extraction of a single source and subsequent deflation of the mixture was proposed in Delfosse and Loubaton (1995). Neural techniques have been further developed using the extraction and deflation techniques (Malouche and Macchi, 1996; Hyvarinen and Oja, 1996; Cichocki, Thawonmas and Amari, 1996).

6.5 Kurtosis Extrema

Let us now reconsider the constrained contrast of ICA (Comon, 1994) written as

$$\Phi(\mathbf{W})_{Max} = \sum_{i=1}^{N} \kappa_4(y_i)^2$$

Such that $\mathbf{W}\mathbf{W}^T = \mathbf{I}$ and the output $\mathbf{y} = \mathbf{W}\Lambda^{2}\mathbf{U}\mathbf{x}$. As (6.6) provides an orthogonal rotation to maximise the objective function

$$J(\mathbf{W}) = \mathbf{1}^T E\{g(\mathbf{W}^T\mathbf{x})\}$$

with a suitable choice of the function $g(\ldots)$ it can be made equivalent to the sum of squares of fourth order marginal cumulants. Note that the sum of the absolute values of kurtosis will yield similar optimal weight parameters for function maximisation as the sum of squared values. We will see that the sum of absolute values of kurtosis is a more convenient objective function for developing a stochastic maximisation algorithm. Using the given definition of kurtosis we see that for a whitened vector, $\mathbf{x}$, orthonormal transformation and projection $\mathbf{y} = \mathbf{W}^T\mathbf{x}$, such that $\mathbf{W}^T\mathbf{W} = \mathbf{I}$, and noting that

$$E\{\mathbf{y}\mathbf{y}^T\} = \mathbf{W}^T E\{\mathbf{x}\mathbf{x}^T\}\mathbf{W} = \mathbf{I}$$

then setting $g(y) = \left|y^4 - 3\right|$ will yield the following

$$
\begin{aligned}
J(\mathbf{W}) &= \mathbf{1}^T E\left\{g\left(\mathbf{W}^T\mathbf{x}\right)\right\} \\
&= \sum_{i=1}^{N} E\left\{g\left(\mathbf{w}_i{}^T\mathbf{x}\right)\right\} \\
&= \sum_{i=1}^{N} \left|\kappa_4\left(\mathbf{w}_i{}^T\mathbf{x}_i\right)\right|
\end{aligned}
$$

without the constraint term (we shall return to the full-constrained cost function (4.48) in the next section). Taking the instantaneous gradient and using compact matrix notation we have

$$
\frac{d\,J(\mathbf{W})}{d\,\mathbf{W}} \propto signum\left(\mathbf{K}_4\right)\mathbf{x}\left(\mathbf{x}^T\mathbf{W}\right)^3
$$

The *signum* operator returns +1 for arguments greater than zero and –1 for an argument less than zero. The term $signum\left(\mathbf{K}_4\right)$ is the diagonal matrix whose elements are the sign of the kurtosis value of all the $\mathbf{w}_i{}^T\mathbf{x}$ terms, so $f(y) = signum\left(\kappa_4(y)\right)y^3$. This indicates that if there are independent sources in the mixed vector $\mathbf{x}$ which have positive kurtosis, the non-linear function to be used for maximisation of the sum of squares of fourth order cumulants is $f(y) = +y^3$ and for negatively kurtotic sources $f(y) = -y^3$. However, this is a decreasing function which introduces numeric instability into (6.6) and practically is unsuitable, as discussed in Chapter 5. The hyperbolic tangent has been used extensively as the non-linearity for (6.6) and other non-linear PCA style algorithms since the truncated Taylor expansion is

$$
\tanh(y) \cong y - \frac{y^3}{3} + \frac{2y^5}{15} - \dots .
$$

As we are considering zero mean data which is white (sphered) and therefore has unit variance, simple numerical calculations show that 95% of the data from a normal distribution lies within the range of -1.93 to +1.93 (Chapter 5, Section 5.3). Noting that by using the hyperbolic tangent as the non-linear term in (6.6) we are effectively seeking to approximately maximise

$$E\left\{\int \tanh(y)dy\right\} \cong E\left\{\int\left(y - \frac{y^3}{3} + \frac{2y^5}{15} - \ldots\right)dy\right\}$$

$$= E\left\{y^2 - \frac{y^4}{12} + \frac{2y^6}{90} - \ldots\right\}$$

$$= 1 - E\left\{\frac{y^4}{12}\right\} + E\left\{\frac{2y^6}{90}\right\} - \ldots$$

The final equality follows as $E\left\{y^2\right\} = 1$

For the given range of data

$$\frac{y^4}{12} > \frac{2y^6}{90}$$

indicating that the use of the hyperbolic tangent causes (6.6) to seek to approximately maximise

$$E\left\{-\frac{y^4}{12}\right\}$$

that is maximise data values of negative kurtosis. The hyperbolic tangent is an increasing function which grows in a manner which will not introduce numeric instability into (6.6) and this non-linearity has been used extensively in ICA type algorithms, e.g Jutten and Herrault (1991), Cichocki *et al* (1995).

Following the above argument, the use of -tanh(y) could be considered for maximising data values of positive kurtosis. This, however, is a decreasing function and causes the weight vectors during adaptation to decrease to zero (as the learning would then be anti-Hebbian) and so is wholly inappropriate for this application. We can use the stable monotonic form of the function proposed and studied in Chapter 5 (5.18)

$$f(y) = y \pm \tanh(y) = y - signum(k_4)\tanh(y)$$

Applying the above arguments we can see that

$$E\left\{\int y \pm \tanh(y) d y\right\} \cong E\left\{\int y \pm\left(y-\frac{y^{3}}{3}+\frac{2 y^{5}}{15}-\ldots\right) d y\right\}$$

So for the form of $y + \tanh(y)$ we will have

$$E\left\{-\frac{y^{4}}{12}\right\}$$

as the dominant term which is similar to the standard hyperbolic tangent which will maximise negative kurtosis. For the form of $y - \tanh(y)$ then the

$$E\left\{-\frac{y^{4}}{12}\right\}$$

term will be dominating in the objective function. This allows maximisation of the kurtosis for super-Gaussian data. However the additional advantage of the function $y - \tanh(y)$ is that it is an approximately linearly increasing function which is numerically stable in the stochastic algorithms (6.6).

We now have identified activation functions which will potentially provide numerically stable ICA contrast maximisation for both sub-Gaussian and super-Gaussian data.

6.6 Finding Interesting and Independent Directions

In this section, we consider the practical application of an Exploratory Projection Pursuit network in identifying the latent causes of a series of observations. It has been demonstrated by (Fyfe, 1995; Fyfe and Baddeley, 1995) that the feedback network and learning will pursue interesting directions within multivariate data. However, if we now consider the restricted latent variable model of data observations we should expect that seeking kurtotic structure in the data would identify relevant latent variables. Two illustrative simulations are performed to confirm our conclusions. A mixture of three independent sources of data is generated to provide us with the observations. Each source is a zero-mean and negatively kurtotic sequence of one thousand data points. The independent sources are respectively uniformly distributed noise, a sinusoid and a sawtooth waveform.

The observations are created by mixing the three sources using a well conditioned 3 $\times$ 3 scalar matrix. The mixture was pre-whitened using the whitening transformation discussed in Chapter 3, Section 3.1. Adaptive neural methods of pre-whitening shall be considered in Section 6.8.

In Figure 6.1, we see one hundred sequential samples of the original sources, the observed mixtures, and the whitened mixtures. Table 6.1 gives details of the kurtosis of the sources, the observed mixtures and whitened mixtures. As we are seeking negatively kurtotic structure in the data we utilise the non-linearity of the form $f(y) = y + \tanh(y)$ as the activation function. The whitened mixture is presented sequentially to a three input, single output feedback network and the weights are updated using the learning rule (6.5). The learning rate was set at a small constant value of 0.001.

SOURCE	K_4	MIXTURE	K_4	WHITE MIX	K_4
Noise	-1.12	1	-0.69	1	-0.79
Sinusoid	-1.50	2	-1.17	2	-0.85
Sawtooth	-1.18	3	-0.955	3	-0.82

Table 6.1: Kurtosis Values of the Sources, Mixture and Whitened Mixture.

Figure 6.1 shows the original signals the observed mixtures and the whitened input to the network. It is clear that the whitening operation alone is not sufficient in identifying the independent sources. The whitened mixture is then sequentially presented to the network until the learning converges to a steady state, after each presentation of the data set the kurtosis of the network output is computed. A short series of six simulations were performed each starting with a randomly generated initial weight matrix. Figure 6.2 shows the graph of the output data kurtosis at each learning epoch (that is, complete data set presentation) for the simulations.

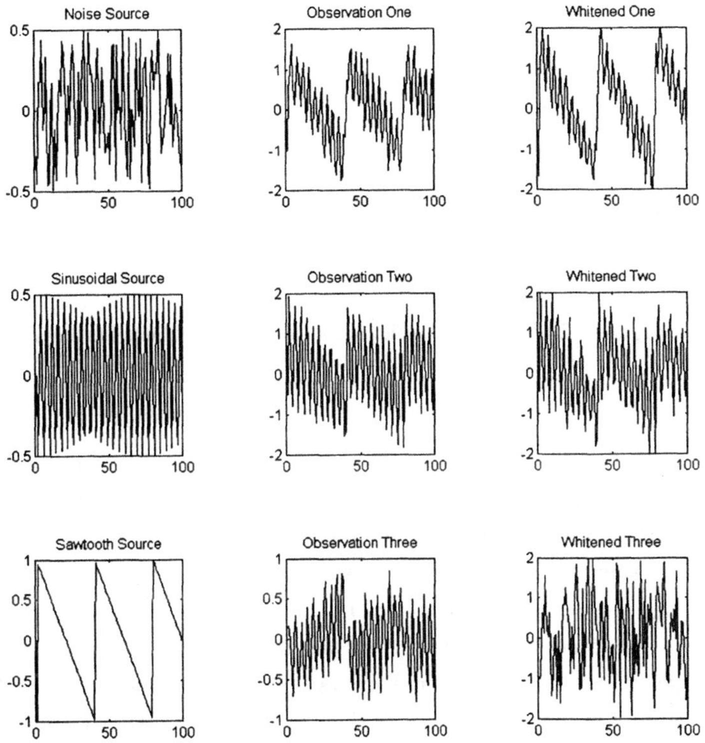

Figure 6.1: One Hundred Sequential Samples of the Three Independent Sources: The observed mixtures and the spatially whitened mixtures are shown here.

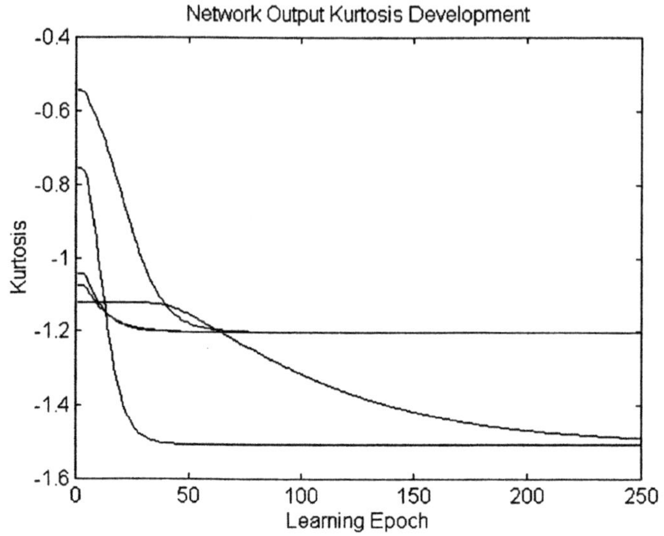

Figure 6.2: Kurtosis Development of the Output Data During Learning.

We can see from Figure 6.2 that the learning does indeed converge to stable values of the kurtosis. Note however that the convergence is not guaranteed to find the point of lowest possible kurtosis. Delfosse and Loubaton (1995) show that the local minima will all be separating solutions and this is the finding here. Figure 6.3 shows the output data for a number of simulations. What is clear however, is that this particular scheme cannot enforce the certain convergence to find the global minima or the source with minimal (maximal negative) kurtosis. This is not an issue in this particular study, however; Cichocki, Thawonmas and Amari (1997) have subsequently developed a deflationary algorithm for sequential extraction of sources in order of the absolute value of kurtosis. It is demonstrated by simulation that the use of a decaying noise term in the adaptation ensures extraction of the source with the maximal absolute value of kurtosis.

What is clear from Figure 6.3 is that the convergence of the algorithm (6.1 - 6.5) is not guaranteed to find the global extremal point of the objective function. It is interesting to note that the noise source was not extracted in the short series of simulations. It is conjectured that the initial weights were repeatedly set within the basins of attraction for the sawtooth source and the sinusoidal source. A similar simulation was carried out with super-Gaussian sources (natural speech) with similar results.

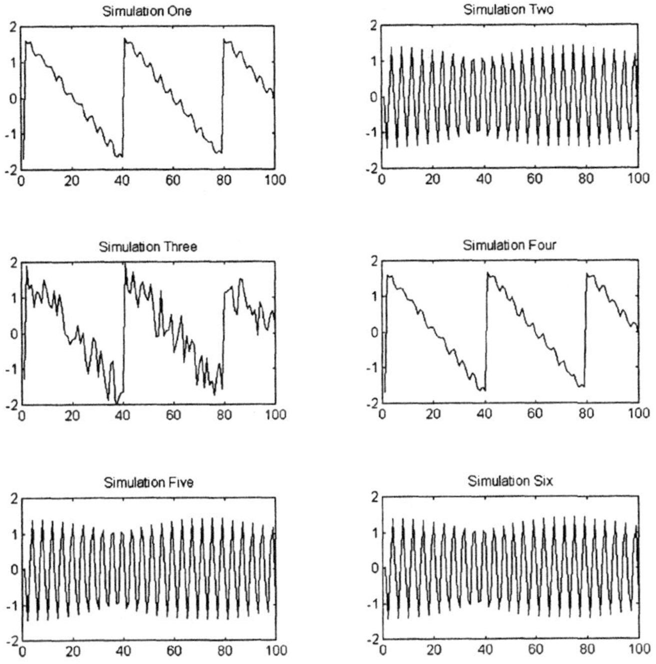

Figure 6.3: The Network Output for a Series of Six Simulations. Each simulation was initialised with a randomly generated weight matrix.

We can conclude from this section that the use of a single output Exploratory Projection Pursuit network will allow extraction of a single independent source from a mixture of such sources. Extracting a single source from a mixture in a stochastic manner will not guarantee which particular source is extracted. If we wish to separate the mixture into the individual independent components then in addition to extraction a form of deflation is required, where the extracted source is then removed from the mixture prior to extraction of subsequent sources. Sequential methods have been investigated by (Malouche and Macchi, 1996; Hyvarinen and Oja, 1996; Cichocki, Thawonmas and Amari, 1996). It is interesting to note that the square matrix form of the EPP algorithm (6.6) is derived under constraints of orthonormality $\mathbf{W}^T\mathbf{W} = \mathbf{I}$ indicating that each column of the matrix $\mathbf{W}$ will be linearly independent. We can then use this property in performing a complete source separation as an alternative to sequential separation. This technique presupposes that the numbers of sources are known *a priori*.

6.7 Finding Multiple Interesting and Independent Directions Using Symmetric Feedback and Adaptive Whitening

Oja's Robust PCA algorithm (6.6) has also been used by Karhunen *et al* (1995) for BSS, and has met with limited success. There are two major shortcomings of the algorithm as it stands at present. It has been empirically found that the orthonormal constraints are satisfied rapidly and so $\mathbf{I} - \mathbf{W}\,\mathbf{W}^T \rightarrow \mathbf{0}$. As the constraint is multiplicative further learning is inhibited. The algorithm is therefore highly susceptible to sub-optimal convergence in terms of stationary points for BSS. We have found this to be the case during extensive simulations. Empirical studies carried out by Karhunen *et al* (1997) have also led to this conclusion and as such have limited the applicability of (6.6) to ICA and BSS. However, the strict orthonormality and computational simplicity of the algorithm make (6.6) attractive for ICA, as the algorithm is precisely an online adaptive technique for orthogonal ICA contrast maximisation, (Comon, 1994).

The second major perceived shortcoming of the algorithm is that the independent components which can be separated are restricted to sub-Gaussian (leptokurtic) pdf's (Karhunen *et al,* 1997). This is largely a problem of algorithmic stability as detailed in Chapter 5, and has been dealt with by the introduction of the compound activation function. What has yet to be addressed is the method of data whitening. In the simulations carried out thus far the spatial whitening has been performed using the numerical eigenvalue decomposition method (Chapter 3, Section 3.1) which is a batch method and runs counter to the objective of seeking online adaptive methods. Fyfe and Baddeley (1995) have used PCA networks to perform the decorrelation for whitening, with a subsequent normalisation using the eigenvalue information. Two points should be made here: firstly it is not necessary to establish the PCA subspace for decorrelation. Secondly this procedure is not satisfactory for continuous whitening in non-stationary environments, as local eigenvalue information needs to be computed and stored locally at each neuron.

6.7.1 Adaptive Spatial Whitening

Foldiak (1989) proposed a simple form of normalised decorrelation network (Chapter 4, Section 4.1.3, Figure 4.2). The output in vector / matrix notation is

$$\mathbf{z} = \mathbf{x} + \mathbf{U}\mathbf{y} \Rightarrow \mathbf{y} = (\mathbf{I} - \mathbf{U})^{-1}\mathbf{x} \tag{6.7}$$

Foldiak gives the weight updates as

$$\Delta\mathbf{U} = \eta\left(\mathbf{I} - \mathbf{y}\mathbf{y}^T\right) \tag{6.8}$$

so that in the expectation the covariance matrix of the transformed data tends to an identity matrix, $E\{\mathbf{y}\mathbf{y}^T\} \rightarrow \mathbf{I}$. From the perspective of numerical computation we can improve this model by considering the computation of the output (6.7). Firstly, we require a matrix inversion to compute the output due to the lateral feedback of the output. Computationally it is desirable to remove the matrix inversion when computing the output of the network. An alternative structure, is given in Figure 6.4. This can be implemented as a feed-forward model with additional non-learning direct connections. The inputs rather than the outputs drive the lateral inhibition and this gives output activation

$$\mathbf{y} = (\mathbf{I} + \mathbf{U})\mathbf{x} \tag{6.9}$$

We use an objective function which gives a measure of how close the covariance matrix $\mathbf{C_{yy}}$ of the N dimensional output vector $\mathbf{y}$ is to the identity matrix and this is a function of the weight matrix $\mathbf{U}$ (Cardoso, 1997).

$$\Phi(\mathbf{U}) \equiv \mathrm{trace}(\mathbf{C_{yy}}) - \log\left[\det(\mathbf{C_{yy}})\right] - N \tag{6.10}$$

To ensure that the learning of $\mathbf{U}$ gives an identity covariance matrix $\mathbf{C_{yy}}$ the objective function (6.10) needs to be minimised. By taking a first order expansion of (6.10) we then have

$$\Phi(\mathbf{U} + \Delta\mathbf{U}) = \Phi(\mathbf{U}) - 2(\mathbf{I} - \mathbf{C_{yy}})\Delta\mathbf{U}^T + o\left(\Delta\mathbf{U}^2\right) \tag{6.11}$$

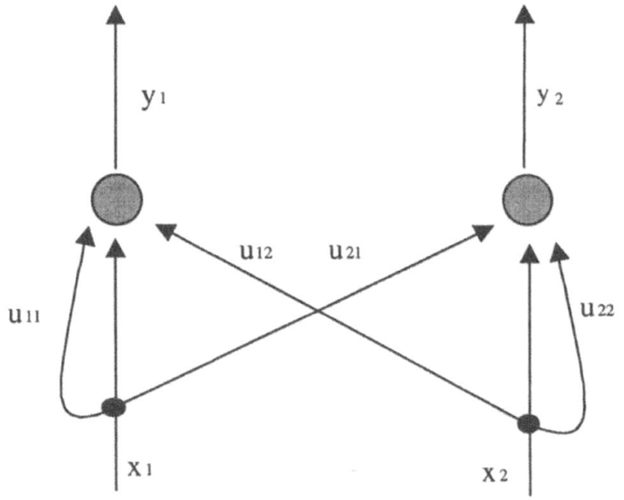

Figure 6.4: Modified Laterally Connected Model.

At a minimum of the objective function when $\mathbf{C_{yy}} = \mathbf{I}$, then $\left(\mathbf{I} - E\{\mathbf{y}\mathbf{y}^T\}\right) = 0$, by removing the expectation we can then use the stochastic version as a whitening algorithm which is identical to (6.8). Using the alternate structure (6.8) and (6.9) yields

$$\mathbf{C_{yy}} = (\mathbf{I} + \mathbf{U})\mathbf{C_{xx}}(\mathbf{I} + \mathbf{U})^T$$

As $\mathbf{C_{yy}} = \mathbf{I}$ then

$$\mathbf{C_{xx}} = \left[(\mathbf{I} + \mathbf{U})^{-1}\right]^2$$

$$\Rightarrow \mathbf{U} = \mathbf{C}_{\mathbf{xx}}^{-\frac{1}{2}} - \mathbf{I} = \mathbf{C}\Lambda^{-\frac{1}{2}}\mathbf{C}^T - \mathbf{I}$$

The eigenvalue decomposition of the input covariance matrix, $\mathbf{C_{xx}} = \mathbf{C}\Lambda\mathbf{C}^T$, shows that the input covariance needs to be positive definite in this case for the matrix $\mathbf{U}$ to be real valued. Haykin (1991) shows that for naturally occurring signals, the positive definite covariance requirement is satisfied. Convergence to an identity covariance matrix in most cases is assured as the value 1 is a stable attractor for the diagonal terms

$$y_i y_i > 1 \Rightarrow \Delta u_{ii} < 0$$

and

$$y_i y_i < 1 \Rightarrow \Delta u_{ii} > 0$$

We shall now employ this modified form of normalising decorrelation network to whiten input data in an online adaptive manner. In Section 6.3 we considered the EPP network as proposed originally by Fyfe and Baddeley (1995), placing the normalising decorrelating layer at the input of the EPP network we arrive at an interesting architecture shown in Figure 6.5.

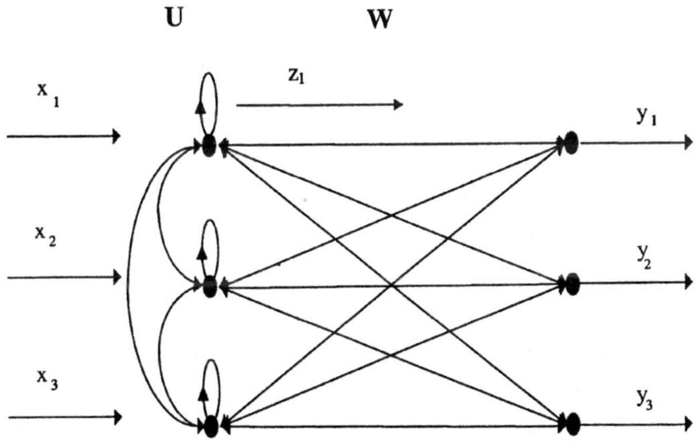

Figure 6.5: Linear Feedback Network with Additional Input Whitening Layer.

The output of the first layer of neurons is given as **z** and so with the linear lateral connections at the input for an N dimensional input vector, the symmetric local activations are

$$\mathbf{z} = [\mathbf{I} + \mathbf{U}]\mathbf{x} \tag{6.12}$$

and the linear summation of the feedforward weights is, in matrix format

$$\mathbf{r} = \mathbf{W}^T [\mathbf{I} + \mathbf{U}]\mathbf{x} = \mathbf{W}^T \mathbf{z} \tag{6.13}$$

The weight of the input layer will be adapted using (6.8) and the feedforward weights will be adapted using the standard adaptation rule (6.6). As the feedforward weights of the network will be orthonormal we then know that this will force the output neurons to converge to differing independent sources. The problem of algorithmic stability has been removed with the introduction of the compound activation function (Chapter 5). An algorithmically simpler method of adaptive data pre-whitening has been proposed and forms the input layer of the EPP network. We now test the performance of the network using the mixtures of sub-Gaussian sources (images), super-Gaussian sources (natural speech) and combined sub- / super-Gaussian sources which are all used in Chapter 5.

6.7.2 Simulations

In each simulation the elements of the initial weight matrix are set to small, normally distributed random numbers. For the results reported here the mixing matrices in each data set are identical to those used within the simulations of Chapter 5. Many other simulations using differing mixing matrices have been performed; however, to enable a comparison of the algorithms a unified data set is utilised throughout the simulations. In generating performance curves a series of five simulations, each with randomly generated initial weight matrices, were performed. Each of the five performance curves are shown on a graph to verify the consistency of the adaptation method. The chief measure of separation performance used is the Performance Index, PI, (Amari, Cichocki and Yang, 1995). To monitor the development of the feedforward matrix and its distance from orthogonality we use the following divergence measure (Cover and Thomas, 1991)

$$KI = \log \prod_{i=1}^{N} \left(\mathbf{W}\,\mathbf{W}^T\right)_{ii} - \log\left|\det\left(\mathbf{W}\mathbf{W}^T\right)\right|$$

This divergence will always be positive and tends to zero as the weight matrix approaches orthonormality. For convenience we will refer to this measure as a Kullback divergence. In simulation number one we consider the separation of a mixture of super-Gaussian sources using the mixture of natural speech (Chapter 5). The results (Figure 6.6) show quite clearly that the adaptive decorrelation works well. The converged full whitening weight matrix was

$$\mathbf{U} = \begin{bmatrix} 15.957 & 3.113 & -3.033 & 3.793 & -1.643 \\ 3.113 & 11.651 & 0.817 & 4.165 & -2.956 \\ -3.033 & 0.817 & 2.246 & -0.183 & 0.969 \\ 3.794 & 4.165 & -0.183 & 11.716 & 2.164 \\ -1.643 & -2.956 & 0.969 & 2.164 & 9.549 \end{bmatrix}$$

and the optimal whitening weight matrix as computed by $\breve{\mathbf{U}} = \mathbf{C}_{\mathbf{xx}}^{-\frac{1}{2}} - \mathbf{I}$ (Section 6.7) where the matrix $\mathbf{C}_{\mathbf{xx}}$ is the covariance matrix of the mixture is computed as

$$\breve{\mathbf{U}} = \begin{bmatrix} 15.852 & 3.136 & -3.078 & 3.962 & -1.839 \\ 3.136 & 11.337 & 0.801 & 4.491 & -2.994 \\ -3.078 & 0.801 & 2.532 & -0.246 & 1.005 \\ 3.962 & 4.491 & -0.246 & 11.410 & 2.264 \\ -1.839 & -2.994 & 1.005 & 2.264 & 9.297 \end{bmatrix}$$

It is instructive to view charts 2 and 4 of Figure 6.6. It is clear that once the feedforward weights are orthogonal there is no further adaptation of the feedforward weights. This occurs after approximately 200,000 iterations (an iteration corresponds to the presentation of one data sample). It is interesting to note that the whitening weights continue to develop after 200,000 iterations, which indicates there is still correlation between the inputs. The chart of the performance index shows that there is no real level of separation and once the weight development ceases there are only fluctuations about a steady value of the performance index. This confirms the major shortcoming of using a standard multiple output EPP network for BSS. Simulations two and three are carried out using the other data sets and from Figures 6.7 and 6.8 it is apparent that this sub-optimal convergence is common over all three types of mixtures.

Simulation 1
Mixtures of Super-Gaussian Sources

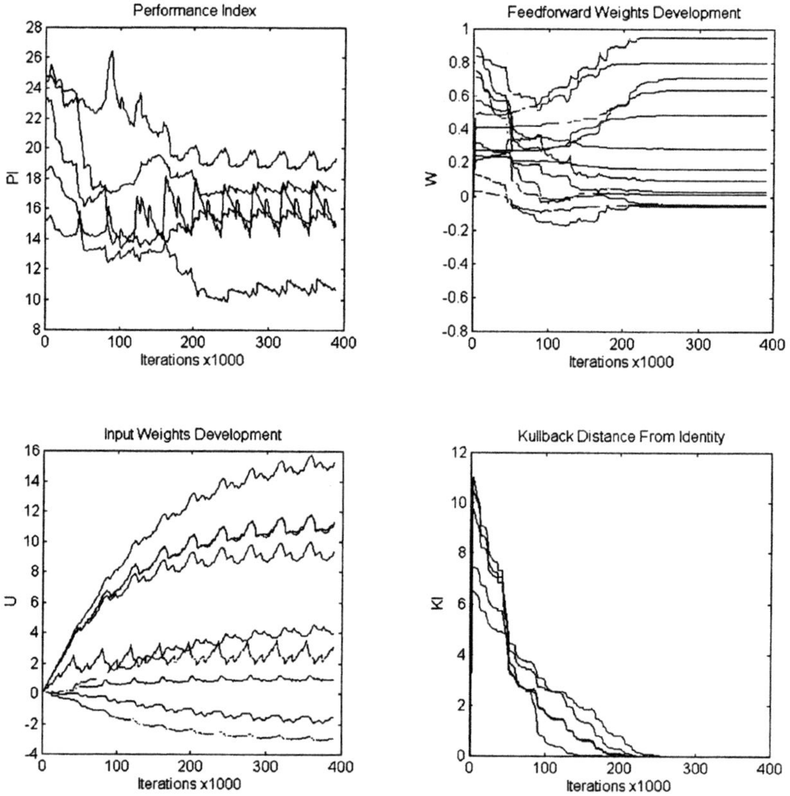

Figure 6.6: Chart 1 Shows the Performance Index for this Simulation. It shows that in all cases separation has not occurred. The development of the feedforward weights is shown in Chart 2, clearly the weights stop developing after 200,000 iterations. Chart 3 shows the development of the whitening weights. Chart 4 shows the Kullback divergence of the feedforward weights from orthogonality. It is clear that once the weights are orthogonal further adaptation of the feedforward weights ceases.

Simulation 2
Mixtures of Sub-Gaussian Sources

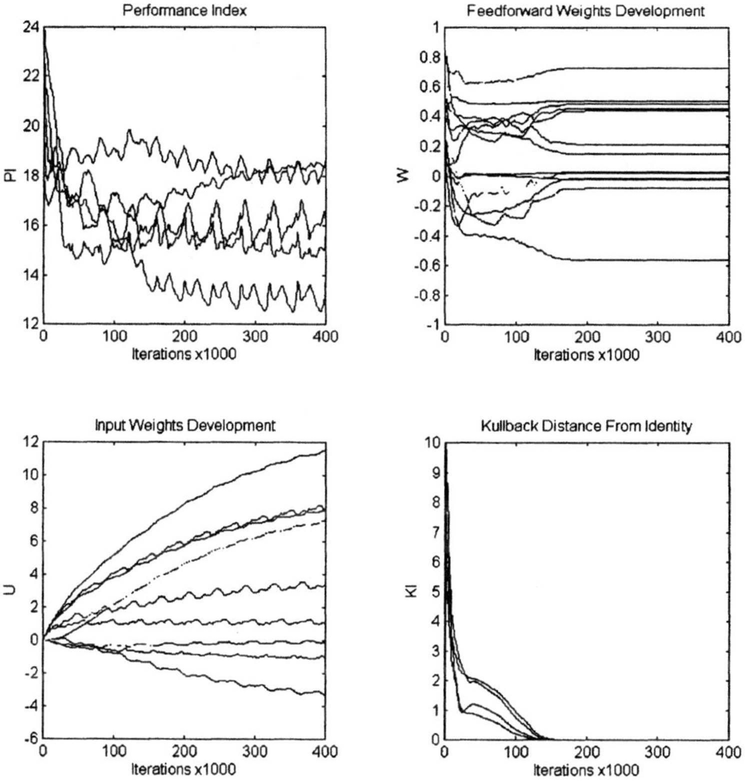

Figure 6.7: As Figure 6.6.

Simulation 3
Mixtures of Sub-Gaussian and Super-Gaussian Sources

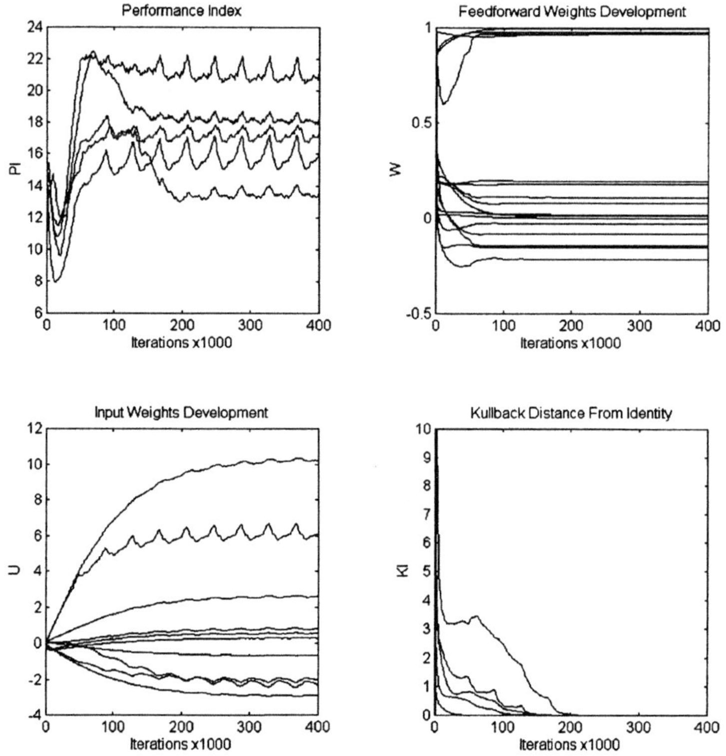

Figure 6.8: As Figure 6.6.

We now have to address the problem of the orthonormality term rapidly converging to the zero matrix and inhibiting further adaptation of the weights, that is $\mathbf{I} - \mathbf{W}\mathbf{W}^T \rightarrow \mathbf{0}$.

6.7.3 An Extended EPP Network with Non-linear Output Connections

To remove the problem of $\mathbf{I} - \mathbf{W}\mathbf{W}^T \rightarrow \mathbf{0}$ so rapidly as to inhibit further learning we can reconsider the original objective function (4.49) and the solely feedforward nature of the associated network. Motivated by the linear self-organising network for PCA of Rubner and Tavan (1989) we first consider the addition of anti-Hebbian connections at the output of the network. Rubner and Tavan utilise a form of lateral anti-Hebbian connections at the output of their self-organising network to constrain the convergence of the feedfoward weights to the distinct eigen-vectors of the data covariance. The lateral weights and the anti-Hebbian learning decorrelate the output units. The feedforward weights will each tend to converge to the first principal component of the data. However, the organisation of the feedforward weights is distorted due to the anti-Hebbian learning, which is taking place at the output, thus forcing the weights to the subsequent principal components of the data. Although the anti-Hebbian connections at the output tend to zero in the limit, the interplay during self-organisation between the lateral and feedforward weights is critical for convergence to the unique principal eigenvectors.

In the case of ICA, the addition of anti-Hebbian lateral connections may also be viewed as introducing another time dependent matrix variable into the form of the objective function (4.49). This will have the effect of altering the stochastic updating of the variable $\mathbf{W}$, as in the linear case, although the stationary points will remain the same. We shall now consider lateral fully connected non-linear anti-Hebbian connections at the output of the EPP network.

We now re-write the objective function (4.49) as

$$J(\mathbf{W}) = \mathbf{1}^T(\mathbf{I} + \mathbf{V})E\left\{g\left(\mathbf{W}^T\mathbf{x}\right)\right\} + \tfrac{1}{2}\mathrm{tr}\left(\Lambda\left(\mathbf{W}^T\mathbf{W} - \mathbf{A}\right)\right) \qquad (6.14)$$

If the matrix $\mathbf{V}$ is diagonal and $\mathbf{I}$ is the identity matrix, then the first term on the right hand side is simply a weighted sum of the elements of g(...). When $\mathbf{V} = \mathbf{0}$ then (6.14) is just simply the original objective function (4.49). From the derivation presented in Karhunen and Joutsensalo (1995) we will then have, taking instantaneous derivatives,

$$\frac{d\,J(\mathbf{W})}{d\,\mathbf{W}} = \mathbf{x}\,g'\left(\mathbf{x}^T\mathbf{W}\right)\left(\mathbf{I} + \mathbf{V}\right)^T + \mathbf{W}\,\Lambda \tag{6.15}$$

Differentiating with respect to the Lagrangian multipliers gives the condition $\mathbf{W}^T\mathbf{W} = \mathbf{A}$ at convergence. Simple manipulation of (6.8) then gives

$$\mathbf{W}^T\frac{d\,J(\mathbf{W})}{d\,\mathbf{W}} = \mathbf{W}^T\mathbf{x}\,g'\left(\mathbf{x}^T\mathbf{W}\right)\left(\mathbf{I} + \mathbf{V}\right)^T + \mathbf{W}^T\mathbf{W}\,\Lambda = 0$$

$$= \mathbf{W}^T\mathbf{x}\,g'\left(\mathbf{x}^T\mathbf{W}\right)\left(\mathbf{I} + \mathbf{V}\right)^T + \mathbf{A}\,\Lambda = 0$$

$$\Rightarrow \Lambda = -\mathbf{A}^{-1}\mathbf{W}^T\mathbf{x}\,g'\left(\mathbf{x}^T\mathbf{W}\right)\left(\mathbf{I} + \mathbf{V}\right)^T \tag{6.16}$$

Substituting (6.16) into (6.15) for $\mathbf{A} = \mathbf{I}$, finally gives

$$\frac{d\,J(\mathbf{W})}{d\,\mathbf{W}} = \left(\mathbf{I} - \mathbf{W}\mathbf{W}^T\right)\mathbf{x}\,g'\left(\mathbf{x}^T\mathbf{W}\right)\left(\mathbf{I} + \mathbf{V}\right)^T \tag{6.17}$$

This can now be used in the stochastic weight update for the $\mathbf{W}$ weights such that

$$\Delta\mathbf{W} = \left(\mathbf{I} - \mathbf{W}\mathbf{W}^T\right)\mathbf{x}\,g'\left(\mathbf{x}^T\mathbf{W}\right)\left(\mathbf{I} + \mathbf{V}\right)^T \tag{6.18}$$

The key difference between (6.18) and (6.6) is the additional post multiplication of the time dependent matrix $\left(\mathbf{I} + \mathbf{V}\right)^T$. Prior to considering the form of update for the additional matrix term, we now introduce a neural structure suitable for the implementation of (6.18) when utilising simple Hebbian learning.

The activation and linear feedback are equivalent to those of the EPP network 6.1, 6.2, 6.3. We now have the laterally connected extension at the output and so the inhibitory symmetric feedback, (Fyfe, 1995) occurs as in (6.2). So

$$\mathbf{z}(t+1) \leftarrow \mathbf{z}(t) - \mathbf{W}\mathbf{W}^T\mathbf{z}(t) \tag{6.19}$$

The non-linear activation in this case is laterally fed forward to give the final network output of

$$\mathbf{y} = [\mathbf{I} + \mathbf{V}] f\left(\mathbf{W}^T \mathbf{z}\right) \tag{6.20}$$

Simple Hebbian learning again is used to update the feedfoward weights

$$\Delta \mathbf{W} = \eta \mathbf{z} \mathbf{y}^T$$

Finally giving

$$\Delta \mathbf{W} = \eta \left(\mathbf{I} - \mathbf{W}\mathbf{W}^T\right)\mathbf{z} f\left(\mathbf{z}^T \mathbf{W}\right)(\mathbf{I} + \mathbf{V})^T \tag{6.21}$$

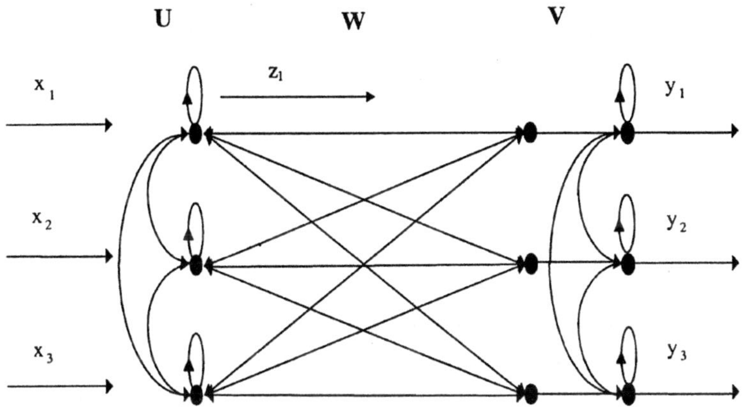

Figure 6.9: The Extended Exploratory Projection Pursuit Network.

We now consider the update of the lateral output weights **V**, the derivation of (6.21) assumed a diagonal matrix **V**. Further utilising anti-Hebbian learning at the output, that is

$$\Delta \mathbf{V} = \mu \left(\mathbf{I} - \mathbf{y}\mathbf{y}^T\right) \tag{6.22}$$

noting however, that we now have a non-linear learning term here due to the activation functions and so

$$\mathbf{I} + \mathbf{V} \rightarrow \mathbf{C}_{ff}^{-\frac{1}{2}} \text{ where } \mathbf{C}_{ff} = E\left\{f(\mathbf{y})f\left(\mathbf{y}^T\right)\right\}.$$

Using the form of non-linear term proposed in Section 6.5, $f(r) = r \pm \tanh(r)$ where the sign is determined by the type of source to be separated, and $\mathbf{r} = \mathbf{W}^T\mathbf{z}$, then

$$\mathbf{C}_{ff} = E\left\{\mathbf{r}\,\mathbf{r}^T \pm \tanh(\mathbf{r})\mathbf{r}^T \pm \mathbf{r}\tanh\left(\mathbf{r}^T\right) + \tanh(\mathbf{r})\tanh\left(\mathbf{r}^T\right)\right\}$$

$$= E\left\{\mathbf{W}^T\mathbf{z}\,\mathbf{z}^T\mathbf{W} \pm \tanh(\mathbf{r})\mathbf{r}^T \pm \mathbf{r}\tanh\left(\mathbf{r}^T\right) + \tanh(\mathbf{r})\tanh\left(\mathbf{r}^T\right)\right\}.$$

Utilising the conclusions from Section 6.5, regarding the hyperbolic tangent for whitened data allows the approximation given below.

$$\mathbf{C}_{ff} \cong k_1\mathbf{I} \pm k_2 E\left\{\mathbf{r}^3\mathbf{r}^T\right\} \pm k_3 E\left\{\mathbf{r}\left(\mathbf{r}^3\right)^T\right\} + k_4 E\left\{\mathbf{r}^3\left(\mathbf{r}^3\right)^T\right\}$$

Where the constant values are collected from the approximative Taylor expansion. Now the non-linear Hebbian learning (6.21) of the feedforward weights will maximise the sum of squares of fourth order cumulants, and so by implication minimise the sum of squares of all cross cumulants of fourth order. The non-linear anti-Hebbian learning of (6.22) will explicitly remove the cross cumulants which can be considered as higher order decorrelation and so $\pm E\left\{r_i^3 r_j\right\} \rightarrow 0$ and $\pm E\{r_i^3 r_j^3\} \rightarrow 0 \quad \forall\ i \neq j$. Higher order moments which are even (4th, 6th, etc) are strictly positive and, taking into account the details regarding suitably scaled white data in Section 6.6, for the diagonal terms we have $k_1 \pm (k_2 + k_3)E\left\{r_i^4\right\} + k_4 E\left\{r_i^6\right\} > 0$ thus indicating indicating that the matrix ($\mathbf{I} + \mathbf{V}$) will be diagonal with positive terms. Extensive numerical simulations confirm this to be the case with data drawn from a number of both sub-Gaussian and super-Gaussian distributions (Girolami and Fyfe, 1996a, b, c, 1997a, b, d, e).

Returning to the new objective function (6.14) where the function g(...) is the absolute value of the fourth order cumulant

$$J(\mathbf{W}) = \mathbf{1}^T(\mathbf{I} + \mathbf{V})E\left\{\left|\kappa_4\left(\mathbf{W}^T\mathbf{x}\right)\right|\right\} + \tfrac{1}{2}\mathrm{tr}\left(\Lambda\left(\mathbf{W}^T\mathbf{W} - \mathbf{A}\right)\right)$$

As ($\mathbf{I} + \mathbf{V}$) develops into a positive diagonal matrix (6.14) is simply now a weighted sum of the expected values which will yield similar optimal parameters as the original non-weighted cost. What is crucial here is that the **V** matrix will also be varying during the self-organisation and so may distort the original trajectory (no lateral connections) of development for the **W** matrix. To test this extension of the EPP network we perform simulations on the three data sets used in Section 6.7.2. The results are given in Figures 6.10, 6.11 and 6.12.

Consider first the results for the separation of a mixture of super-Gaussian sources simulation 4, (Figure 6.10). From the chart of the Kullback divergence of the **W** weight matrix from orthonormality it is clear that convergence to an orthonormal weight matrix has been delayed significantly. The development of the performance index follows a similar erratic path to that followed by the Kullback measure. However, in comparison to simulation 1, where the original EPP network was unable to separate mixtures of super-Gaussian sources, the final value of the performance index is small and indeed a good level of separation is given as noted by the final matrix product given below.

$$\mathbf{W}^T(\mathbf{I} + \mathbf{U})\mathbf{A} = \begin{bmatrix} 2.590 & 0.043 & 0.468 & \mathbf{-27.680} & -0.280 \\ \mathbf{30.905} & -0.136 & 0.546 & 2.794 & -0.808 \\ -3.663 & -0.305 & 1.228 & 1.849 & \mathbf{-26.829} \\ 0.347 & -0.043 & \mathbf{23.121} & -0.065 & 0.275 \\ -0.937 & \mathbf{-14.374} & 1.523 & -1.605 & -0.626 \end{bmatrix}$$

Simulation 4
Mixtures of Super-Gaussian Sources

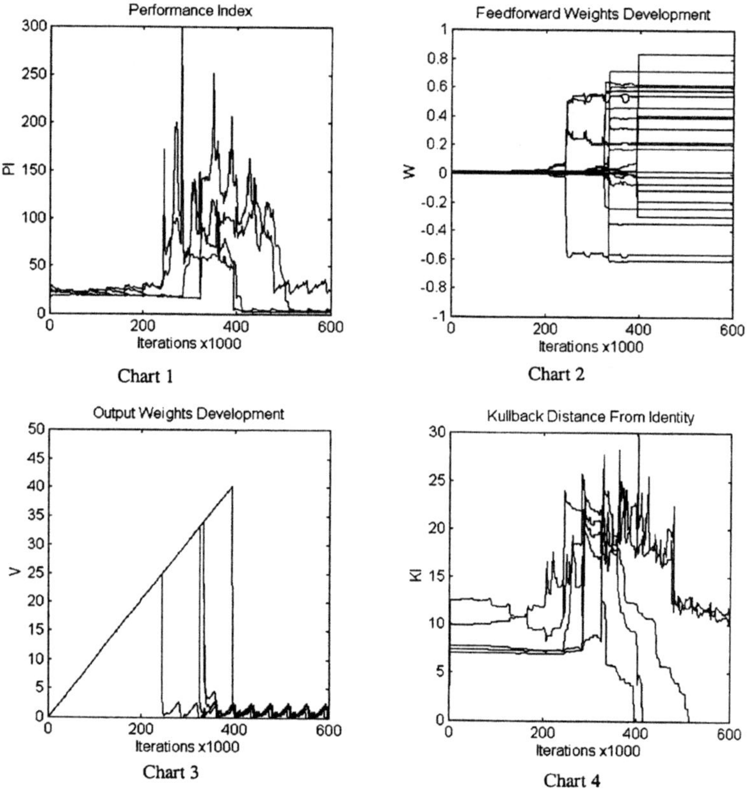

Figure 6.10: Chart 1 Shows the Performance Index for this Simulation. It shows that in all cases separation has occurred. The development of the feedforward weights is shown in Chart 2. Chart 3 in the second row shows the development of the output weights. Chart 4 shows the Kullback divergence of the feedforward weights from orthogonality.

Simulation 5

Mixtures of Sub-Gaussian Sources

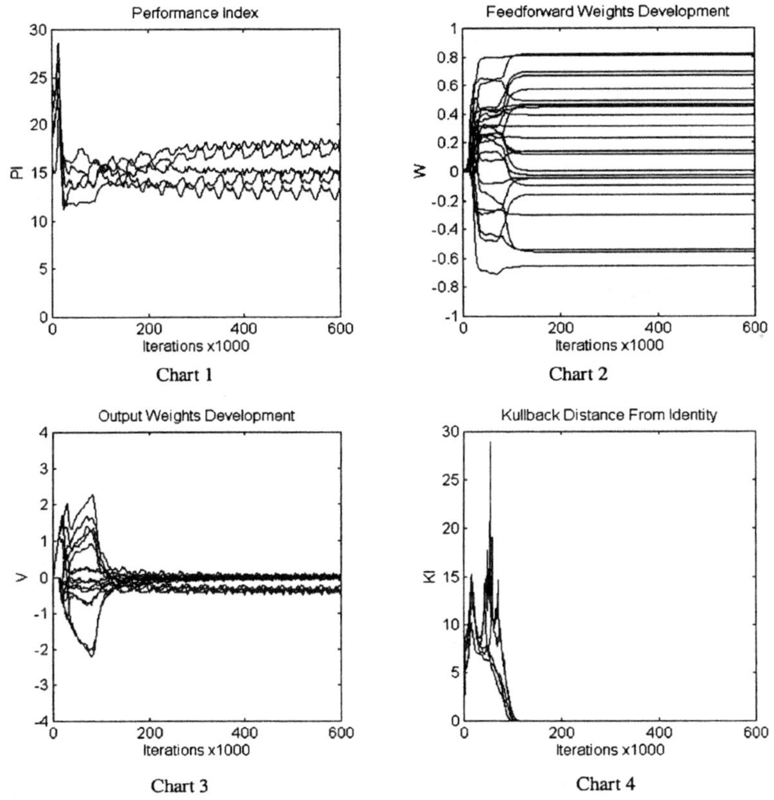

Figure 6.11: Chart 1 Shows the Performance Index for this Simulation. It shows that in all cases separation has not occurred. The development of the feedforward weights is shown in Chart 2, and clearly the weights stop developing after 200,000 iterations. Chart 3 shows the development of the ouput weights. Chart 4 shows the Kullback divergence of the feedforward weights from orthogonality. It is clear that once the weights are orthogonal, further adaptation of the feedforward weights ceases.

Simulation 6
Mixtures of Sub-Gaussian and Super-Gaussian Sources

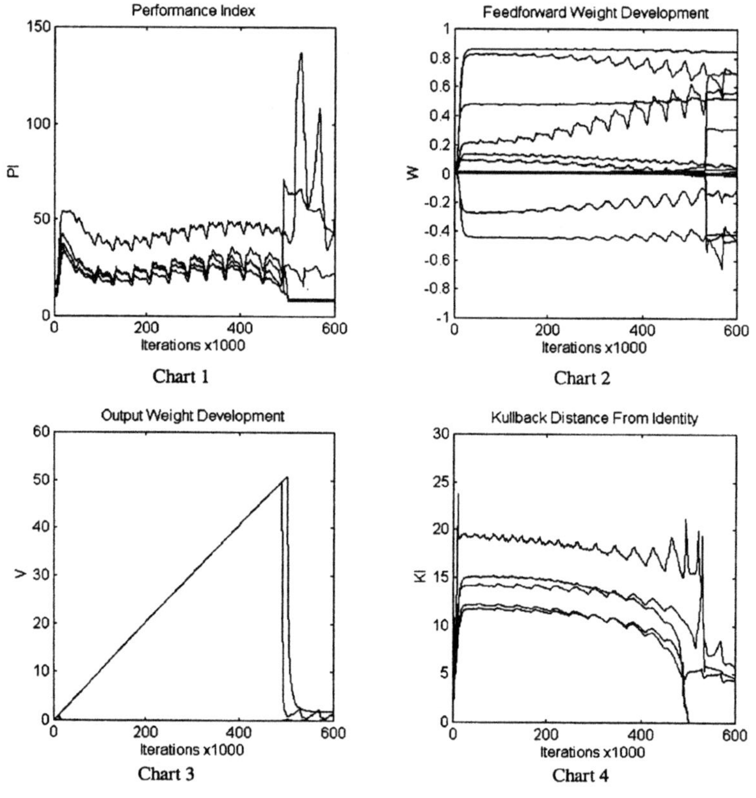

Figure 6.12: As Figure 6.11.

It is clear that the general matrix product of the network transformation is a permutation and scaling matrix with only one dominant term existing in each row and column. The addition of the output connections appears to have delayed the convergence of the weight matrix to orthonormality sufficiently to allow convergence to separating solutions. Extensive simulations confirm the performance of the network architecture for mixtures of super-Gaussian sources. The development of the feedforward weights and the output weights highlights clearly how the convergence to sub-optimal solutions is avoided using this particular architecture. If we consider the development of the output weights at the start of the learning when the weights are set to relatively small values, the non-linearity for super-Gaussian sources will take on small values

$$f(y) = y - \tanh(y) \rightarrow 0$$

This then initially inhibits development of the feedforward weights (6.21). The coupling of the output weights, however, means that at each iteration the output weights will be updated by $\Delta \mathbf{V} = \mu (\mathbf{I})$ and so the self-connections will grow in an almost linear manner (Figure 6.10). This acts as a form of amplification for (6.21) and can be considered as performing the normalisation discussed in (Amari, Cichocki and Yang, 1995b; Cichocki, Unbehauen, Moszczynski and Rummert, 1995; Cichocki and Moszczynski, 1994). As the feedforward weights develop, the anti-Hebbian learning starts to act on the self-connections causing them to diminish in strength whilst the feedforward weights associated with each output neuron develop in strength. The drop in self-connection strength appears dramatic, however, each point on each chart is computed every one thousand iterations. What is clear is that the self-connections act to allow each neuron to develop and extract each source in a phased manner. The conjectured time varying distortion of the trajectory of the **W** weights convergence has largely been driven by the self-connections. This extended form of EPP learning also works well for large mixtures of super-Gaussian sources.

Investigation of the results of simulation 5, (Figure 6.11) shows similar behaviour to that seen in simulation 2, (Figure 6.7). The **W** weights achieve orthonormality rapidly and so the performance index converges to a non-separating value. Simulation 6 shows that the super-Gaussian sources can be separated but the sub-Gaussian sources are not fully extracted. It is clear that the extension of the EPP network under consideration performs BSS well for mixtures of super-Gaussian sources but fails with sub-Gaussian sources. Considering the performance shown in Figure 6.10 it is clear that a phased series of extractions is occurring. This observation leads us now to consider a hierarchic, or deflationary, form of feedback in the EPP network.

6.8 Finding Multiple Interesting and Independent Directions Using Hierarchic Feedback and Adaptive Whitening

For the network considered (Figure 6.5) the feedback of activation was symmetric. We now consider introducing asymmetry to the weight update algorithm

$$\Delta \mathbf{W} = \eta \left(\mathbf{I} - \mathbf{W}\mathbf{W}^T \right) \mathbf{z} f\left(\mathbf{z}^T \mathbf{W} \right)$$

which in the symmetric linear case will converge to some arbitrary orthogonal basis vectors of a PCA subspace. Sanger (1989) proposed the Generalised Hebbian Algorithm (GHA) by introducing a form of asymmetry into the learning of the subspace rule. The individual weights are updated as

$$\Delta w_{ij} = \eta_t f\left(\sum_{p=1}^{N} w_{ip} z_p(t) \right) \left\{ z_j(t) - \sum_{k=1}^{i} w_{kj} \sum_{q=1}^{N} w_{kq} z_q(t) \right\} \tag{6.23}$$

We can see from (6.23) that the feedback of the activation occurs in a hierarchic manner. It is shown (Sanger, 1989) that the GHA will converge to the actual principal components of the observed data covariance matrix. This hierarchy can be considered as a form of deflation. As the first neuron captures the first principal component (PC), the residual used in the Hebbian learning for the weights of the second neuron will have the first PC removed and so the second neuron will capture the second PC, and so on. This can be related to BSS and indeed sequential deflationary extraction has been proposed by various authors (Delfosse and Loubaton, 1995; Cichocki, Thawonmas and Amari, 1997; Hyvarinen and Oja, 1996). Karhunen and Joutsensalo (1995) consider that for non-linear and robust PCA algorithms, hierarchy is not so important because non-linearities break complete symmetry during learning. This is not the case however when applying hierarchy to EPP learning as shall be demonstrated in Section 6.9. The introduction of hierarchy into the EPP network will then introduce a deflationary aspect to the learning. The feedforward weight update of (6.6) can now be written in matrix notation as

$$\Delta \mathbf{W} = \eta\left(\mathbf{z} f\left(\mathbf{z}^T \mathbf{W}\right) - \mathbf{W} \times \text{upper}\left(\mathbf{W}^T \mathbf{z} f\left(\mathbf{z}^T \mathbf{W}\right)\right)\right) \tag{6.24}$$

The operator upper[.] makes its matrix argument upper triangular. The phased or hierarchic feedback may distort the development of the feedfoward weights. Consider the rightmost term in (6.23) in componential form

$$\left\{ z_j(t) - \sum_{k=1}^{i} w_{kj} \sum_{q=1}^{N} w_{kq} z_q(t) \right\} =$$

$$z_j(t) - \sum_{k=1}^{i} w_{kj} y_k =$$

$$z_j(t) - \sum_{k=1}^{i} w_{kj} \hat{s}_k$$

We can see that the linear network activation, which can be considered as an approximation to each independent source is fed back in a hierarchic manner. The residual that is formed is used in the simple non-linear Hebbian learning (6.23). As each linear output converges to an approximation of one of the underlying sources, the subsequent neurons in the hierarchy will have their weights updated using residuals which have had weighted approximations of the previously extracted sources removed. Simulations will show that the hierarchic extension to EPP learning is of significant importance.

6.9 Simulations

The three data sets used in this simulation were those used in the previous simulations. The network shown in Figure 6.5 is employed. We continue to use the whitening rule (6.8): however, a hierarchic form of feedback is employed and so the feedforward weight update is given as (6.24). The simulation results are shown in Figures 6.13, 6.14 and 6.15. Consider the separation of a mixture of super-Gaussian sources in simulation 7. What we see immediately is that the performance index achieves a far lower value than that achieved in simulation 1 although the number of iterations required is greater by, approximately, a factor of three. The most significant result found here is that the feedforward weights do not cease developing once orthonormality is achieved. Simulation 8 (Figure 6.14) shows this far more clearly where the development of one feedforward weight is charted.

This result has been overlooked in the past for BSS and presents an important extension to the EPP network or more generally Oja's non-linear Generalised Hebbian Algorithm. Although the strict orthonormality causes further weight development to cease in the case of strict symmetric feedback, hierarchic feedback allows the weights to continue development. The hierarchic feedback introduces an elegant and simple form of sequential deflation of the mixture. In the linear form of the GHA where the converged solution will be the principal eigenvectors, the deflation will be almost exact. Due to the inherent indeterminacy and scaling of source extraction at best an approximate deflation will be achieved.

6.10 Adaptive BSS Using a Deflationary EPP Network

A final large-scale simulation is given to demonstrate the performance of the deflationary EPP network with adaptive whitening. *A priori* knowledge of the source signal statistics has been required to choose the sign for the compound nonlinearity $f(y) = y - signum(\kappa_4)\tanh(y)$ and with this knowledge, mixtures of both sub-Gaussian and super-Gaussian signals have been able to be separated. In keeping with the 'blind' form of the proposed separation we can estimate online the kurtosis of each neuron using a simple moving average estimator (Cichocki, Kasprzak and Amari, 1996)

$$\hat{m}_p\left[y_i(t+1)\right] = \left[1 - \eta(t)\right]\hat{m}_p\left[y_i(t)\right] + \eta(t)y_i^p(t) \tag{6.25}$$

$$\hat{\kappa}_4\left[y_i(t+1)\right] = \frac{\hat{m}_4\left[y_i(t)\right]}{\hat{m}_2^2\left[y_i(t)\right]} - 3 \tag{6.26}$$

(6.25) estimates online the pth order moments of the data, $\eta(t)$ is a small learning constant. (6.26) is an estimate of the kurtosis for zero mean data.

Simulation 7

Mixtures of Super-Gaussian Sources

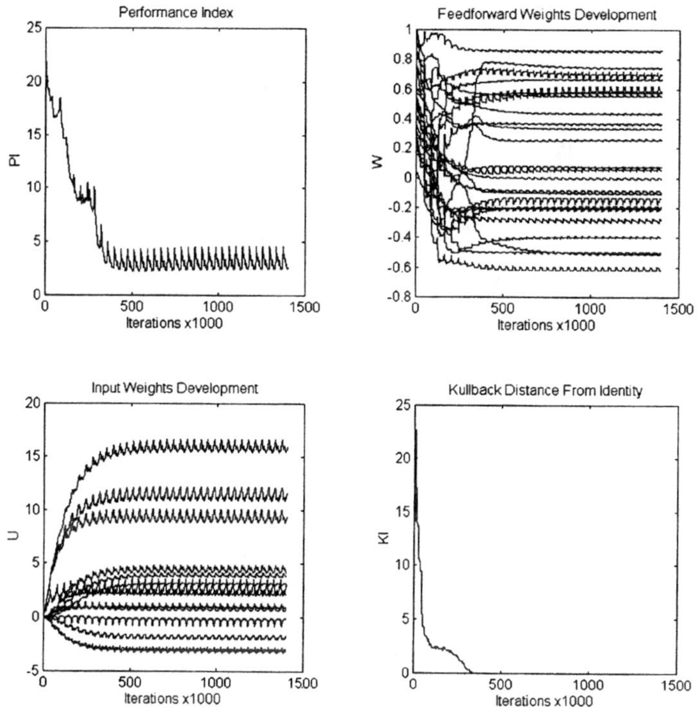

Figure 6.13: Chart 1 Shows the Performance Index for this Simulation. It shows that in this case separation has occurred. The development of the feedforward weights is shown in Chart 2 and clearly the weights continue developing after 200,000 iterations. Chart 3 shows the development of the whitening weights. Chart 4 shows the Kullback divergence of the feedforward weights from orthogonality. It is clear that once the weights are orthogonal further adaptation of the feedforward weights continues. Reducing the learning rate can dampen the oscillations out.

Simulation 8
Mixtures of Sub-Gaussian Sources

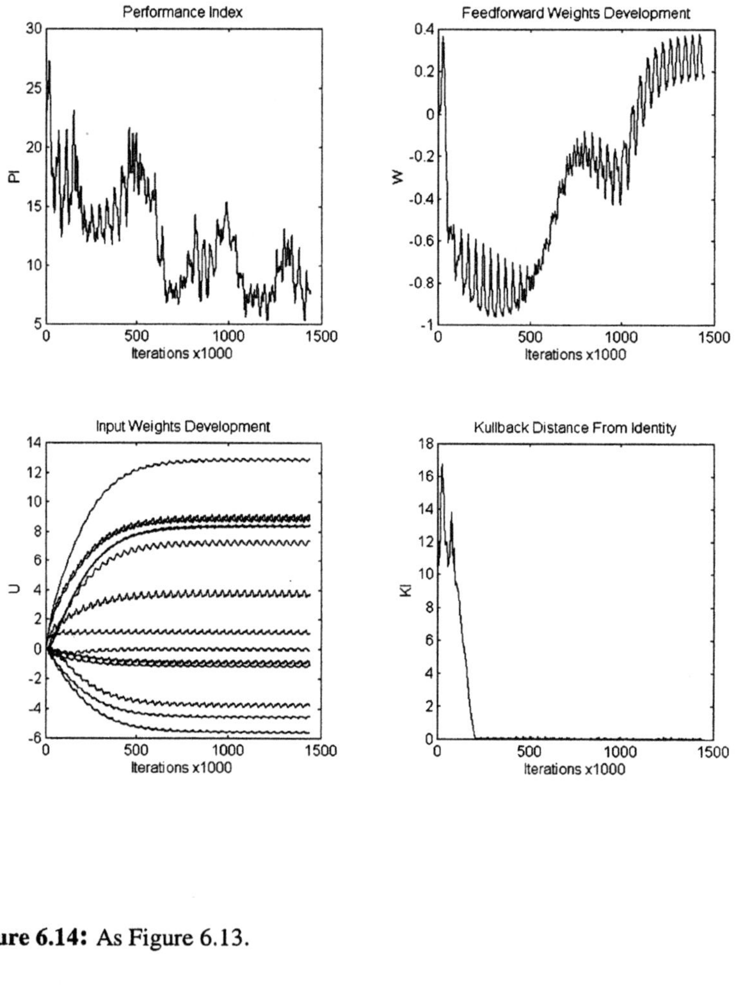

Figure 6.14: As Figure 6.13.

Simulation 9
Mixtures of Super-Gaussian and Sub-Gaussian Sources

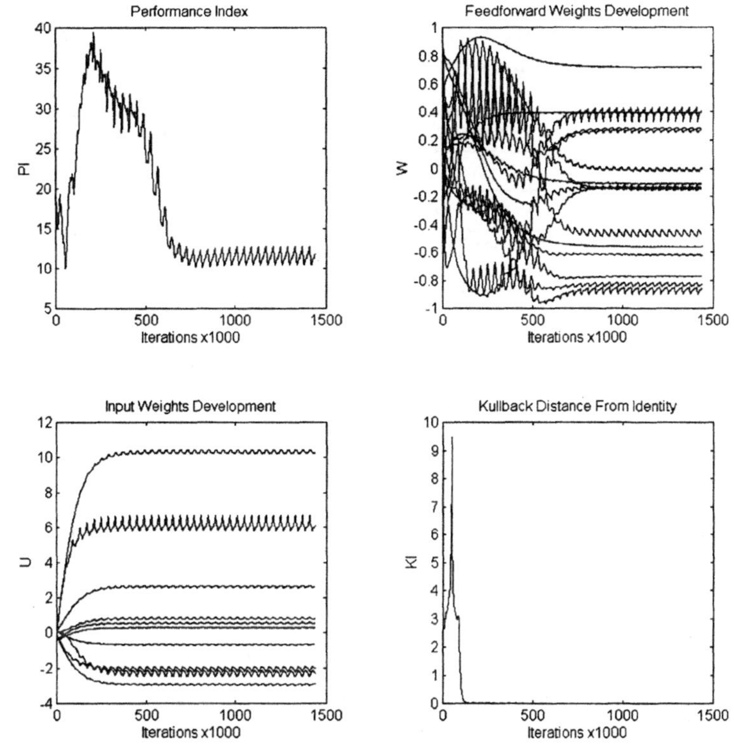

Figure 6.15: As Figure 6.13.

We can then use the adaptive non-linearity of

$$f[y_i(t)] = y_i(t) - signum(\hat{\kappa}_4[y_i(t)])\tanh[y_i(t)] \qquad (6.27)$$

as the output neuron activation function at each pre-specified time step t. Ten greyscale images were chosen based on the kurtosis values of each. Each image was 202×202 pixels in size, with each pixel greyscale using an eight bit representation. Figure 6.16 shows the original images and the final recovered images from the mixture. Table 6.2 gives a listing of both the original and mixed data statistics.

Image	Mean	Kurtosis	Skew	Mixed Images	Kurtosis
Mulder	0.370	-1.245	0.0014	Mix 1	-0.0806
Turing	0.470	+1.467	0.0016	Mix 2	-0.3562
Lena	0.690	-0.730	-0.0049	Mix 3	-0.2652
Noise	0.000	-1.193	0.00063	Mix 4	-0.3479
Finger	0.590	-1.285	-0.00056	Mix 5	-0.2688
Peppers	0.460	-0.878	-0.0023	Mix 6	-0.3458
Scully	0.420	-1.144	0.0023	Mix 7	-0.3999
Stripe	0.730	-1.484	-0.0018	Mix 8	-0.3939
Worm	0.350	+2.031	0.0015	Mix 9	-0.3319
Virus	0.320	-1.279	0.0014	Mix 10	-0.3211

Table 6.2: Original and Mixed Image Statistics.

From Table 6.2 it is clear that the majority of the images are negatively kurtotic; however, the images of Turing and Worm both have positive values of kurtosis. The images have negligible skew in their histograms indicating an almost symmetric pdf. A randomly generated 10×10 matrix carried out the mixing. Figure 6.16 shows the mixed images. As is apparent from Table 6.2, the values of kurtosis have all tended to small values and the corresponding histograms show quite clearly the onset of central limit effects with each mixed image having almost Gaussian statistics. From Figure 6.16 we can see that the mixing has caused significant degradation of the images making them almost indistinguishable. Each mixture had the mean value removed prior to presenting the data to the network. The input weights were initially set to zero, whilst the feedforward weights were randomly set to values between -1 and +1. The sign of kurtosis appearing in the nonlinearity were updated at the end of each epoch in this simulation. We use the sum of squares of fourth order marginal cumulants as a measure (or contrast) of the overall separating performance of the network. Figure 6.18 shows the development of the contrast at the end of each learning epoch. The overall contrast reaches a maximal value of 80% of the original value. Two aspects of the learning that are of particular interest are the kurtosis sign development and the residuals once the output neurons converge to the optimal values. Inspection of the sign of the kurtosis at each learning epoch shows the switching from positive to negative at certain outputs until stability is reached. If we consider the kurtosis development of each individual output, it is clear that a phased extraction of the sources is occurring (Figure 6.19).

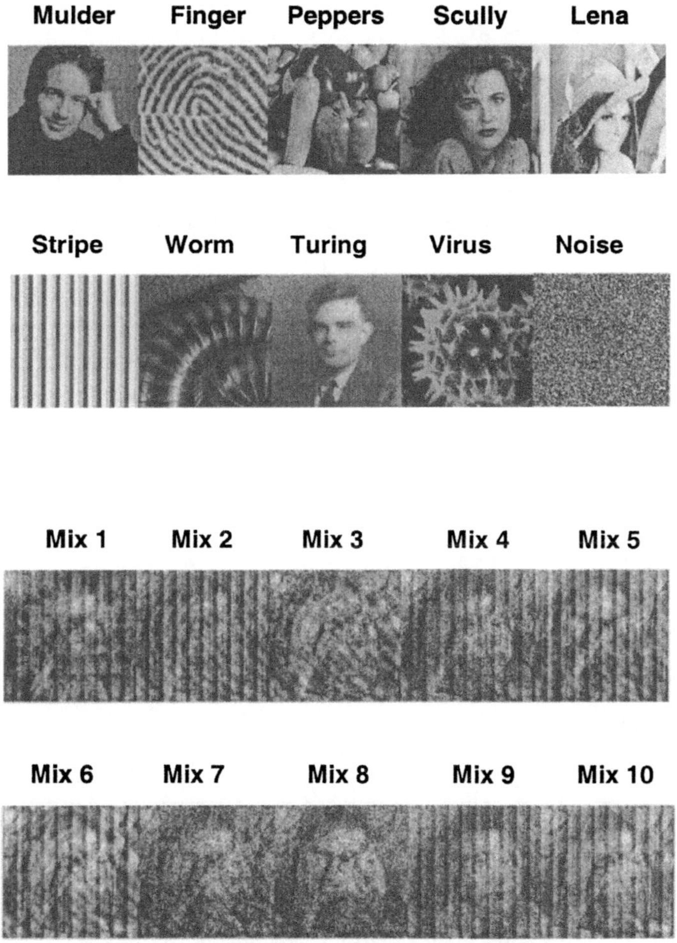

Figure 6.16: Original Source Images and Mixed Images.

Figure 6.17: Network Output and Restored Images.

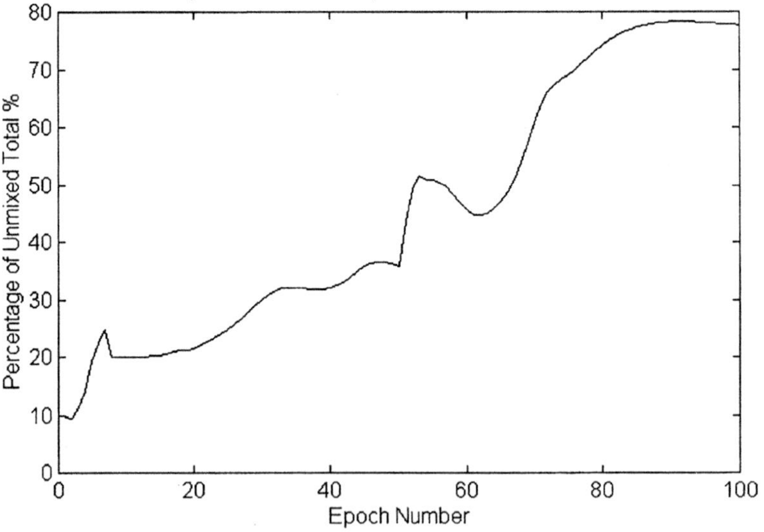

Figure 6.18: Contrast Development During Learning.

A number of points now need to be highlighted. Firstly the number of epochs or complete passes through the data set is in the order of one hundred, which is a substantial number. The hierarchic feedback now allows the network to continue learning when the weights are fully orthonormal. Inspection of Figure 6.19 indicates that the extraction of the sources does not necessarily follow a sequential manner. The manner of the extraction is dependent on the correct development of the kurtosis sign at each output. If the kurtosis sign for a particular neuron is incorrect at some point of the learning then the neuron will pursue an inappropriate direction for maximisation. However, as the weight matrix **W** is strictly orthonormal during the learning period, the linear independence of the weight matrix columns will force a change of the kurtosis sign. This changes the direction of pursuit and ensures the strict orthonormal nature of the weight matrix. Figure 6.20 shows the sign of the non-linear term at each neuron and how these have changed during learning.

6.11 Conclusions

This chapter has presented the strong link with BSS and EPP when kurtotic projections are being pursued. The negative feedback network proposed by Fyfe (1995) was considered as an implementation of EPP and therefore BSS. The weight update for the linear feedback network can be derived from the stochastic maximisation of a non-linear criterion (Chapter 4, Section 4.2.3.2). When the criterion is the absolute value of the kurtosis then we can extract single sources from a mixture. Extending the single output network to an $N \times N$ separation network we have demonstrated this will provide an exact orthogonal transformation in maximising the sum of the squared marginal cumulants. The non-linear PCA algorithm studied in Chapter 5 only gives an approximate orthogonal transformation. An adaptive whitening layer has been proposed with a simple normalised anti-Hebbian learning algorithm which simplifies the method of spatial whitening and also allows online adaptive whitening. The shortcoming of the EPP network when employing symmetric feedback is that of weight adaptation ceasing when the weights are orthonormal. An additional layer of lateral weights at the output neurons delays the attainment of strict orthonormality and allows separation of super-Gaussian sources. This technique does not perform satisfactorily for sub-Gaussian sources, but it has indicated that the hierarchic form of learning may be more significant than previously considered. Although originally proposed by Karhunen and Joutsensalo (1994) the importance of hierarchy had not been fully appreciated or

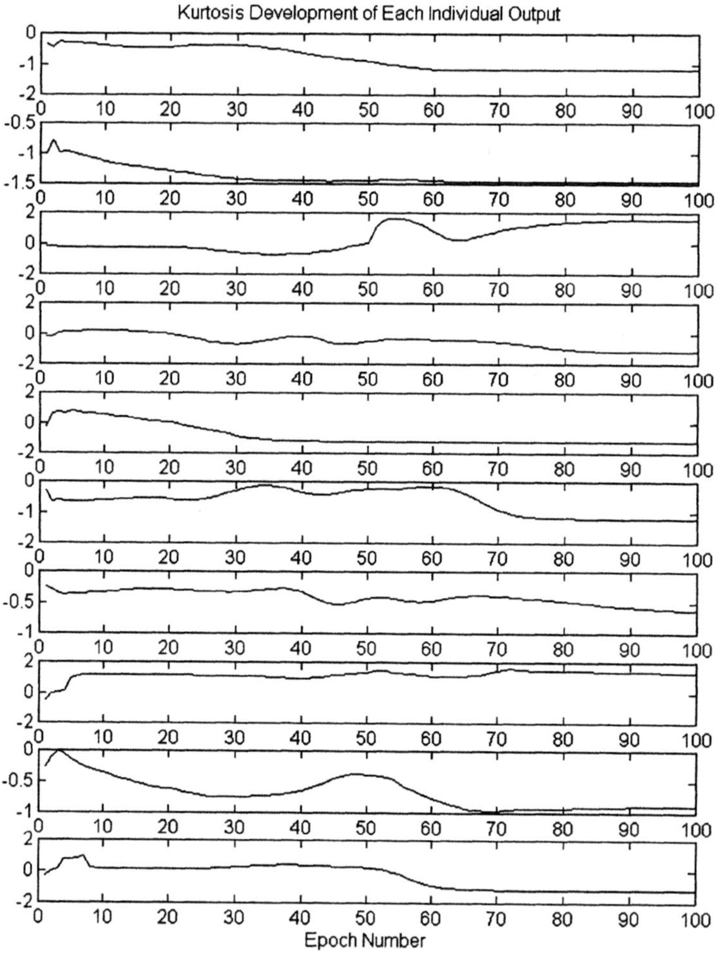

Figure 6.19: Development of the Data Kurtosis at Each Output Neuron.

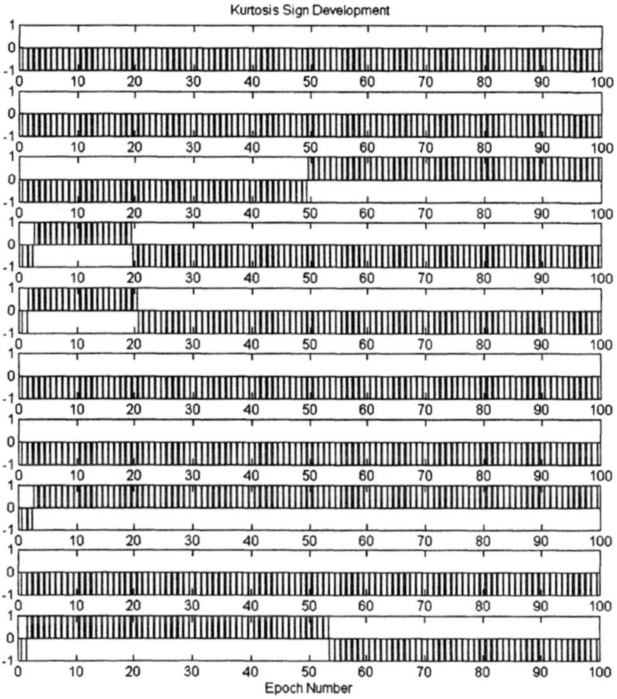

Figure 6.20: Development of the Kurtosis Sign at Each Output Neuron. The rows signify the nonlinearity sign(k_4) term at each one of the output neurons. The changes of sign during learning can be seen at neurons 3, 4, 5, 8, and 10.

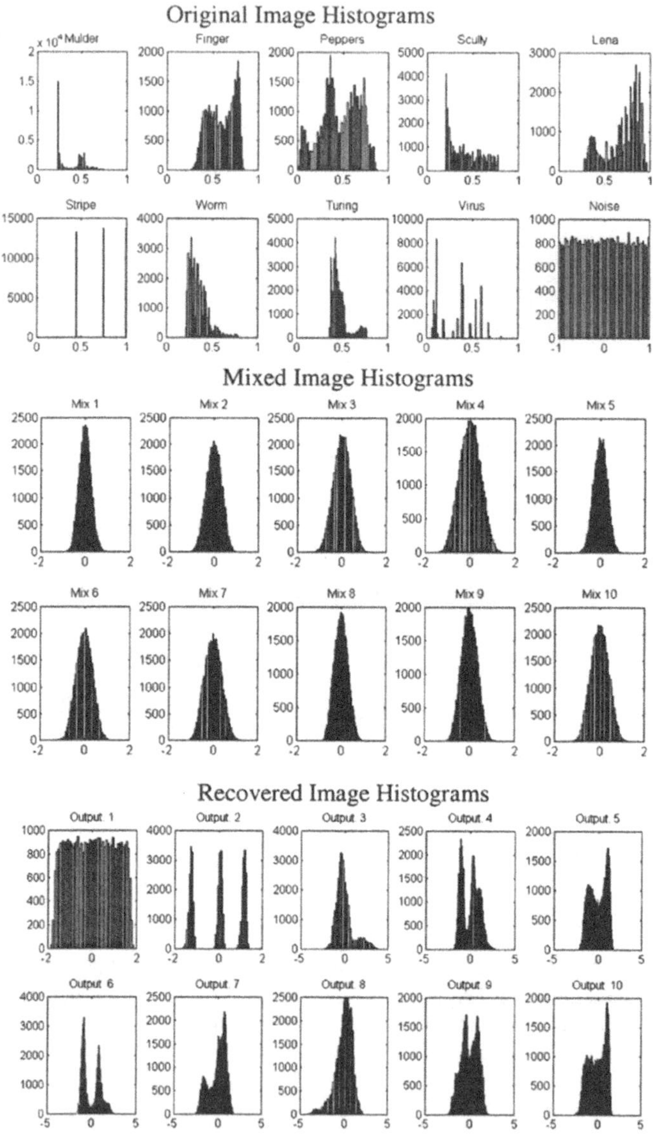

Figure 6.21: The Original, Mixed and Recovered Image Histograms. The permutation of the outputs is apparent.The recovered histograms are shown as zero-mean.

exploited when applied to BSS. It has been shown that a simple hierarchic feedback EPP network with an adaptive whitening layer is capable of separating mixtures of both sub-Gaussian and super-Gaussian sources. The introduction of online kurtosis estimation provides a method of dispensing with the requirement for *a priori* knowledge of the types of sources forming the mixture.

The two-stage process of BSS developed in this chapter suffers from the same problem as that considered in Chapter 5, i.e., slow convergence. The requirement for pre-whitening is an additional processing overhead, with which we would like to dispense. However, as the non-linear PCA and EPP algorithms provide approximate and exact orthogonal transformations only pre-whitened mixtures can be separated. We now reconsider the information theoretic basis of BSS in attempting to develop alternative structures and improved learning algorithms for BSS.

7. *Information Theoretic Non-Linear Feature Extraction and Blind Source Separation*

In this chapter we consider an information theoretic index for EPP and BSS. We develop an adaptive algorithm for EPP based on the maximisation of the negentropy of the transformed data. There is an equivalence between EPP and Blind Source Separation, as shown in Chapter 6. In this chapter the strong equivalence between EPP and BSS is identified using information theory directly.

7.1 Introduction

The adaptive ICA style algorithm developed in this chapter is shown to be a generalisation of the Infomax algorithm (Bell and Sejnowski, 1995). The enhanced versatility of the algorithm is demonstrated both analytically and with corroborating simulations. A comparison between the proposed maximum negentropy algorithm for BSS is made with both Oja's non-linear PCA algorithm and the Hierarchic Exploratory Projection Pursuit Network learning.

7.2 Information Theoretic Indices for EPP

In Chapter 6 we considered EPP indices based on higher order moments and cumulants (Jones and Sibson, 1987). From a statistical perspective the use of indices based on higher order moments are sensitive to outliers within the data. The use of simple polynomial functions within the non-linear and robust PCA algorithms has also been shown to give algorithmic instability (Karhunen and Joutsensalo, 1994).

This particular problem can be circumvented by the use of the hyperbolic tangent in generating higher order moments (Chapters 5, 6). Marriot notes (Jones and Sibson, 1987) indices based on third or fourth order moments will not identify clustered projections which are approximately symmetrical and mesokurtic (almost Gaussian). Motivated by this observation the entropy of the projection is proposed as a measure of non-normality (Jones and Sibson, 1987). However, differential entropy is an inappropriate index for maximisation as it may not be bounded (Chapter 2, Section 2.2.1). A more appropriate index would be a difference between two entropies; this would overcome the problem of unbounded divergence. One measure of non-normality would be the negentropy of the projection. Negentropy was introduced in Chapter 2, Section 2.2.2, as the Kullback divergence of a distribution from a Gaussian distribution with identical mean and variance.

$$D\left(p \,\|\, p_{Gaussian}\right) = \int p_x\left(x\right) \log \frac{p_x\left(x\right)}{p_G\left(x\right)} \, dx$$

The negentropy of the projection will always be greater than zero and only vanishes when the distribution $p_x\left(x\right)$ is normally distributed. This will then lend itself to stochastic gradient ascent techniques (Robbins and Munro, 1951).

Adaptation algorithms have been developed for the self-organisation of neural networks based on linear and non-linear Hebbian and anti-Hebbian learning. Most notable are the criterion based algorithms introduced by (Oja, 1982; Karhunen and Joutsensalo, 1994; Bell and Sejnowski, 1995; Amari, Cichocki and Yang, 1995). If we consider a single neuron implementation of EPP based on negentropy maximisation then we have a neuron which will be seeking maximally non-normal structure within the observed data. What we would like to have is a series of neurons which would each be sensitive to different non-normal structures within the data. Of course this is precisely the nature of the networks considered in Chapter 6; it is desired to improve on the performance of these algorithms and structures. The development of a simple single layer structure and a fast learning algorithm is the goal of this chapter. Motivated by the equivalence, in certain cases, of EPP and BSS we now seek to develop a direct link with the search for non-normal projections and BSS. We now consider developing the maximum negentropy learning algorithms for a linear single layer network.

7.3 Maximum Negentropy Learning

7.3.1 Single Neuron Maximum Negentropy Learning

We first of all consider the single linear output neuron case. The observed data at time t will be an N dimensional zero-mean vector

$$\mathbf{x}(t) = [x_1(t) \ldots x_N(t)]^T .$$

The output of the neuron will then be $y(t) = \mathbf{w}^T\mathbf{x}$ where the corresponding weight vector of the neuron is $\mathbf{w} = [w_1 \ldots w_N]^T$ (Chapter 4, Section 4.1). The negentropy of the output as a function of the weight parameters is then

$$D(\mathbf{w}) = \int p_y(y) \log \frac{p_y(y)}{p_G(y)} dy$$

$$= \int p_y(y) \log p_y(y) dy - \int p_y(y) \log p_G(y) dy$$

$$\Rightarrow D(\mathbf{w}) = E\{\log p_y(y)\} + \frac{1}{2}\log\left(2\pi e E\{y^2\}\right)$$

Taking gradients with respect to the weight parameters gives

$$\frac{d D(\mathbf{w})}{d \mathbf{w}} = E\left\{\frac{p_y'(y)}{p_y(y)}\mathbf{x}\right\} + \frac{d}{d\mathbf{w}}\left(\frac{1}{2}\log\left(2\pi e\left(\mathbf{w}^T\mathbf{C}_{xx}\mathbf{w}\right)\right)\right)$$

If the input data is spatially white and $\mathbf{C}_{xx} = \mathbf{I}$ then we have, for the case of instantaneous gradients

$$\frac{d D(\mathbf{w})}{d \mathbf{w}} = \frac{p_y'(y)}{p_y(y)}\mathbf{x} + \frac{\mathbf{w}}{\|\mathbf{w}\|^2} \quad (7.1)$$

The L_2 norm of the weight vector is given as $\|\mathbf{w}\| = \sqrt{\mathbf{w}^T\mathbf{w}}$. This can then be used in a stochastic gradient ascent algorithm for maximising the negentropy of the output data.

$$\mathbf{w}_{n+1} = \mathbf{w}_n + \eta \frac{d\,D(\mathbf{w}_n)}{d\,\mathbf{w}_n}$$

$$\mathbf{w}_{n+1} = \mathbf{w}_n + \eta \left(\frac{p_y'(y)}{p_y(y)} \mathbf{x} + \frac{\mathbf{w}}{\| \mathbf{w} \|^2} \right) \tag{7.2}$$

It is clear to see that (7.2) is an unconstrained learning rule and as such requires some form of constraint for stabilisation. The most natural form of constraint is to ensure that the norm of the weight vector is kept constant during adaptation. To ensure that the weight vector development follows a path on the surface of a hypersphere of constant radius the constraint technique proposed by Wang and Karhunen (1996) is employed. In developing the bigradient algorithm (Wang and Karhunen, 1996) propose two objective functions which have to be optimised. The first is a general non-linear optimisation criterion similar to that studied in Chapter 6. The second is a weight normalisation criterion and can be taken as

$$J(\mathbf{w}) = \frac{1}{2}\left(k - \mathbf{w}^T \mathbf{w}\right)^2 \tag{7.3}$$

The criterion will be minimised when the norm of the weight vector equals $|\sqrt{k}\,|$. The gradient term of (7.3) can be used to iteratively update the weight vector to achieve and maintain the constant norm. Denoting the weight vector prior to normalisation as $\breve{\mathbf{w}}$ then

$$\frac{\partial J(\mathbf{w})}{\partial \mathbf{w}} = -\mathbf{w}\left(k - \mathbf{w}^T \mathbf{w}\right)$$

$$\Rightarrow \mathbf{w}_{n+1} = \breve{\mathbf{w}}_{n+1} + \mu\, \breve{\mathbf{w}}_{n+1}\left(k - \breve{\mathbf{w}}_{n+1}^T \breve{\mathbf{w}}_{n+1}\right) \tag{7.4}$$

The weight update from (7.2) can then be denoted as

$$\breve{\mathbf{w}}_{n+1} = \mathbf{w}_n + \eta \left(\frac{p_y'(y)}{p_y(y)} \mathbf{x} + \frac{\mathbf{w}_n}{\| \mathbf{w}_n \|^2} \right) \equiv \mathbf{w}_n + \eta\, \Phi$$

and so substituting into (7.4) gives

$$\mathbf{w}_{n+1} = \mathbf{w}_n + \eta\Phi + \mu(\mathbf{w}_n + \eta\Phi)\left(k - (\mathbf{w}_n + \eta\Phi)^T(\mathbf{w}_n + \eta\Phi)\right)$$

$$\Rightarrow \mathbf{w}_{n+1} = \mathbf{w}_n + \eta\Phi + \mu\mathbf{w}_n\left(k - \mathbf{w}_n^T\mathbf{w}_n\right)$$

$$+ o(\mu\eta) + o\left(\mu\eta^2\right) + o\left(\mu\eta^3\right)$$

As the learning rates are small the higher order terms can be neglected then

$$\mathbf{w}_{n+1} = \mathbf{w}_n + \eta\frac{p_y'(y)}{p_y(y)}\mathbf{x}_n + \mathbf{w}_n\left(\mu\left(k - \mathbf{w}_n^T\mathbf{w}_n\right) + \frac{\eta}{\|\mathbf{w}_n\|^2}\right) \tag{7.5}$$

By considering simply the unit hypersphere where $k = 1$ and letting $\mu = \eta$ the final difference equation is

$$\mathbf{w}_{n+1} = \mathbf{w}_n + \eta\left[\frac{p_y'(y)}{p_y(y)}\mathbf{x}_n + \mathbf{w}_n\left(1 + \frac{1}{\mathbf{w}_n^T\mathbf{w}_n} - \mathbf{w}_n^T\mathbf{w}_n\right)\right] \tag{7.6}$$

It is instructive to consider the maximum negentropy learning rule for the single output neuron. The rightmost term in (7.6) is the weight constraint term and acts to ensure that the norm is kept at a constant value. This can then be used in performing EPP by parameterising the derivative of the log density to reflect the pdf of the non-linear structure to be identified. Parameterisation of the derivative of the log pdf will be considered in detail in Section 7.4. To illustrate the utility of the maximum negentropy learning rule a simple simulation demonstrates the ability of (7.6) to perform EPP.

Ten dimensional data is generated by drawing the marginal components independently from zero-mean Gaussian distributions. Two of the marginals, however, are drawn from a double exponential density (Stuart and Ord, 1987) and a uniform density respectively. Figure 7.1 shows the marginal distributions of the data, clearly component 4 and 8 deviate from Gaussian and represent higher order structure within the observed data.

As discussed in Chapter 6 (Sections 6.2, 6.3 and 6.4) the observed data is sphered. The single output neuron learning rule (7.6) is used to update the weights of the neuron at each presentation of the data. The learning rate was set at a constant value of 0.01. To monitor the development of the weights the direction cosine of the current weight vector is computed relative to the interesting direction under consideration. The first simulation considered the double exponential marginal density as interesting structure to be identified, in which case the derivative of the log density is set to the signum function. Figure 7.2 shows the development of the direction cosine and the weight vector norm during learning. The multivariate data comprised of one thousand data points.

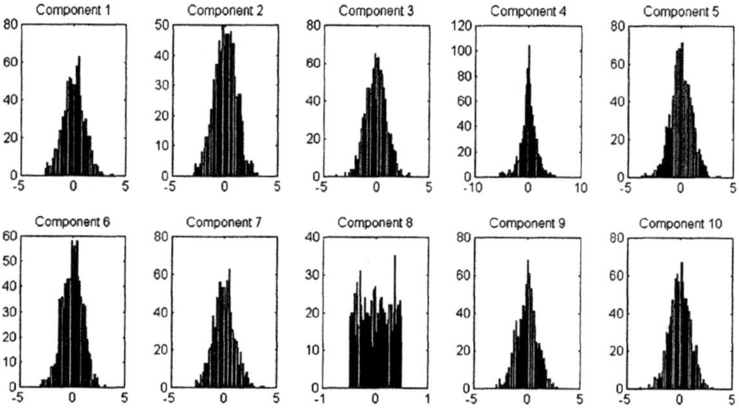

Figure 7.1: Histograms of the Marginal Densities of the Ten Dimensional Observed Data. All marginal components are distributed normally with the exception of component 4 and component 8. These components are distributed according to the double exponential and uniform densities respectively.

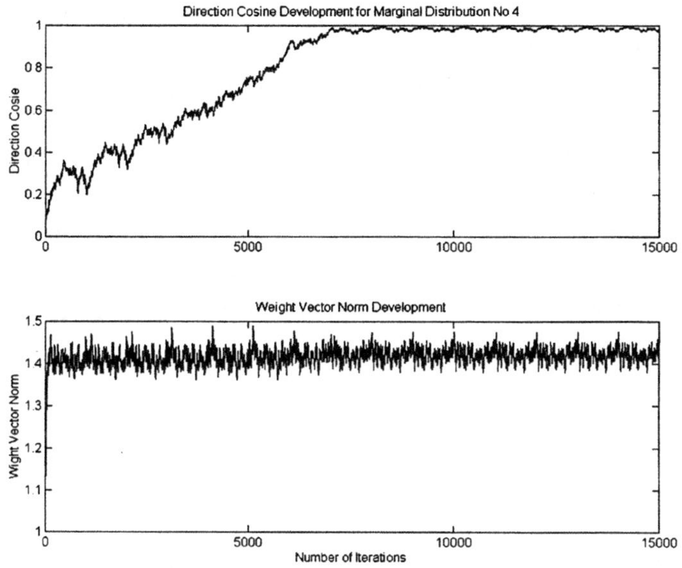

Figure 7.2: The Top Chart Shows the Development of the Direction Cosine Between the Weight and the Interesting Direction No 4. Convergence to the particular direction takes place after approximately six epochs.

To identify the alternate direction of interest, that is component eight, there is a slight problem. Although the pdf is known, the derivative of the log pdf does not exist. Approximations such as the arc-sine could be used (Stuart and Ord, 1987) or an approximate pdf expansion could be considered. However for this simulation we simply note that marginal density of interest is sub-Gaussian and so use the simple hyperbolic tangent approximation (Chapter 6). This also is successful in identifying the direction of interest.

This simulation has only considered EPP, but (7.6) will also extract independent components from their mixtures. With that we now consider a multiple output version of the maximum negentropy learning rule.

7.3.2 Multiple Output Neuron Maximum Negentropy Learning

In this specific case we shall constrain the dimensionality of the output to be equal to that of the input. We are attempting to stochastically maximise the negentropy of the output neurons, in other words we are seeking to drive the distribution of the data from each output neuron maximally from a normal distribution. We know that this will perform an exploratory projection pursuit on the data, however, we can now show that this will also be equivalent to BSS in a more general sense than moment-based EPP (Chapter 6).

We then use the factorial parametric form for the density of the network output where $\mathbf{y} = \mathbf{W}\mathbf{x}$ and $\mathbf{W} \in \Re^{N \times M}, N \leq M$. Each output neuron will be parameterised individually as it is our intention that each neuron will respond optimally to different features within the data. We then use the factorial parametric form for the density of the network output in which case the proposed divergence measure to be maximised is

$$D\left(p_F \,\|\, p_{Gaussian}\right) = \int p_{\mathbf{y}}(\mathbf{y}) \log \frac{\prod_{i=1}^{N} p_i(y_i)}{p_G(\mathbf{y})} d\mathbf{y} \tag{7.6}$$

Where the subscript F denotes a parametric factorial pdf representation. It is instructive to consider (7.6) written as

$$D\left(p_F \,\|\, p_{Gaussian}\right)$$

$$= E\left\{\log \prod_{i=1}^{N} p_i(y_i)\right\} + \frac{1}{2}\log\left((2\pi e)^N \det\left(\mathbf{C}_{\mathbf{yy}}\right)\right)$$

$$= -\sum_{i=1}^{N} H(y_i) + \frac{1}{2}\log\left(\det\left(\mathbf{C}_{\mathbf{yy}}\right)\right) + \frac{1}{2}\log\left((2\pi e)^N\right) \tag{7.7}$$

Due to the Hadamard inequality (Deco and Obradovic, 1996) $\det\left(\mathbf{C}_{\mathbf{yy}}\right) \leq \prod_{i=1}^{N}\left(\mathbf{C}_{\mathbf{yy}}\right)_{ii}$, the term $\log\left(\det\left(\mathbf{C}_{\mathbf{yy}}\right)\right)$ appearing in (7.7) will be maximised once the covariance matrix has been diagonalised i.e. the second order redundancy has been minimised. The term $\sum_{i=1}^{N} H(y_i)$ will be maximal once the data approximately conforms to a factorial density (2.28). This indicates that the single algorithm that maximises (7.6) will perform both the whitening and the higher order redundancy reduction.

Taking gradients over the weight matrix:

$$\frac{d}{d\mathbf{W}} D\left(p_F \,\|\, p_{Gaussian}\right) =$$

$$\frac{d}{d\mathbf{W}}\left[E\left\{ \log \prod_{i=1}^{N} p_i\left(y_i\right)\right\} + \frac{1}{2}\log\left(\left(2\pi e\right)^N \det\left(\mathbf{C}_{\mathbf{yy}}\right)\right)\right]$$

$$= \frac{d}{d\mathbf{W}}\left[\sum_{i=1}^{N} E\left\{ \log p_i\left(y_i\right)\right\} + \frac{1}{2}\log\left(\det\left(\mathbf{W}\mathbf{C}_{\mathbf{xx}}\mathbf{W}^T\right)\right)\right] + \frac{N}{2}\log\left(2\pi e\right)$$

The rightmost term is not a function of the weights and will not affect the value of the instantaneous gradients. It is also interesting to note that the term

$$\log\left(\det\left(\mathbf{W}\mathbf{C}_{\mathbf{xx}}\mathbf{W}^T\right)\right)$$

ensures that the rank of $\mathbf{W}$ is equal to N and so each of the columns of $\mathbf{W}$ will be linearly independent. This is a naturally occurring term which ensures that each output neuron will seek mutually independent directions, and can be viewed as a generalisation of the constraints of orthonormality imposed on the non-linear forms of the PCA algorithm. Now it is a standard result that

$$\frac{d}{d\mathbf{W}}\log\left(\det\left(\mathbf{W}\mathbf{C}_{\mathbf{xx}}\mathbf{W}^T\right)\right) = \frac{\operatorname{adj}\left(\mathbf{W}\mathbf{C}_{\mathbf{xx}}\mathbf{W}^T\right)^T}{\det\left(\mathbf{W}\mathbf{C}_{\mathbf{xx}}\mathbf{W}^T\right)}\mathbf{W}\mathbf{C}_{\mathbf{xx}}$$

$$= \left(\mathbf{W}\mathbf{C}_{\mathbf{xx}}\mathbf{W}^T\right)^{-1}\mathbf{W}\mathbf{C}_{\mathbf{xx}}$$

and so

$$\frac{d}{d\mathbf{W}} D\left(p_F \,\|\, p_G\right) = \frac{d}{d\mathbf{W}}\sum_{i=1}^{N} E\left\{\log p_i\left(y_i\right)\right\} + \left(\mathbf{W}\mathbf{C}_{\mathbf{xx}}\mathbf{W}^T\right)^{-1}\mathbf{W}\mathbf{C}_{\mathbf{xx}}$$

Taking the instantaneous gradient of the output entropy gives

$$\frac{d}{d w_{ij}}\log\left(p_{\mathbf{y}}\left(\mathbf{y}\right)\right) = \frac{p_i'\left(y_i\right)x_j\prod_{k\neq i} p_k\left(y_k\right)}{\prod_{k=1}^{N} p_k\left(y_k\right)} = \frac{p_i'\left(y_i\right)}{p_i\left(y_i\right)}x_j$$

$$\frac{d}{d\mathbf{W}}\log\left(p_{\mathbf{y}}(\mathbf{y})\right)=\left[\frac{p'(y_1)}{p(y_1)},\ \ldots,\ \frac{p'(y_i)}{p(y_i)},\ \ldots,\ \frac{p'(y_N)}{p(y_N)}\right]^T\mathbf{x}^T$$

$$\Rightarrow\frac{d}{d\mathbf{W}}\log\left(p_{\mathbf{y}}(\mathbf{y})\right)=f(\mathbf{y})\mathbf{x}^T$$

The final gradient term is then

$$\frac{d}{d\mathbf{W}}D\left(p_F\,\|\,p_{Gaussian}\right)=$$

$$f(\mathbf{y})\mathbf{x}^T+\left(\mathbf{W}\mathbf{C}_{\mathbf{xx}}\mathbf{W}^T\right)^{-1}\mathbf{W}\mathbf{C}_{\mathbf{xx}} \tag{7.8}$$

The weight update is finally given as

$$\Delta\mathbf{W}_n=\eta\left(f(\mathbf{y}_n)\mathbf{x}_n^T+\left(\mathbf{W}_n\mathbf{C}_{\mathbf{xx}}\mathbf{W}_n^T\right)^{-1}\mathbf{W}_n\mathbf{C}_{\mathbf{xx}}\right) \tag{7.9}$$

We note that (7.9) has a similar form to the algorithm of Bell and Sejnowski (1995). Pearlmutter and Parra (1996) derive a similar algorithm from a maximum likelihood perspective. Now, let us re-consider the divergence measure for the case where $M = N$ and then re-write (7.6) as

$$\int p_{\mathbf{y}}(\mathbf{y})\log\frac{\prod_{i=1}^{N}p_i(y_i)}{p_{\mathbf{y}}(\mathbf{y})}d\mathbf{y}+\int p_{\mathbf{y}}(\mathbf{y})\log\frac{p_{\mathbf{y}}(\mathbf{y})}{p_G(\mathbf{y})}d\mathbf{y}$$

$$=-I(\mathbf{y})+\int p_{\mathbf{y}}(\mathbf{y})\log p_{\mathbf{y}}(\mathbf{y})d\mathbf{y}-\int p_{\mathbf{y}}(\mathbf{y})\log p_G(\mathbf{y})d\mathbf{y}$$

$$=-I(\mathbf{y})-H(\mathbf{y})+\frac{1}{2}\log\left((2\pi e)^N\det\left(\mathbf{C}_{\mathbf{yy}}\right)\right)$$

As the output of the network is $\mathbf{y} = \mathbf{W}\mathbf{x}$ and $M = N$, we can the use the pdf transformation equality (2.41) giving

$$-I(\mathbf{y}) - H(\mathbf{x}) - \log\left(\left|\det(\mathbf{W})\right|\right) + \frac{1}{2}\log\left((2\pi e)^N \det\left(\mathbf{C}_{\mathbf{yy}}\right)\right)$$

$$= -I(\mathbf{y}) - H(\mathbf{x}) - \log\left(\left|\det(\mathbf{W})\right|\right) +$$

$$\frac{1}{2}\log\left((2\pi e)^N\right) + \frac{1}{2}\log\left(\det\left(\mathbf{W}\,\mathbf{C}_{\mathbf{xx}}\,\mathbf{W}^T\right)\right)$$

$$= -I(\mathbf{y}) - H(\mathbf{x}) - \log\left(\left|\det(\mathbf{W})\right|\right) +$$

$$\frac{1}{2}\log\left((2\pi e)^N\right) + \frac{1}{2}\log\left(\det\left(\mathbf{C}_{\mathbf{xx}}\right)\right) + \log\left(\left|\det(\mathbf{W})\right|\right)$$

$$= -I(\mathbf{y}) - H(\mathbf{x}) + \frac{1}{2}\log\left((2\pi e)^N\right) + \frac{1}{2}\log\left(\det\left(\mathbf{C}_{\mathbf{xx}}\right)\right)$$

Using the instantaneous gradient we can seek a maximal value by stochastic gradient ascent and so

$$\frac{d}{d\mathbf{W}} D\left(p_F \,\|\, p_{Gaussian}\right) =$$

$$\frac{d}{d\mathbf{W}}\left(-I(\mathbf{y}) - H(\mathbf{x}) + \frac{1}{2}\log\left((2\pi e)^N\right) + \frac{1}{2}\log\left(\det\left(\mathbf{C}_{\mathbf{xx}}\right)\right)\right)$$

Note that the input data entropy and the non-linear function of the input data covariance matrix are not functions of the weight parameters and so

$$\frac{d}{d\mathbf{W}} D\left(p_F \,\|\, p_{Gaussian}\right) = -\frac{d}{d\mathbf{W}} I(\mathbf{y}) \tag{7.10}$$

This shows that maximising the form of output data divergence (7.6) is identical to minimising the mutual information of the output data. Minimisation of the mutual information is the direction which Bell and Sejnowski (1995) and Amari, Cichocki and Yang (1995) take when developing their BSS algorithms. It should be noted that this is a general equivalence unlike the specific equivalence of moment-based EPP. The fundamental difference with Bell and Sejnowski's Infomax algorithm is that the non-linear term in (7.9) is formed by the marginal derivatives of the logarithm of the output probability density functions.

7.3.3 Maximum Negentropy Learning and Infomax Equivalence

In Section 7.3.2 it was shown that the maximisation of (7.6) and minimisation of mutual information are identical, with the differential equality of (7.10) being valid. Note that the objective function to be maximised does not have explicit constraints imposed on the weight matrix such as the orthonormality and unit norm constraints used in the development of the robust PCA algorithm (Chapter 4, Section 4.2.3.2). Restricting the transformation to a rotation requires the mixture to be spatially whitened. The transformation considered here is not constrained to a rotation and so the mixture does not need to be pre-whitened. This is a significant simplification for online adaptive processing. Consider the simple form of the Bell and Sejnowski Infomax algorithm

$$\Delta \mathbf{W}_n = \eta_n \left(-2 \tanh(\mathbf{y}_n)\mathbf{x}_n^T + \left(\mathbf{W}_n^T\right)^{-1} \right)$$

The equivalent and more general stochastic negentropy[1] maximisation algorithm is,

$$\Delta \mathbf{W}_n = \eta_n \left(f(\mathbf{y}_n)\mathbf{x}_n^T + \left(\mathbf{W}_n \mathbf{C}_{\mathbf{xx}} \mathbf{W}_n^T\right)^{-1} \mathbf{W}_n \mathbf{C}_{\mathbf{xx}} \right)$$

Bell and Sejnowski base the development of their algorithm on the maximisation of information forced through a bounded monotonic nonlinearity, which matches the cumulative distribution function of the data. In the case of the hyperbolic tangent activation function then

$$\int_0^y p_{\hat{s}}(x)dx = -2\tanh(y) \Rightarrow p_{\hat{s}}(x) = 2\operatorname{sech}^2(x)$$

which is proportional to the Hyperbolic-Cauchy probability density distribution. The algorithm as it stands is then capable of maximising noiseless information transfer if the received data is approximately distributed according to the Hyperbolic-Cauchy distribution. Taking the non-linear term within the maximum-negentropy update rule (7.9) it is clear that the derivative of the logarithm of a Hyperbolic-Cauchy distribution is simply the negative hyperbolic tangent.

---

[1] We shall now refer to the maximisation of the divergence measure (7.6) as negentropy maximisation.

$$\frac{p(y)}{p(y)} = \frac{-4\operatorname{sec}h^{3}(y)\sinh(y)}{2\operatorname{sec}h^{2}(y)} = -2\tanh(y)$$

It is reported in (Bell and Sejnowski, 1995) that the Infomax algorithm fails to minimise the mutual information and so separate mixtures of uniformly or sub-Gaussian distributed sources. It is clear that this failing is largely a pdf mismatch problem. Applying the Infomax algorithm to the separation of a mixture of five images, whose pixel values are distributed in a sub-Gaussian manner, (Chapter 5, Chapter 6) we can see an example of this phenomenon. Figure 7.3 shows the performance index computed every 100 iterations for a series of five simulations using the Info-max algorithm to separate the mixture of five images. This is a similar problem to that found in the non-linear PCA algorithm and the EPP network learning algorithm.

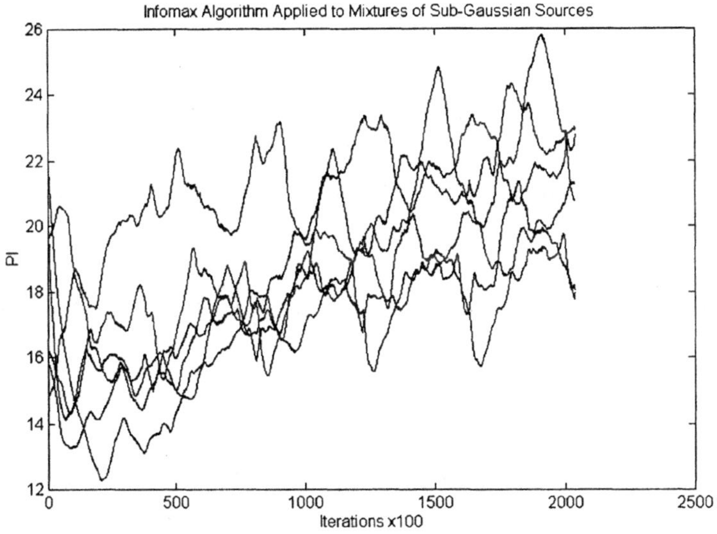

Figure 7.3: Traces of the Performance Index for Five Simulations Using the Infomax Algorithm on Mixtures of Sub-Gaussian Sources. The learning rate was set at a constant value of 0.0001, the initial weight matrix was randomly set between the values -1 and $+1$ for each simulation.

7.3.4 The Natural Gradient and Covariant Learning

From a computational perspective the maximum negentropy rule is costly due to the matrix inversion required at each iteration. This matrix inversion appears in all adaptive gradient based information theoretic source separation algorithms. However there is a more fundamental weakness with these gradient based algorithms as discussed in Section 2.5.1. These of course can be overcome by the use of the natural gradient. The natural gradient operator within the parameter space of arbitrary square matrices is equivalent to the Euclidean gradient operator post multiplied by the product of the matrix transpose and matrix. It is clear that the natural gradient removes the dimensional inconsistency of the non-covariant gradient operator and so will provide uniform performance irrespective of the matrix scaling. In particular for the general case where $N \leq M$ the square matrix term $\mathbf{W}_n^T \mathbf{W}_n$ will be positive semidefinite so the standard natural gradient formula (2.107) cannot be used directly. The modified formula below is proposed

$$\Delta \mathbf{W}_n = \eta_n \frac{d}{d\,\mathbf{W}_n} D\left(p_F \,\|\, p_{Gaussian}\right) \left(\mathbf{W}_n^T \mathbf{W}_n + \varepsilon_n \mathbf{I}\right)$$

where ε_n is a small positive constant which ensures that the term $(\mathbf{W}_n^T \mathbf{W}_n + \varepsilon_n \mathbf{I})$ is always positive definite. This approach is similar to that used in many optimisation methods to keep the Hessian positive definite. Utilising this term in (7.9) then gives

$$\Delta \mathbf{W}_n = \eta_n \left(f(\mathbf{y}_n)\mathbf{x}_n^T + \left(\mathbf{W}_n \mathbf{C}_{\mathbf{xx}} \mathbf{W}_n^T\right)^{-1} \mathbf{W}_n \mathbf{C}_{\mathbf{xx}} \right) \left(\mathbf{W}_n^T \mathbf{W}_n + \varepsilon_n \mathbf{I}\right)$$

$$= \eta_n \left(f(\mathbf{y}_n)\mathbf{y}_n^T + \mathbf{I} \right)\mathbf{W}_n +$$

$$\varepsilon_n \eta_n \left(f(\mathbf{y}_n)\mathbf{x}_n^T + \left(\mathbf{W}_n \mathbf{C}_{\mathbf{xx}} \mathbf{W}_n^T\right)^{-1} \mathbf{W}_n \mathbf{C}_{\mathbf{xx}} \right)$$

For small values of ε_n then $O(\eta_n) \gg O(\eta_n \varepsilon_n)$ and the rightmost term will have a negligble effect on the weight update so the learning equation can be approximated by

$$\Delta \mathbf{W}_n = \eta_n \left(f(\mathbf{y}_n)\mathbf{y}_n^T + \mathbf{I} \right)\mathbf{W}_n \tag{7.12}$$

As the algorithm is now covariant we would expect to see almost Newton-like convergence properties in the vicinity of a solution. To demonstrate the performance improvement we compare the original Infomax BSS algorithm (Bell and Sejnowski, 1995) with the natural gradient equivalent, that is, the updates

$$\Delta \mathbf{W}_n = \eta_n \left(\left(\mathbf{W}_n^T\right)^{-1} - 2\tanh\left(\mathbf{y}_n\right)\mathbf{x}_n^T \right)$$

and

$$\Delta \mathbf{W}_n = \eta_n \left(\mathbf{I} - 2\tanh\left(\mathbf{y}_n\right)\mathbf{y}_n^T\right)\mathbf{W}_n .$$

As we have shown that this algorithm will only separate mixtures of super-Gaussian sources (Section 7.3.3) we consider the mixture of five sources of natural speech. A total of seven simulations were carried out and an initial weight matrix was generated. The Infomax and natural gradient Infomax algorithms were then both run for five epochs each. The learning rate was kept at a constant value of 0.0001 in both cases. A new initial weight matrix was generated and the process repeated. The performance index of separation was computed every fifty iterations. Figure 7.4 shows the results which clearly demonstrate the superiority of the natural gradient, in terms of convergence speed, over the standard gradient.

From Figure 7.2 we note that the performance index reaches a minimum value of almost zero after 100,000 iterations. In Figure 6.13, we see that the extension of EPP with adaptive whitening and hierarchic feedback requires 500,000 iterations prior to reaching a separating solution. This indicates a five fold increase in the speed of convergence when using the natural gradient based algorithm. This simulation confirms the benefits, in terms of speed of convergence, of using the natural gradient as opposed to the standard Euclidean gradient for information theoretic BSS algorithms. In other words the use of covariant algorithms can allow convergence speeds which approach Newton convergence, in the vicinity of a solution.

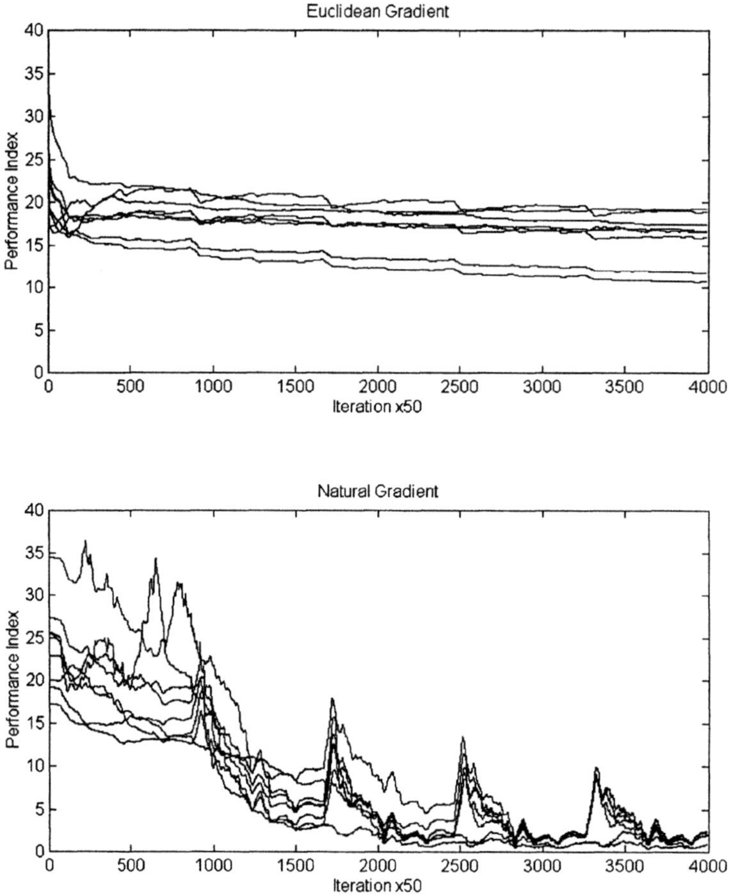

Figure 7.4 : Traces of the Performance Index for Seven Simulations Using the Infomax Algorithm on Mixtures of Super-Gaussian Sources. The learning rate was set at a constant value of 0.0001, the initial weight matrix was randomly set between the values −1 and +1 for each simulation. The top graph shows the development of separation when using the Infomax algorithm based on the Euclidean gradient with the bottom graph highlighting the performance using the natural gradient.

7.4 General Maximum Negentropy Learning

It is clear that the general form of the source separation algorithm originally proposed by Cichocki *et al* (1994)

$$\Delta \mathbf{W} = \eta\left(\mathbf{I} - f(\mathbf{y})g\left(\mathbf{y}^T\right)\right)\mathbf{W}$$

provides a generalisation of the covariant algorithms for source separation. What has been shown in deriving the maximum negentropy rule is that the optimal functions are the derivative of the log pdf, parameterised according to the original sources and the identity function. So we have

$$f(y) = -\frac{p_s'(y)}{p_s(y)} \text{ and } g(y) = y$$

Cichocki, Kasprzak and Amari (1996) show experimentally that for mixtures of super-Gaussian sources the functions $f(y) = \tanh(y)$ and $g(y) = y^3$ perform well. Mixtures of sub-Gaussian sources can be separated by the use of $f(y) = y^3$ and $g(y) = \tanh(y)$. Mixtures that contain both types of source will require the sequence of the non-linearities to be changed, which effectively requires a change of the algorithm form.

It is clear that we require a valid approximation for the derivative of the log pdf. Methods such as mixtures of densities have been proposed in parameterising a pdf for BSS and inferring the mixture parameters from the observed data (Pearlmutter and Parra, 1996; Pham, Garrat and Jutten, 1992). We are motivated by algorithmic simplicity and note that essentially the requirement is not a parameterised approximation of the sources' pdf but an approximation of the derivative of the log pdf. Consider the case where we use a standardised Gaussian distribution of zero mean and unit variance

$$p_G(y) = \frac{1}{\sqrt{2\pi}} e^{-\frac{y^2}{2}} \text{ therefore } f(y) = -\frac{p_s'(y)}{p_s(y)} = y$$

Using this term in (7.11) then gives

$$\Delta \mathbf{W}_n = \eta\left(\mathbf{I} - \mathbf{y}_n \mathbf{y}_n^T\right)\mathbf{W}_n \tag{7.13}$$

This can then be interpreted as minimising the mutual information between the components of the vector **y** assuming only Gaussian statistics. In other words this rule is acting to decorrelate the signals. Cardoso (1997) derives this particular form of whitening using the relative gradient. As the source separation model deals with non-Gaussian sources then we need to consider a more general form for the underlying pdf.

Density functions can be approximated by expansions of derivatives of the normal distribution. Two significant density expansions are the Gram-Charlier and the Edgeworth expansions (Stuart and Ord, 1987). We shall only consider the Gram-Charlier expansion here; however, both expansions are identical when truncated at fourth order. The Gram-Charlier expansion is chosen purely for reasons of clarity and simplicity of presentation. The Gram-Charlier expansion about a normal density $p_G(y)$ for a density $p_y(y)$ can be written as

$$p_y(y) = \sum_{i=0}^{\infty} c_i H_i(y) p_G(y) \tag{7.14}$$

The term $H_i(y)$ is the orthogonal Hermite polynomial defined as

$$(-1)^k \frac{d^k p_G(y)}{dy^k} = H_k(y) p_G(y) \tag{7.15}$$

which can be computed in a recursive manner

$$H_0(y) = 1,\ H_1(y) = y$$

$$H_k(y) = yH_{k-1} - (k-1)H_{k-2}$$

The coefficients within the expansion are computed as

$$c_i = \frac{1}{i!} \int_{-\infty}^{\infty} p_y(y) H_i(y) dy \tag{7.16}$$

The expansion as shown in (7.14) is infinite; however, in many practical applications the expansion is truncated at fourth order (Stuart and Ord, 1987; Masters, 1995). Once the series expansion includes polynomials of higher than fifth order then severe oscillations can start to manifest themselves in the approximation.

The fourth order expansion of a zero-mean distribution is then explicitly given as

$$p_y(y) = p_G(y)\Big[1 + \frac{1}{2!}(\mu_2 - 1)(y^2 - 1) + \frac{1}{3!}\mu_3(y^3 - 3y) + \frac{1}{4!}(\mu_4 - 6\mu_2 + 3)(y^4 - 6y^2 + 3)\Big] \tag{7.17}$$

The kth order moments of the density $p_y(y)$ are denoted as μ_k within the expansion. We can make some constraints on the expansion to simplify (7.17). Let us assume that the density has unit variance and is symmetric; that is, $\mu_2 = 1$ and $\mu_3 = 0$. This is a reasonable assumption made by many researchers (Comon, 1994) and (Amari, Cichocki and Yang, 1995). Denoting the fourth order cumulant as κ_4 the truncated density expansion is simplified to

$$p_y(y) = p_G(y)\left[1 + \frac{\kappa_4}{4!}(y^4 - 6y^2 + 3)\right]$$

$$= p_G(y)\left[\left(1 + \frac{\kappa_4}{8}\right) + \frac{\kappa_4 y^4}{4!} - \frac{\kappa_4 y^2}{4}\right]$$

Denoting the expansion $\left(1 + \frac{\kappa_4}{8}\right) + \frac{\kappa_4 y^4}{4!} - \frac{\kappa_4 y^2}{4}$ by $\Phi(y)$ then

$$p_y(y) = p_G(y)\Phi(y)$$

The derivative of the log density is then simply

$$\frac{p'(y)}{p(y)} = \frac{\Phi'(y)}{\Phi(y)} - y$$

$$\Rightarrow \frac{p'(y)}{p(y)} = \frac{\kappa_4}{2\Phi(y)}\left(\frac{y^3}{3} - y\right) - y \tag{7.18}$$

It is clear from (7.18) that the derivative of the log density appearing in (7.9) and (7.12) will be composed of linear and non-linear terms. We are then required to identify a suitable form for $\Phi'(y)/\Phi(y)$. Consider first the case where the source data has a sub-Gaussian distribution. One method that we propose for modelling a symmetric zero-mean sub-Gaussian density is to use a simplified Gaussian mixture model as proposed by Pearson (1894).

MLE approaches to data clustering (Everitt, 1993) employ mixtures of Gaussian (MOG) models to seek transition regions of high and low density and so identify data clusters. An early MOG model for data clustering was proposed in (Pearson, 1894) which took the form of

$$p(s) = (1-a) f_1(s) + a f_2(s)$$

where

$$f_1(s) = \frac{1}{\sigma_1 \sqrt{2\pi}} \exp \frac{-(s-\mu_1)^2}{2\sigma_1^2}$$

and

$$f_2(s) = \frac{1}{\sigma_2 \sqrt{2\pi}} \exp \frac{-(s-\mu_2)^2}{2\sigma_2^2}$$

are Gaussians with mean values and variances defined as μ_1, μ_2 and σ_1^2, σ_2^2 respectively. The wieghting coefficient a serves to create levels of skewness in the distribution. Figure 7.5a shows the range of densities which can be formed by this model for values of a within the valid range [0 ... 1] and the parameter $\mu_1 = -\mu_2 = 2$, $\sigma_1^2 = \sigma_2^2 = 1$. It is clear that the distribution is symmetric possessing two distinct modes when $a = ½$. The cumulant generating function (CGF) for the density and the related cumulants are now computed.

The cumulant generating function for the proposed density model where $\mu_1 = -\mu_2 = \mu$ and $\sigma_1^2 = \sigma_2^2 = \sigma^2$ admits

$$\phi(w) = \log(\varphi(w))$$

where

$$\varphi(w) = \int_{-\infty}^{+\infty} p(s) \exp(iws)\, ds$$

$$= \int_{-\infty}^{+\infty} ((1-a) f_1(s) + a f_2(s)) \exp(iws)\, ds$$

This then gives a cumulant generating function of

$$\phi(w) = \log((1-a)\exp(A) + a\exp(B))$$

where $A = i\mu w - \dfrac{\sigma^2 w^2}{2}$ and $B = i\mu w + \dfrac{\sigma^2 w^2}{2}$

The related cumulants can be computed as

$$\kappa_n = (-i)^n \frac{d^n\phi(w)}{dw^n}\Big|_{w=0}$$

The first four cumulants of the density can now be computed and so

$$\kappa_1 = (-i)\frac{d\phi(w)}{dw}\Big|_{w=0} = -i^2\mu(1-2a) = \mu(1-2a)$$

$$\kappa_2 = (-i)^2\frac{d^2\phi(w)}{dw^2}\Big|_{w=0} = (-i)^2\left(4a\mu^2(a-1) - \sigma^2\right)$$

$$= \left(4a\mu^2(1-a) + \sigma^2\right)$$

$$\kappa_3 = (-i)^3\frac{d^3\phi(w)}{dw^3}\Big|_{w=0} = (-i)^3\, 8ia\mu^3(a-1)(2a-1)$$

$$= 8a\mu^3(a-1)(2a-1)$$

$$\kappa_4 = (-i)^4\frac{d^4\phi(w)}{dw^4}\Big|_{w=0} =$$

$$(-i)^4\, 16a\mu^4(1-a)\left(6a^2 - 6a + 1\right)$$

$$= 16a\mu^4(1-a)\left(6a^2 s - 6a + 1\right)$$

For the strictly symmetric case where $a = ½$ then

$$\kappa_1 = \text{Mean Value} = 0$$

$$\kappa_2 = \text{Variance} = \left(\mu^2 + \sigma^2\right)$$

$$\kappa_3 = \text{Skew} = 0$$

$$\kappa_4 = \text{Unnormalised Kurtosis} = -2\mu^4$$

The kurtosis of the symmetric density model is then

$$\text{Kurtosis} = \frac{\kappa_4}{(\kappa_2)^2} = \frac{-2\mu^4}{\left(\mu^2 + \sigma^2\right)^2}$$

The kurtosis takes on strictly negative values for all $\mu > 0$.
Using the expressions for the second and fourth order cumulants the second chart on Figure 7.5 is created and it shows the levels of kurtosis for varying values of μ and a. For small values of skewness i.e. when $a = 0.2 \sim 0.8$ the kurtosis is negative; interestingly, high levels of skewness drive the kurtosis of the distribution to positive values. However for the strictly symmetric case then the kurtosis of the distribution is negative. This mixture model may then serve as a suitable density for computing the score function of symmetric sub-Gaussian sources.

Computing the score function for the density in the general case yields

$$\frac{p'(s)}{p(s)} = \frac{s - \mu_1 - \left(\zeta / \sigma_2^2\right)(s - \mu_2)\Gamma}{\zeta\Gamma - \sigma_1^2}$$

where

$$\Gamma = \exp -\left(\alpha s^2 - \beta s - \gamma\right); \qquad \zeta = \varphi\left(\sigma_1^2\right)^2 / \sigma_2^2$$

$$\varphi = a/(a-1); \qquad \alpha = \left(\sigma_2^2 - \sigma_1^2\right) / 2\sigma_1^2\sigma_2^2;$$

$$\beta = \left(\mu_2\sigma_1^2 - \mu_1\sigma_2^2\right) / \sigma_1^2\sigma_2^2;$$

$$\gamma = \left(\mu_1^2\sigma_2^2 - \mu_2^2\sigma_1^2\right) / 2\sigma_1^2\sigma_2^2$$

Consider the case where $|\mu_1| = |\mu_2| = |\mu|$ and $\sigma_1^2 = \sigma_2^2 = \sigma^2$ then

$$\frac{p'(s)}{p(s)} = \frac{s - \mu - \varphi(s + \mu)\exp(-2cs)}{(\varphi \exp(-2cs) - 1)\sigma^2}$$

where $c = \frac{\mu}{\sigma^2}$ and after some manipulation

$$\frac{p'(s)}{p(s)} = \frac{-s}{\sigma^2} + \frac{\mu(1 + \varphi\exp(-2cs))}{\sigma^2(1 - \varphi\exp(-2cs))} = \frac{-s}{\sigma^2} + \frac{\mu_1}{\sigma^2} f(s)$$

Figure 7.6, shows the shape of the nonlinear term *f(s)* for varying values of the mixing coefficient *a*. This family of curves can be considered as a series of shifted hyperbolic tangents, indeed for a fully symmetric distribution where $a = 1/2$ the score function takes on a very simple form

$$\frac{p'(s)}{p(s)} = \frac{-s}{\sigma^2} + \frac{\mu(1 - \exp(-2cs))}{\sigma^2(1 + \exp(-2cs))}$$

$$= \frac{-s}{\sigma^2} + \frac{\mu}{\sigma^2}\tanh\left(\mu s / \sigma^2\right) \tag{7.19}$$

Finally, for the case where $\sigma^2 = \mu = 1$, the kurtosis equals –1/2 and so the score function boils down to

$$\frac{p'(s)}{p(s)} = -s + \tanh(s)$$

It is clear then that $\Phi'(y)/\Phi(y) = (\mu/\sigma^2)\tanh(\mu s / \sigma^2)$ in this instance, however, $\Phi'(y)/\Phi(y)$ does not represent a truncated expansion of Hermite polynomials but an exact representation of the non-linear part of the derivative of the log density for this particular mixture model.

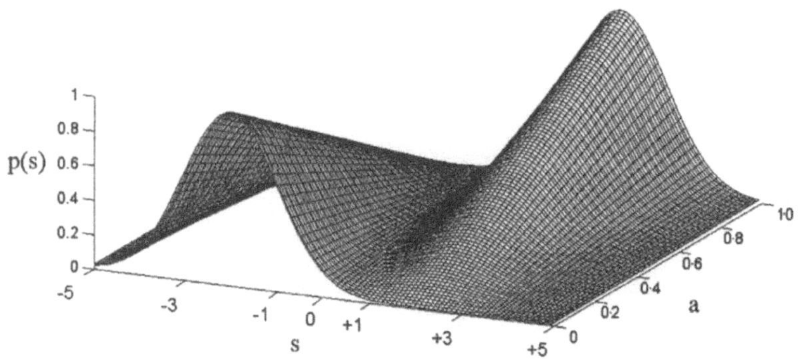

Figure 7.5a: The Sub-Gaussian Density Generated with the Use of a Mixture of Two Unit Variance Gaussians.

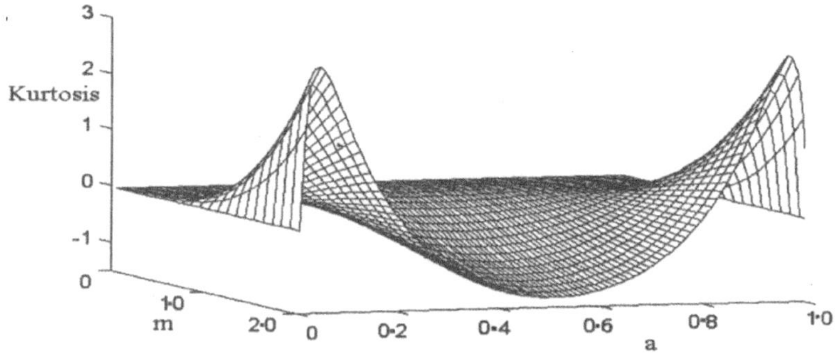

Figure 7.5b: The Range of Kurtosis Values for Varying Values of Mixing Coefficient.

For the case of super-Gaussian sources it is clear from the discussion in Section 7.3.3 that a Hyperbolic-Cauchy distribution can be used to parameterise the derivative of the log density. Another possible variant is

$$p_y(y) \propto p_G(y)\,\mathrm{sech}^2(y)$$

which is charted in Figure 7.7. The derivative of the log density in this particular case is now

$$\frac{p'(y)}{p(y)} = -\tanh(y) - y \tag{7.20}$$

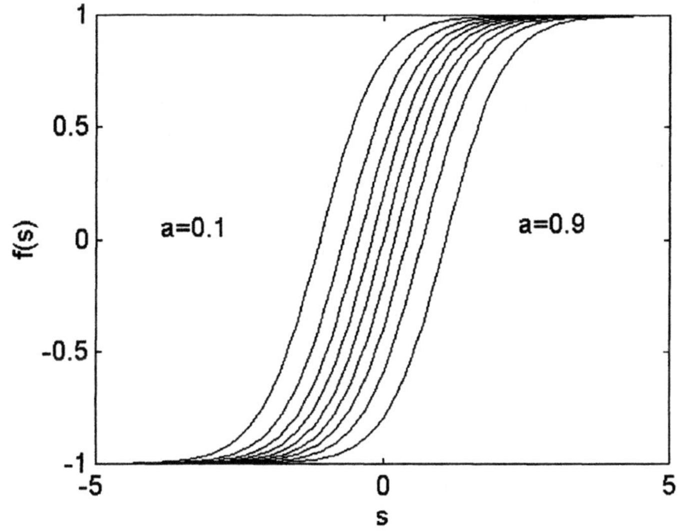

Figure 7.6: The Plot of the Non-linear Term Appearing in the Score Function for the Pearson Density Model for Varying Values of Mixing Coefficient.

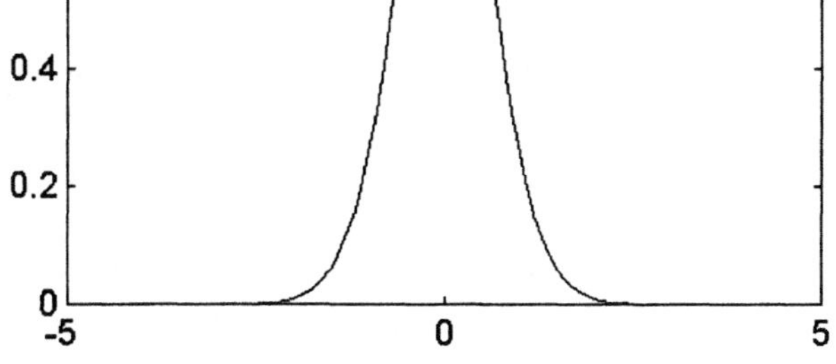

Figure 7.7: The Chart of $p_y(y) \propto p_G(y)\,\mathrm{sec}h^2(y)$.

We can then generalise (7.19) and (7.20) as

$$\frac{p'(y)}{p(y)} = -signum(\kappa_4)\tanh(y) - y \tag{7.21}$$

Note the similarity between (7.21) and the generic non-linearities introduced in Chapter 5 (5.18) and Chapter 6 (6.27). Section 7.5 will examine the asymptotic stability of the maximum negentropy algorithm for ICA using (7.21) as a generic non-linear term. The expression for (7.21) can be written in vector format as

$$f(\mathbf{y}) = -\mathbf{K}_4 \tanh(\mathbf{y}) - \mathbf{y} \tag{7.22}$$

where $\mathbf{K}_4$ is the square diagonal matrix which contains the individual kurtosis signs, defined as

$$\mathbf{K}_4 = diag\left[sign(\kappa_4(1)),\ sign(\kappa_4(2))\ \ldots,\ sign(\kappa_4(N))\right]$$

The generic term (7.22) can be substituted into the covariant gradient term for maximising data negentropy (7.12) finally giving

$$\Delta \mathbf{W}_n = \eta_n\left(\mathbf{I} - \mathbf{K}_4 \tanh(\mathbf{y}_n)\mathbf{y}_n^T - \mathbf{y}_n\mathbf{y}_n^T\right)\mathbf{W}_n \tag{7.23}$$

From the structure of (7.23) it is anticipated that it will be possible to separate scalar mixtures of both sub- and super-Gaussian sources. Note that if the sources are Gaussian then $\mathbf{K}_4 = \mathbf{0}$ and the update algorithm is simply a covariant spatial whitener (7.13).

We shall now show that these approximations will yield asymptotically stable stationary points of the algorithm, which are separating solutions. This does not say anything regarding the efficiency of the algorithm in reaching these solutions. It remains an open area of research as to the sufficiency of the pdf estimates. Analysis of the stability of each of the stationary points is now required. Amari, Chen and Cichocki (1997) have recently given the necessary and sufficient conditions for algorithms of the form $\Delta \mathbf{W} = \eta(\mathbf{I} - f(\mathbf{y})\mathbf{y}^T)\mathbf{W}$ to achieve stable separating solutions where $f(y_i) = -p_i'(y_i)/p_i(y_i)$.

7.5 Stability Analysis of Generalised Algorithm

The stability analysis consists of introducing a small perturbation to the points of stability and considering the behaviour of the system around these points (Minorsky, 1962). By developing expressions for the time averaged behaviour around the stationary points the stability can then be studied. The following must hold

$$\frac{d}{dt}\delta \mathbf{W} = \mathbf{J}\delta \mathbf{W} \rightarrow 0$$

where the Jacobian of the time averaged weight update is given as

$$\mathbf{J} = \frac{d}{d\mathbf{W}} E\{\Delta \mathbf{W}\}.$$

When the real parts of the eigenvalues of the Jacobian are negative, then the stationary points are asymptotically stable. It can be shown (Amari, Chen and Cichocki, 1997) that for all i, j $(i \neq j)$ then the following must hold for asymptotic stability

$$E\{y_i^2 f_i'(y_i)\} + 1 > 0 \tag{7.24}$$

$$E\{f_i'(y_i)\} > 0 \tag{7.25}$$

$$E\{y_i^2\}E\{y_j^2\}E\{f_i'(y_i)\}E\{f_j'(y_j)\} > 1 \tag{7.26}$$

Applying these conditions to (7.23) yields

$$E\{sign(\kappa_4(i))y_i^2 \operatorname{sec}h^2(y_i)\} + E\{y_i^2\} + 1 > 0 \tag{7.27}$$

$$E\{sign(\kappa_4(i))\operatorname{sec}h^2(y_i)\} + 1 > 0 \tag{7.28}$$

$$\begin{aligned} E\{y_i^2\}E\{y_j^2\}E\{sign(\kappa_4(i))\operatorname{sec}h^2(y_i) + 1\}\times \\ E\{sign(\kappa_4(j))\operatorname{sec}h^2(y_j) + 1\} > 1 \end{aligned} \tag{7.29}$$

Clearly we can see that the sign returned by the $sign(\kappa_4(i))$ operator and the distribution of the data sample used in computing the expectations determine the stability of the separating solutions. Numerical computation of 7.27 to 7.29 for varying non-Gaussian distributions shows that for pairwise independent super-Gaussian sources stability is achieved when $sign(\kappa_4(i)) = +1$ and for sub-Gaussian sources $sign(\kappa_4(i)) = -1$. For independent data where the ith source is sub-Gaussian and the jth source is super-Gaussian then $sign(\kappa_4(i)) = -1$ and $sign(\kappa_4(j)) = +1$ give stable stationary solutions, as would be expected. We should note that this does not guarantee that this algorithm will converge to the desired separating solution.

We now have a generic algorithm, which, by maximising the divergence measure proposed in (7.6), will provide an approximation to minimisation of the mutual information. The key difference between this particular method and the non-linear PCA and orthogonal EPP algorithms is that the transformation is not restricted to a rotation. This then removes the prior requirement of spatial whitening of the mixtures. The optimal nonlinearity is identified as the derivative of the log pdf. If we have prior knowledge as to the form of the underlying data pdf this can then be embedded within the algorithm to yield the optimally efficient estimator. In Chapter 8 we shall utilise this observation when developing separation algorithms for mixtures of convolved sources of natural speech. As with the online adaptation of the nonlinearity in Chapter 6 the same technique can be applied in this case to the identification of the diagonal elements of the $\mathbf{K}_4$ matrix. The similarity in form between (7.23) and the EASI (Equivariant Adaptive Separation by Independence) algorithm of Cardoso (1997) (Chapter 3, Section 3.3) should be noted.

7.6 Simulation Results

A number of simulations are now carried out to assess the performance of (7.23) and a comparison with the non-linear PCA algorithm (Chapter 5) and the hierarchic moment-based EPP algorithm (Chapter 6) is made. The three standard simulations, which have been utilised in Chapters 5 and 6 will be used here. The performance index (5.22) is used as a measure of the algorithm performance during adaptation. The learning continues for a series of five presentations of the data. Each simulation is repeated seven times with each run being initialised with a randomly generated weight matrix.

The level of separation is computed at every one hundred iterations. Figure 7.8 charts the performance index for each of the three data sets. The learning rate was set to a constant value of 0.0001 in all three cases. It is clear that convergence to a separating solution is achieved within the five presentations of the data.

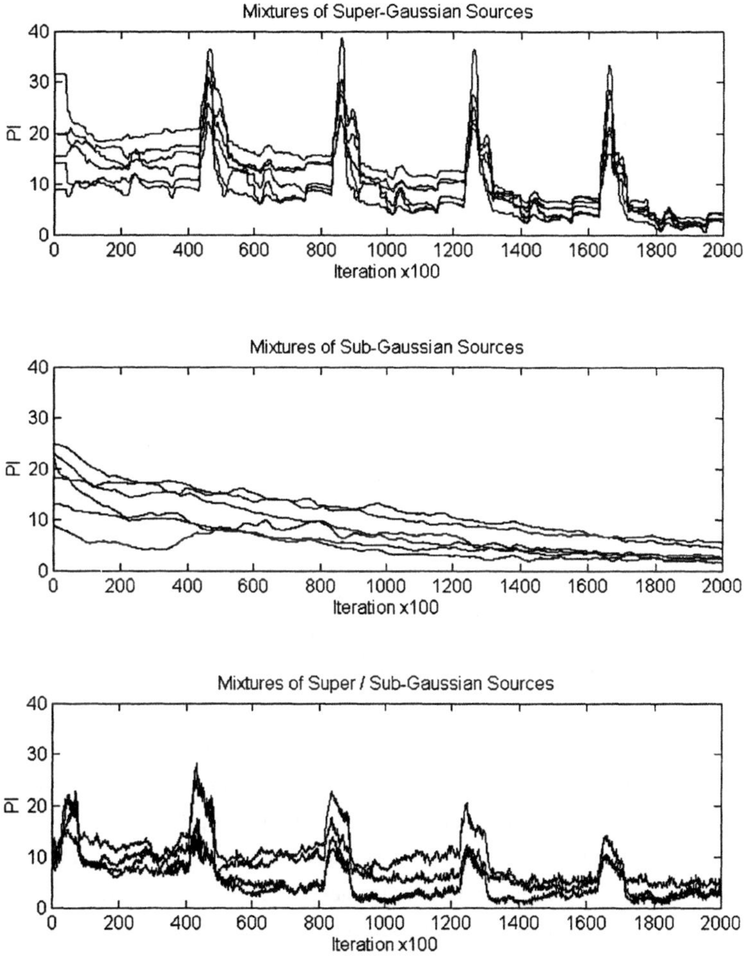

Figure 7.8: Performance Index for Seven Runs Through each Mixture of Independent Sources Using the Approximate Maximum Negentropy Algorithm.

Consider the development of the performance index for the mixture of super-Gaussian data. The distinct peak at the beginning and end of each epoch requires some comment. The traces generated by the non-linear PCA and hierarchic

EPP algorithms for mixtures of super-Gaussian sources (Figures 5.13 and 6.13) do not exhibit this peak. The mixtures of speech have periods of silence at the beginning and end of each record (Figure 5.12), the super-Gaussian images exhibit similar non-stationary characteristics. During periods where the data values are negligible the covariant form of the algorithm (7.23) will then have weight updates

$$\mathbf{x}_n \cong \mathbf{0}$$

$$\Rightarrow \mathbf{W}_{n+1} = \mathbf{W}_n + \eta\left(\mathbf{I} - \mathbf{K}_4 \tanh\left(\mathbf{y}_n\right)\mathbf{y}_n^T - \mathbf{y}_n\mathbf{y}_n^T\right)\mathbf{W}_n$$

$$\rightarrow \mathbf{W}_n + \eta\,\mathbf{W}_n$$

The weights will then continue to update in a linear manner driven by the learning rate. The non-linear PCA and EPP form of weight update, in periods where the amplitude of the observed data is almost zero, will have insignificant weights updates. This is a potential shortcoming of this form of algorithm where inappropriate updating may take place for non-stationary data. Monitoring the power of the incoming signals to the network would allow decisions to be made regarding whether an update should take place or not. Arbitrarily permuting the sequence of data will completely remove the temporal structure within the data but will preserve the gross statistics (Figure 7.9). By presenting the permuted versions of the mixture to the network we can see the 'smoother' convergence to a separating matrix during adaptation (Figure 7.10).

Over all simulations the convergence to a separating solution is achieved substantially faster with (7.23) in comparison to the non-linear PCA and hierarchic EPP methods (Table 7.1). The algorithm (7.23) requires approximately 20% of the total number of iterations over the other methods under consideration. The lack of requirement for spatial whitening is a major benefit saving of the order of 500,000 iterations. The fact that the algorithm is covariant (Equivariant) due to the use of the natural gradient is of great significance to the enhanced speed of convergence.

This final simulation focuses on image enhancement and is used here to demonstrate the algorithm performance when applied to ICA. The problem consists of three original source images which are mixed by a non-square linear memoryless mixing matrix such that the number of mixtures is greater than the number of sources.

The mixing matrix is given below

$$\mathbf{A} = \begin{bmatrix} -0.9846 & -0.8609 & 0.4024 \\ -0.2332 & 0.6923 & 0.8206 \\ -0.4557 & 0.0539 & 0.4239 \\ -0.1650 & -0.8161 & -0.8751 \\ 0.6735 & 0.8078 & -0.9051 \end{bmatrix}$$

The pixel distribution of each image is such that two of them are sub-Gaussian with negative values of kurtosis and the other is super-Gaussian with a positive value of kurtosis. The values of kurtosis for each image are computed as 0.3068, -1.3753 and –0.2415. It is interesting to note that two of the images (Figure 7.10) have relatively small absolute values of kurtosis and as such are approximately Gaussian. This is a particularly difficult problem due to the non-square mixing and the presence of both sub- and super-Gaussian sources within the mixture. This difficulty is also compounded with the small absolute values of kurtosis of two sources.

The first problem that has to be addressed is identifying the number of sources. Simply computing the rank of the covariance matrix of the mixture can do this. It is considered as future work to adaptively estimate the number of sources. However, for this simulation we assume there is sufficient data available to compute the rank of the mixture covariance matrix; this then indicates the number of outputs the network requires.

Historically the next problem would be two-fold as the mixture consists of a number of sources which are sub-Gaussian and some which are super-Gaussian. This of course affects the choice of the nonlinearity required to successfully separate the sources. However, from (15) all that is required is to 'learn' the diagonal terms of the **K4** matrix, which is now done online using a moving average estimator. Secondly, the problem of a low absolute value of kurtosis is often problematic, however we are considering the sign value and so this is no longer of concern.

Figure 7.11 shows the observations and the final separated sources. Each value is drawn randomly from the mixture and (15) is used to update the network weights. The learning rate is kept at a fixed value of 0.0001, and Figure 7.12 shows the performance index against the number of iterations. Each iteration corresponds to one pixel sample from the mixture. The performance index is based on the distance the overall system matrix **WA** is from a permutation and scaling [8]. The number of iterations in Figure 7.12 corresponds to one pass through the mixture. The **K4** matrix is initialised to a zero matrix and the diagonal terms then take the values computed from the moving average estimator of the output kurtosis. Figure 7.13 shows the development of the values, which achieve stablity (in terms of their sign) rapidly, for the **K4** matrix. We therefore are not required to make any assumptions on the type of non-Gaussian sources present in the mixture, nor is choosing another form of nonlinearity and changing the simple form of the algorithm required. Figure 7.11 shows the final separated images indicating the good performance of the algorithm.

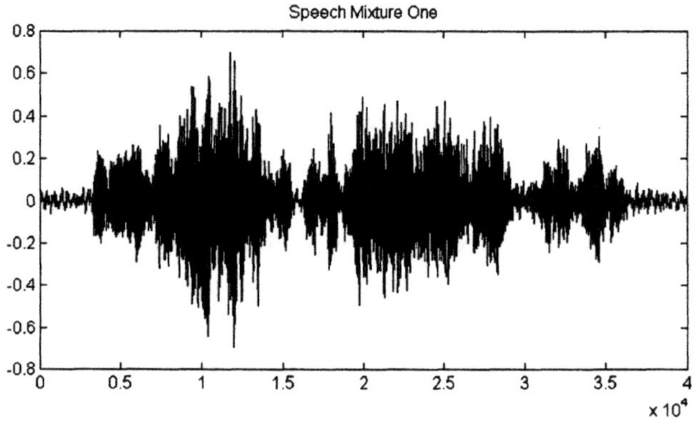

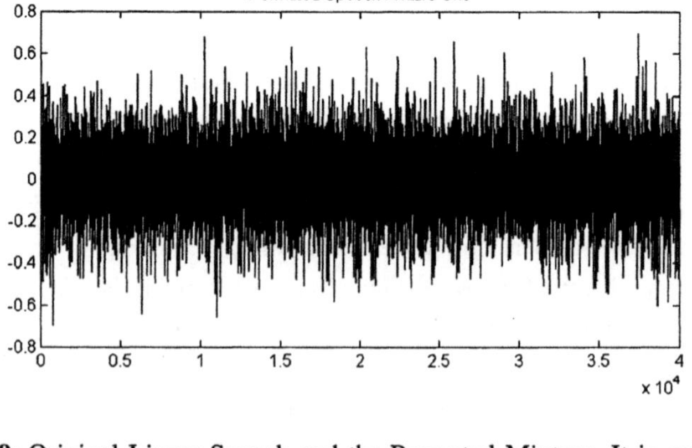

Figure 7.9: Original Linear Speech and the Permuted Mixture. It is quite clear the temporal structure has been completely removed and the permuted trace simply resembles temporally independent noise.

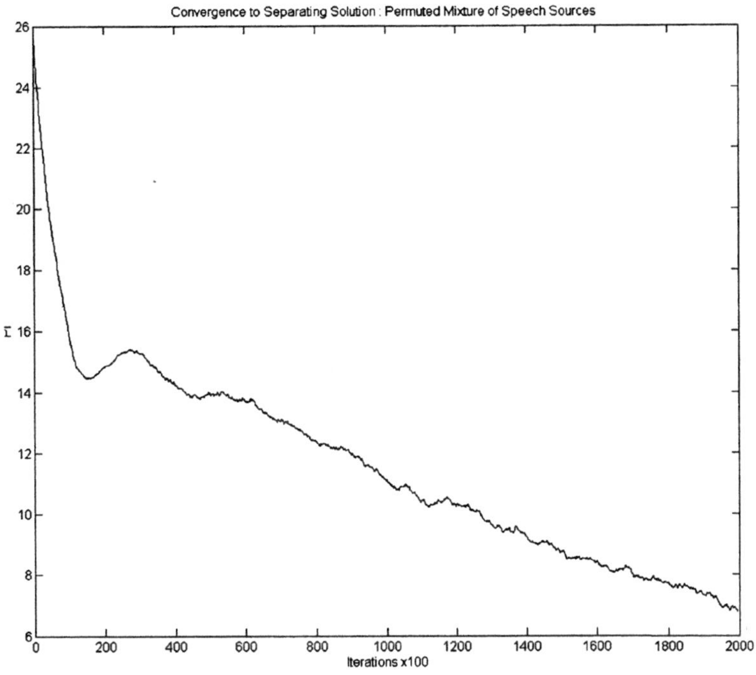

Figure 7.10: Convergence to Separating Solution for Permuted Mixture of Natural Speech.

Algorithm	Sub-Gausian Sources	Super-Gaussian Sources	Sub/Super-Gaussian
Non-linear PCA	800,000	800,000	1,300,000
Hierarchic EPP	1,100,000	500,000	1,000,000
Max Negentropy	180,000	180,000	180,000

Table 7.1: Number of Iterations Taken to Achieve a Separating Solution for Each Algorithm.

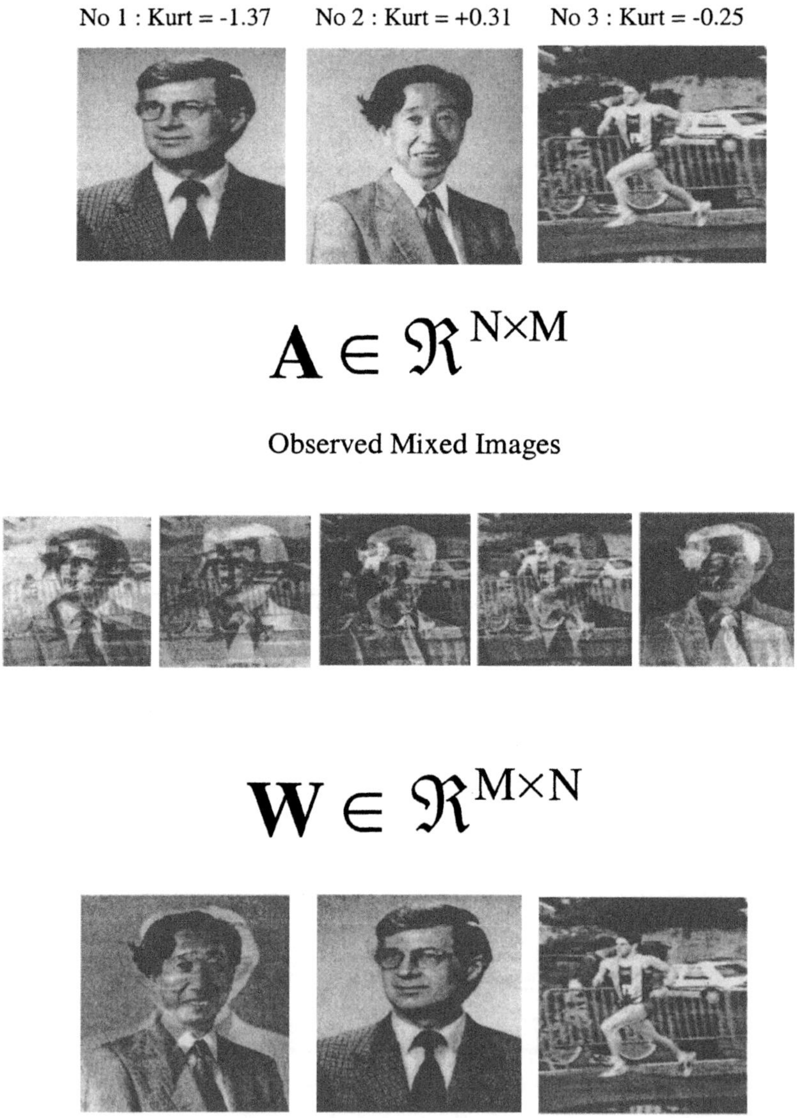

Figure 7.11: Independent Component Analysis performed on a 5 x 3 Mixture of Three Images. One is super-Gaussian with a kurtosis value of + 1.37; another has a very small value of positive kurtosis +0.307, with the third having a negative kurtosis of -0.25. The two images with the small absolute values of kurtosis could be considered as approximately mesokurtic.

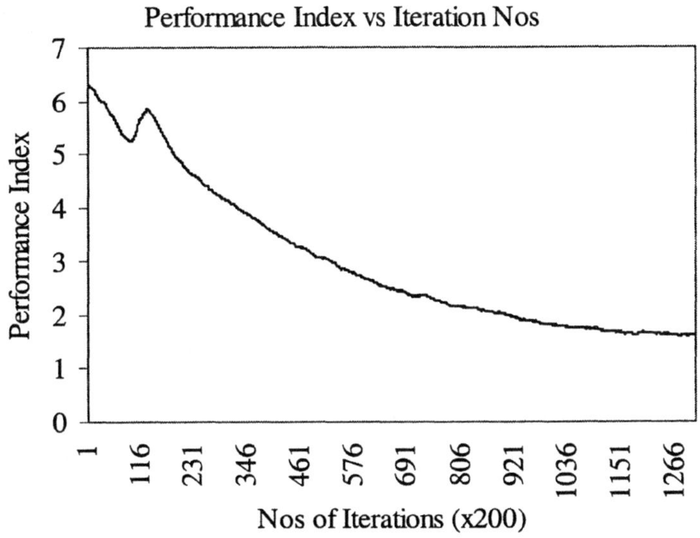

Figure 7.12: Typical Development of Overall Separating Matrix. Perfect separation would be indicated by a residual value for the performance index of zero.

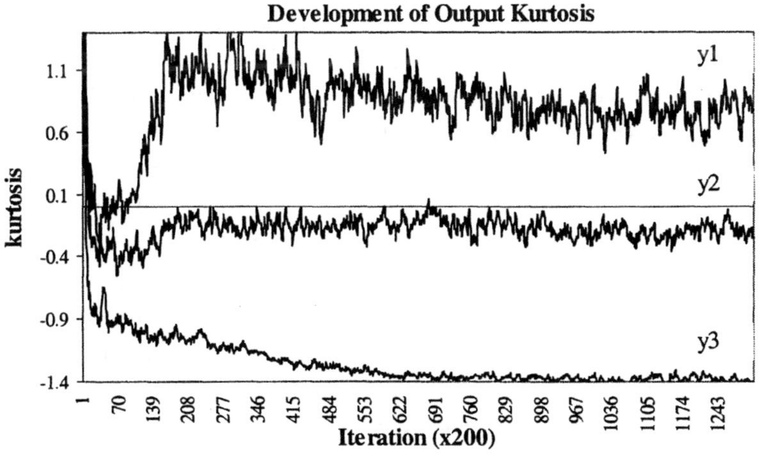

Figure 7.13 : The Development of the Kurtosis Estimates for the Diagonal Terms of the Coefficient Matrix **K4**. It is clear that the correct terms for the diagonal matrix appear and stabilise after approximately 20,000 sample iterations

7.7 Conclusions

In this chapter the equivalence of exploratory projection pursuit and blind source separation has been considered from an information theoretic perspective. It has been shown that a data transformation maximising the proposed divergence measure is identical, in an information theoretic sense, to the minimisation of mutual information. A generalised non-linearity has been proposed which allows separation of non-Gaussian sources with arbitrary unknown densities. The final proposed covariant algorithm will not be optimally efficient due to the density approximations, nevertheless the convergence performance of the algorithm has been shown to be far superior to the non-linear PCA and hierarchic EPP algorithms. The new algorithm proposed can be seen to be a generalisation of the Infomax algorithm of Bell and Sejnowski. This generalisation is important as the optimally efficient non-linearity is identified and the range of source distributions is no longer restricted to super-Gaussian densities. The work in this chapter has enabled us to reconsider our understanding of the EPP algorithm of Chapter 6. The hyperbolic tangent is a more important non-linear term than simply a moment-generating function and is the outcome of the specific density models utilised for sub- and super-Gaussian sources.

Jung *et al* (1997), McKeown *et al* (1997) and Lee *et al* (1999) have successfully applied the developed algorithm (7.23) to the challenging real world problem of removing artefacts from electroencephalograph (EEG) recordings of brain activity. The original infomax algorithm had been shown to be unable to remove artefacts such as muscular, ocular, electrocardiogram (ECG) and mains power line noise (Bell and Sejnowski, 1995) due to their sub-Gaussian statistics. The proposed algorithm (7.23) enables all sub-Gaussian artefacts to be concentrated into single channels and so has been adopted as an efficient tool for EEG signal processing. The focus of this and preceding chapters has been on the linear memoryless mixing model $\mathbf{x} = \mathbf{A}\mathbf{s}$. An important variant is the convolutive mixing model where the mixing matrix is now replaced by a matrix of transfer functions, which then convolve the original sources. This is used to model the distortion which signals, such as speech, experience when transmitted in an acoustic environment, such as a living room, in the presence of noise or other competing speech. The following chapter develops potential solutions to the convolutive mixing problem based on a form of anti-Hebbian learning.

8. Temporal Anti-Hebbian Learning

This chapter studies an extension of anti-Hebbian learning that includes temporal context. This particular chapter highlights the cross fertilisation of the study of self-organising neural networks, statistical signal processing and adaptive filtering.

8.1 Introduction

Up until now the mixing model considered has been linear and memoryless. This model has an extensive range of application in statistical data analysis, array processing, medical instrumentation and image analysis. However, the classical 'Cocktail Party Problem', where wanted speech is separated from unwanted competing speech or noise does not fit the scalar mixing model. To consider the 'Cocktail Party Problem' the scalar mixing model must be extended to a convolutive mixture model. The development of a generalised temporal anti-Hebbian structure and algorithm is presented which provides an improved method of separating wanted speech from unwanted speech or noise within acoustic environments.

8.2 Blind Source Separation of Convolutive Mixtures

Listening to, or recording, a speech signal in a noisy acoustic environment is described as follows. The speech signal *s(t)* is distorted by an acoustic path $a_i(t)$ before it reaches the ear or microphone. This also holds for the competing noise or speech sources $n_{ij}(t)$. The resulting signal at the receiver is then, in the deterministic case where there is no additive noise at the receiver

$$x_i(t) = a_i(t) * s_i(t) + \sum_j a_{ij}(t) * n_j(t) \tag{8.1}$$

The operator * denotes convolution. It is also assumed that that the receiver does not distort the summation of the signals. This would be typified by a flat frequency response over the range of frequency components of the signals. We can then extend the linear ICA model where the mixing model, with no additive noise, is now defined as

$$\mathbf{x}(z) = \mathbf{A}(z)\mathbf{s}(z) \tag{8.2}$$

For convenience, we shall use z-domain notation throughout. The polynomial matrix **A**(z) will have individual entries of the form

$$A_{ij} = \sum_{k=0}^{\infty} a_{ij}(k) z^{-k},$$

indicating that the mixing components are now right sided causal filters of infinite order. We impose stability constraints on each entry of **A**(z) such that bounded inputs produce bounded outputs (BIBO) i.e.

$$\sum_{k=0}^{\infty} \left| a_{ij}(k) \right| < \infty.$$

In the case of acoustic environments the impulse response of a typical room will have a finite decaying duration, typically being of the order of 0.35 seconds (Mackenzie, 1964). This indicates that for a sampling rate of 11.025 kHz the finite causal mixing filter will have a length of typically 4000 taps delays The impulse response of a small hard walled bedroom is shown in Figure 8.1. More reverberent environments, such as a cathedral, will have far longer decaying responses. We can therefore approximate the causal filter by a finite impulse response of order L such that

$$A_{ij} = \sum_{k=1}^{L} a_{ij}(k) z^{-k}.$$

As we are considering an inverse problem, we require that both the finite convolving filter and its inverse are stable and causal. This then requires that all poles and zeros of the mixing filters are within the unit circle (Oppenheim & Shafer, 1989). This requirement is realistic in most simple acoustic situations where there are no excessive levels of reverberation or complicating multi-path signal arrivals.

For illustrative purposes, if we consider an N source / N receiver situation we have, in the z-domain, the observed signals given as :

$$\mathbf{x}_1(z) = A_{11}(z)\mathbf{s}_1(z) + \ldots + A_{1N}(z)\mathbf{s}_N(z)$$
$$\vdots$$
$$\mathbf{x}_N(z) = A_{N1}(z)\mathbf{s}_1(z) + \ldots + A_{NN}(z)\mathbf{s}_N(z)$$

and equivalently in the time domain

$$x_1(t) = \sum_{k=0}^{L} a_{11}(k)s_1(t-k) + \ldots + \sum_{k=0}^{L} a_{1N}(k)s_N(t-k)$$
$$\vdots$$
$$x_N(t) = \sum_{k=0}^{L} a_{N1}(k)s_1(t-k) + \ldots + \sum_{k=0}^{L} a_{NN}(k)s_N(t-k)$$

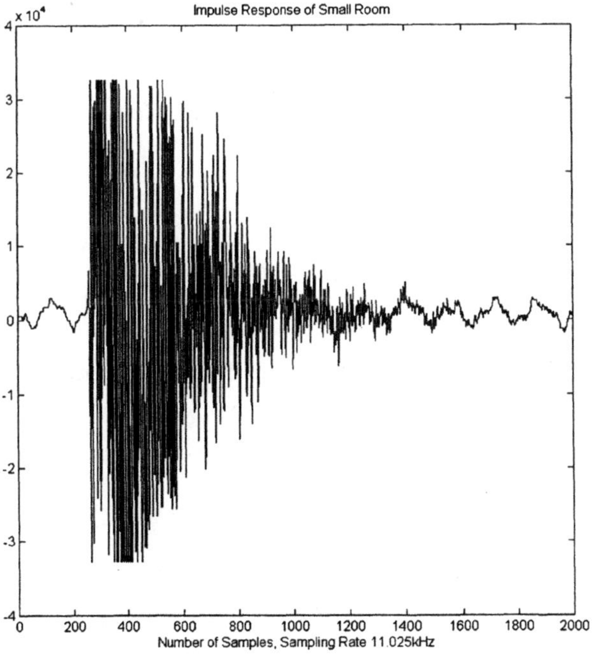

Figure 8.1: The Impulse Response of a Small Room. From this figure it is clear that the impulse decay is approximately 1200 samples which gives a T_{60} of 0.11 seconds.

The notation *x(t)* and *x(t-k)* indicates the instantaneous sample value at time *t* and the lagged value at time *t-k*. As in the linear case we seek a transformation which will approximately invert the effect of the mixing and so in this case seek a filter $\mathbf{W}(z)$

$$\mathbf{y}(z) = \mathbf{W}(z)\mathbf{x}(z) = \mathbf{W}(z)\mathbf{A}(z)\mathbf{s}(z) \qquad (8.3)$$

As in the instantaneous case we seek a polynomial matrix which will tend to satisfy $\mathbf{W}(z) \rightarrow \mathbf{A}^{-1}(z)$ where the inverse of the polynomial matrix is (Barnett, 1971; Chan *et al*, 1996)

$$\mathbf{A}^{-1}(z) = \frac{1}{\det(\mathbf{A}(z))}\left[(-1)^{(i+j)}\det(\mathbf{A}_{ji}(z))\right]_{ij} \qquad (8.4)$$

with the determinant given as the matrix Laplace expansion

$$\det(\mathbf{A}(z)) = \sum_{j=1}^{N}(-1)^{(j-1)}A_{1j}(z)\det(\mathbf{A}_{1j}(z)).$$

The term

$$\left[(-1)^{(i+j)}\det(\mathbf{A}_{ji}(z))\right]_{ij}$$

being the matrix of cofactors of $\mathbf{A}(z)$ as in the standard linear case. If we consider the simplified 2×2 case of (8.3) we then have

$$\mathbf{W}(z) = \mathbf{A}^{-1}(z) =$$

$$\frac{1}{(A_{11}(z)A_{22}(z) - A_{12}(z)A_{21}(z))}\begin{bmatrix} A_{22}(z) & -A_{12}(z) \\ -A_{21}(z) & A_{11}(z) \end{bmatrix} \qquad (8.5)$$

As in the general expression (8.3) we have the additional requirement that for a stable and causal separating solution $\mathbf{W}(z)$ to exist, the determinant of the polynomial mixing matrix must have all poles and zeros within the unit circle. In this section, we have considered the general convolutive mixing model, which consists of stable and causal finite length filters. The inverse system will be causal and stable if the mixing system is minimum phase (Oppenheim and Schafer, 1991), that is all poles and zeros exist within the unit circle region of convergence. It is important to highlight and be aware of the shortcomings of this simplified model. The transfer functions

$$A_{ij} = \sum_{k=1}^{L} a_{ij}(k) z^{-k}$$

describe the point to point acoustic path which will change if the sources or receivers are physically non-stationary. These functions are only approximations of the complex acoustic field. Van Gerven (1996) gives a detailed discussion on the validity of the proposed acoustic mixing model. For our purposes, this model will allow investigation into the signal separating properties of temporal anti-Hebbian learning. We now propose a temporal extension of the initial decorrelating model of anti-Hebbian learning proposed by Foldiak (1989).

8.3. Temporal Linear Anti-Hebbian Model

We take Foldiak's first model, Figure 8.2a, and apply 'memory based' synaptic lateral connections. Figure 8.2b gives the temporal model where the weights are written in the z-transform notation and where the z^{-1} operator is shown explicitly for two tapped delays. Figure 8.2c shows the adaptive filter model equivalent of the temporal anti-Hebbian model. The addition of memory to the synaptic weights reflects the notion that information may be conveyed and therefore extracted from the temporal relations within the data stream. The network output is now given as a time delayed weighted version of (4.13), that is

$$y_i(t) = x_i(t) + \sum_{j=1}^{N} \sum_{k=0}^{M} w_{ij}(t-k) y_j(t-k) \tag{8.6}$$

where N is the number of neurons and M is the total number of delays. Written as a z domain matrix we have the compact form of (8.6)

$$\mathbf{y}(z) = (\mathbf{I} - \mathbf{W}(z))^{-1} \mathbf{x}(z) \tag{8.7}$$

The anti-Hebbian rule given in Chapter 4, Section 4.1.3 has been shown to yield an output with diagonal covariance (Foldiak, 1992). For second order independence the following should be satisfied

$$E\{y_i(t)y_j(t-k)\} = 0 \ \forall \ i \neq j \wedge k = 1 \ldots M$$

and so we require an adaptive algorithm which adapts the dependant variable of the network output (i.e. the weights) to yield temporally decorrelated outputs in the expectation. By utilising the temporally extended anti-Hebbian rule

$$\Delta w_{ij}(k) = -\eta \ y_i(t)y_j(t-k) \ \forall i \neq j \wedge k = 1 \ldots M \qquad (8.8)$$

for each temporal output we can then force the output cross-correlation terms to zero. So the cross weights will grow in an inhibitory fashion if there is correlation between the output $y_i(t)$ and each of the tapped outputs of the neuron $y_j(t-k)$ until the following holds

$$E\{y_i(t)y_j(t-k)\} = 0 \ \forall i \neq j \wedge k = 1 \ldots M .$$

The weight connecting the current output at node i to the historical output at time $(t-k)$ of node j is denoted as $w_{ij}(k)$. Note that in the non-temporal model $\Delta w_{ij} = -\eta \ y_i y_j = -\eta \ y_j y_i = \Delta w_{ji}$ and so the anti-Hebbian learning will give a symmetric weight matrix.

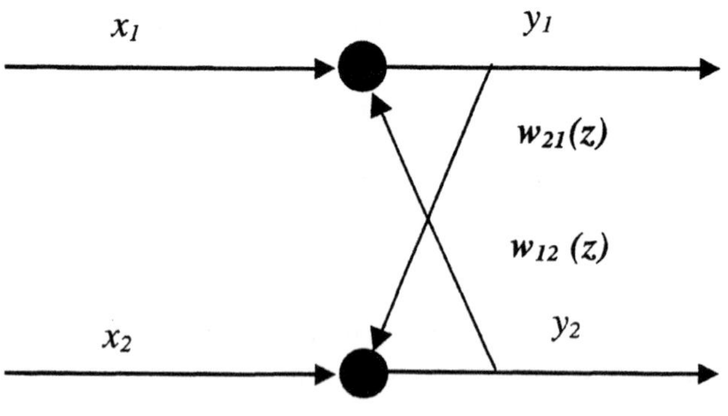

Figure 8.2.a: Instantaneous Lateral Network Model.

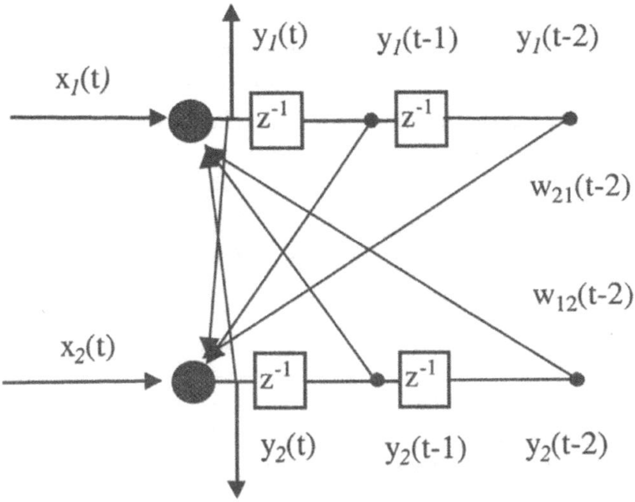

Figure 8.2b: Temporal Extension of Lateral Network Model.

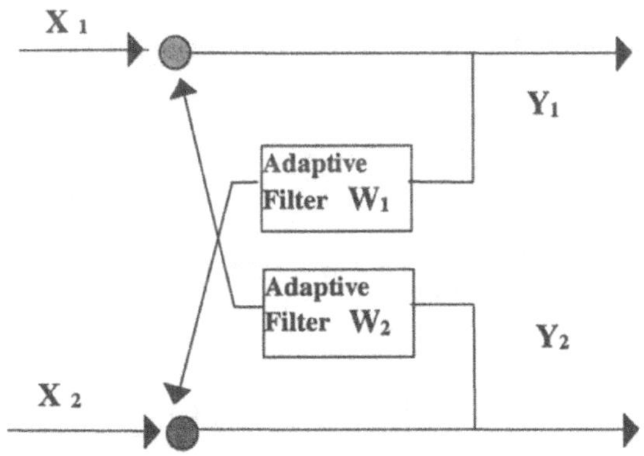

Figure 8.2c: Adaptive Filter Equivalent of Temporal Model.

In the temporal case $\Delta w_{ij}(k) \neq \Delta w_{ji}(k)$: $-\eta\ y_i(t)y_j(t-k)$ will in general not equal $-\eta\ y_j(t)y_i(t-k)$ and so an asymmetric polynomial weight matrix is generated. The linear anti-Hebbian learning decorrelates the delayed outputs of all neurons $i : (i \neq j \ \forall \ i)$ with the instantaneous outputs of neuron j.

Consider two signal sources s_1 and s_2 the signals received at two points displaced in space (x_1 and x_2) from the sources will be given as the matrix multiplication of the transfer function matrix **A(z)** and the source vector vis,

$$\begin{bmatrix} x_1 \\ x_2 \end{bmatrix} = \begin{bmatrix} a_{11}(z) & a_{12}(z) \\ a_{21}(z) & a_{22}(z) \end{bmatrix} \begin{bmatrix} s_1 \\ s_2 \end{bmatrix} \tag{8.9}$$

$$\mathbf{x} = \mathbf{A}\,\mathbf{s} \tag{8.10}$$

For clarity we drop the use of *(z)* as it is now implied in the relevant equations. To recover the original sources then $\mathbf{s} = \mathbf{A}^{-1}\mathbf{x}$ must be satisfied up to an arbitrary filter, using (8.7) , for **y** to approximate **s** at convergence we can write

$$\mathbf{y} = \hat{\mathbf{s}} = (\mathbf{I} - \mathbf{W})^{-1}\mathbf{x} \equiv \mathbf{A}^{-1}\mathbf{x} \tag{8.11}$$

Some algebraic manipulation will yield, in the discrete z domain

$$(1 - w_{12}w_{21})y_1 = (a_{11} + w_{12}a_{21})s_1 + (a_{12} + w_{12}a_{22})s_2 \tag{8.12}$$

$$(1 - w_{12}w_{21})y_2 = (a_{22} + w_{21}a_{12})s_2 + (a_{21} + w_{21}a_{11})s_1 \tag{8.13}$$

and so

$$w_{12}(z) = -a_{12}(z)a_{22}^{-1}(z) \quad \text{and} \quad w_{21}(z) = -a_{21}(z)a_{11}^{-1}(z)$$

The values of the network output will then be a filtered representation of the original uncorrupted signal source as given in the more general case of (8.5).

$$\begin{bmatrix} \hat{s}_1 \\ \hat{s}_2 \end{bmatrix} = (\mathbf{I} - \mathbf{W})^{-1}\mathbf{A}\,\mathbf{s} \cong \begin{bmatrix} s_1 \\ s_2 \end{bmatrix} \tag{8.14}$$

The weights of the network can then be forced to converge to the inverse filters given in (8.13) using a suitable criterion. The criterion which will be considered is initially the cross-correlation between the received signals and is a second order independence criterion. We can use the temporal linear anti-Hebbian learning given in (8.8) to stochastically maximise the second order independence criterion. Matsuoka *et al* (1994) develop a blind separation algorithm for separation of an instantaneous symmetric mixture of time-varying Gaussian signals based on second order statistics. As the signal statistics are non-stationary it is shown that a normalised form of anti-Hebbian learning based on the feedback network (Figure 8.2a) can separate symmetric mixtures of Gaussian sources. The nonstationarity is exploited by online estimation of the signal variance which is time dependent. They then propose a simple algorithm

$$\Delta w_{ij}(t) = -\frac{\eta \; y_i(t) y_j(t)}{E\{y_i^2(t)\}} \equiv -\frac{\eta \; y_i(t) y_j(t)}{\Phi(t)} \quad \forall i \neq j$$

The variance is estimated using a moving average estimator

$$\Phi_i(t+1) = \alpha \Phi_i(t) + (1-\alpha) y_i^2(t)$$

However, by using a temporal form of the Matsuoka *et al* anti-Hebbian rules, statistical independence of the network output, for convolutive mixing, may also be achieved without resorting to higher order statistics.

$$\Delta w_{ij}(k) = -\frac{\eta \; y_i(t) y_j(t-k)}{\Phi_i(t)} \quad \forall i \neq j$$

$$\Phi_i(t+1) = \alpha \Phi_i(t) + (1-\alpha) y_i^2(t) \tag{8.16}$$

This is effectively a normalised version of the temporal anti-Hebbian update rule (8.8). Torkkola (1996) develops an adaptation rule for a feedback network (Figure 8.2b) based on the Infomax algorithm of Bell and Sejnowski (1995). From the experience gained in considering linear mixtures it seems intuitively reasonable that the temporal Infomax algorithm will provide enhanced separation performance over temporal linear anti-Hebbian learning. The algorithm developed (Torkkola, 1996) for a network non-linearity based on the hyperbolic tangent is

$$\Delta w_{ij}(k) = -\eta \tanh(y_i(t))y_j(t-k) \quad \forall i \neq j \wedge k = 1 \dots L \quad (8.17)$$

In developing the Symmetric Adaptive Decorrelation (SAD) algorithm Van Gerven (1996) shows that nulling of the cross-spectrum of mixtures of convolved sources is a necessary condition for separation. The adaptation algorithm of (8.8) or the normalised version (8.16) will then be potentially suitable for separation of mixtures of convolved sources. A preliminary simulation is carried out to compare both the linear and non-linear temporal methods for separation.

8.4. Comparative Simulation

Five seconds of male and female speech was sampled at 8Khz and mixed using the transfer function matrix employed by Torkkola (1996) in his simulations. This is given below

$$\begin{bmatrix} x_1 \\ x_2 \end{bmatrix} = \begin{bmatrix} 1-0.4z^{-25}+0.2z^{-45} & 0.4z^{-20}-0.2z^{-28}+0.1z^{-36} \\ 0.5z^{-10}+0.3z^{-22}+0.1z^{-34} & 1-0.3z^{-20}+0.2z^{-38} \end{bmatrix} \begin{bmatrix} s_1 \\ s_2 \end{bmatrix}$$

We use the Sum of Squares of Fourth Order Normalised Marginal Cumulants (SSFONMC) and Fourth Order Normalised Marginal Cumulant, (FONMC) as a measure of the separation yielded. The impulse response of the ideal inverting filters is graphed along with those of the converged linear temporal network in Figure 8.4. A memory length of 100 sample lags was used.

	FONMC Voice 1	FONMC Voice 2	SSFONMC
Originals	4.46	7.55	76.89
Mixed	2.76	5.10	33.63
Retrieved	4.30	7.42	73.54

Table 8.1: FONMC Measures of Original, Mixed and Retrieved Signals.

We can see from Table 8.1 the drop in the absolute value of the FONMC of each source caused by the onset of central limit effects due to the convolutive mixing. The restored signals FONMC is within 4% of the original values. Scatter plots of the original, mixed and restored signals amplitude are given in Figure 8.3. The characteristic orthogonal cross shape shows clearly the independence of the two original signals; the plot of the mixed signals shows clearly the correlation now existing between the mixtures. The blurring of the plot indicates the colouring of each signal by the other due to the convolved mixing. The plot of the restored signals shows the characteristic orthogonal cross shape, indicating the approximate independence of the output signals.

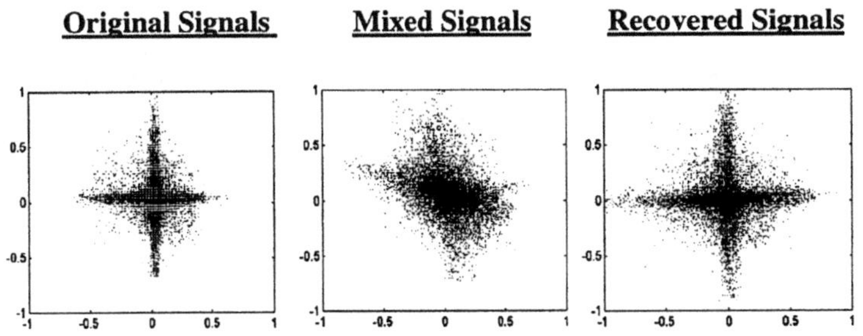

Figure 8.3: Signal Amplitude Scatter Plots.

The impulse response coefficients given by inverting the filters are plotted in Figure 8.4 along with the converged network weight values using the temporal linear anti-Hebbian learning of (8.8) and the Information Maximisation algorithm (8.17). The mean square value of the estimation errors caused by the use of linear anti-Hebbian and information maximisation algorithms were almost identical, (MSE 'Info' Max = 2.28%, MSE Linear Anti-Hebb = 2.91%). The audible results were '*good*' with some echo still remaining in the output signals. Applying the learning of (8.16) gave slightly improved results over those given by the use of (8.8), though the learning parameters required careful selection. It will be shown in subsequent sections why (8.16) yields improved results over (8.8).

The main result from this simulation indicates that the temporal form of the information maximisation algorithm gives little improvement in separation performance than that found with the linear form of anti-Hebbian learning. This result runs counter to our understanding developed in studying the linear memoryless BSS model. A brief review of the methods which have been developed for separation of mixtures of convolved sources will help to elucidate this phenomenon and indicates that a more efficient method can be proposed. Techniques based on classical filter theory will be reviewed along with the more recent methods which have been developed from the study of self-organising neural networks.

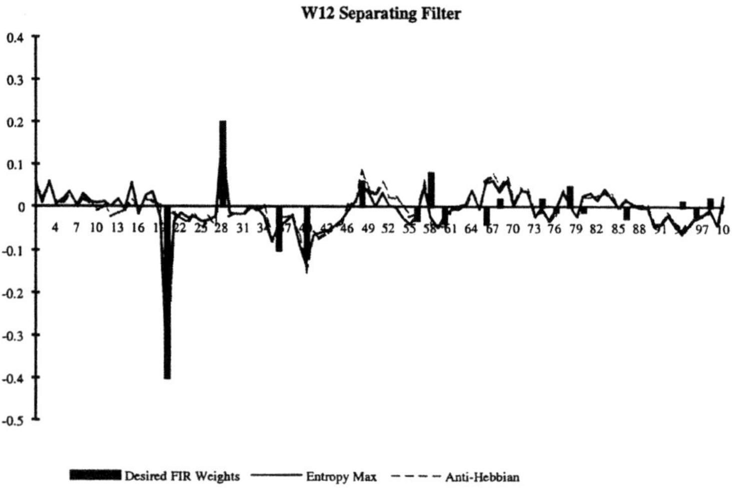

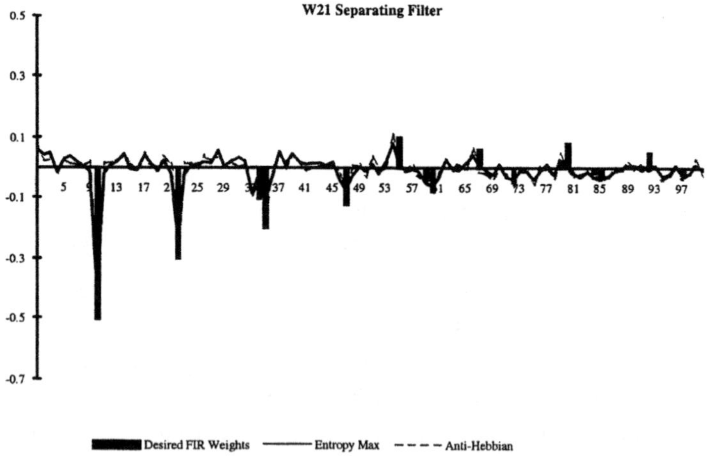

Figure 8.4: Converged Network Weights and Required FIR Coefficients.

8.5 Review of Existing Work on Adaptive Separation of Convolutive Mixtures

A human listener present in a room with several sources of sound is able to concentrate on any one of the particular sounds, this ability is referred to as the 'Cocktail Party' effect (Cherry, 1953). The question, which has been asked historically, is how do humans segregate speech sounds and is it possible to design filters or machines which are capable of this separation? Cherry (1953) investigated what cues within received signals are important for humans to suppress unwanted signals. The important area of contextual cues, information based on language structure and visual gestures (lip reading), was studied in an attempt to assess whether a machine could use this contextual information to separate voices. Indeed, the utilisation of additional information from contextual cues provided the inspiration for the 'contextual independent component analysis' (cICA) algorithm of Pearlmutter and Parra (1996). However, of most significance to the contents of this chapter was the finding that, in a noisy environment, binaural hearing was superior to monaural hearing (Plomp, 1976; Moncur and Dirks, 1967).

The cochlea is the main structure within the inner ear. The processing centres of the auditory brainstem receive, from the cochlea, a two-channel set of time domain signals in contiguous non-linearly spaced frequency bands. Current interpretations of experimental evidence identify the separation of, left from right ear signals, and low from high frequency signals, timing from intensity information, and their re-integration at various processing centres and levels in the hierarchy. It also appears that due to the intermittent nature of the signals windows in either the desired or competing signal can be used to view and estimate the other for interference reduction (Plomp, 1976). Experimental evidence suggests that the auditory system is able to model a communications channel (Darwin *et al*, 1989). This implies that enhancement and source location may be aided by estimation of the differential acoustic transfer function path between the interference and the desired signal.

It had been noted that the ability of an individual to suppress unwanted noise was greatly reduced with monaural hearing. An example is the case of two sources being recorded by one microphone and then played through a single loudspeaker. On listening to the loudspeaker output the individual no longer has the use of the binaural cocktail party effect and so the intelligibility of what is played through the loudspeakers is greatly reduced (Cherry, 1953). A similar effect is evident in hearing impaired individuals (Plomp, 1976; Moncur and Dirks, 1967).

Studies have shown that for ideal conditions the sound detection threshold for binaural hearing exceeds that of monaural by 25dB (Durlach and Colburn, 1978).

Binaural hearing has also been shown superior (Plomp, 1976; Moncur and Dirks, 1967) to monaural at maintaining the intelligibility of speech in the presence of reverberation, continuous speech shaped noise, or competing connected speech. That is, binaural processing does not simply perform coherent addition of the signals at the two ears. The "binaural unmasking" effect (Durlach *et al*, 1986) lowers the hearing threshold, may operate in frequency sub-bands, and appears to utilise binaural correlation properties to de-emphasise an undesired signal. Culling and Summerfield (1995) found that masking release was largely independent of the pattern of interaural correlations across frequency.

Since lateralisation is not necessary for effective binaural masking release, how can correlation aid binaural unmasking if not used for grouping by interaural time? One possibility is that the sub-band signals are being grouped for selective processing dependent on their degree of interaural correlation rather than interaural time delay. Thus the main enhancement advantage of binaural hearing may be in the ability to perform "binaural unmasking", possibly operating as an adaptive noise cancellation process in frequency sub-bands. Adaptive noise cancellation (Toner and Campbell, 1993) is an operation at least superficially analogous to binaural unmasking, as is temporal anti-Hebbian learning (Shields *et al*, 1997). An engineering implementation of anti-Hebbian type adaptive noise cancellation offers the possibility of performing "binaural unmasking" outwith the body, providing signals of improved signal to noise ratio (SNR).

Kaiser and David (1960) first exploited the notion that interaural correlation may be the driving mechanism behind binaural unmasking. They successfully reproduced the binaural cocktail party effect by applying non-linear cross-correlation techniques to the outputs of two microphones. Adaptive filtering techniques employing both wide-band and sub-band processing have been developed to enhance the intelligibility of speech in the presence of corrupting noise (Toner and Campbell, 1993). These techniques rely on noise alone periods to estimate the differential transfer functions related to the unwanted signal sources. Speech / No-Speech detection methods are therefore required and form integral parts of the developed systems.

As information redundancy between network nodes is the adaptation mechanism in anti-Hebbian learning, it is then clear that one simple model of interaural correlation based binaural unmasking may be as shown in Figure 8.2b.

The classical adaptive filter structure (Figure 8.5) which implements the LMS (Least Mean Square) algorithm (Widrow and Stearns, 1985) has been applied to adaptive noise cancellation (ANC) (Widrow, 1975). The LMS algorithm is a stochastic gradient descent method for adaptation of the filter **W** to minimise the mean square error (MSE) at the filter output. The optimal weight parameters are given by the classical Wiener solution (Haykin, 1991). Consider Figure 8.5: the mean square error is given as

$$E\left\{\mathrm{E}^2\right\} = E\left\{\left(\mathrm{P} - \mathbf{W}^T\mathbf{R}\right)^2\right\} \tag{8.18}$$

where P denotes the instantaneous signal at the primary input, $\mathbf{W} = \left[w(t),\ \ldots,\ w(L)\right]^T$ denotes the filter of length L and $\mathbf{R} = \left[R(t),\ \ldots,\ R(L)\right]^T$ denotes the delayed reference inputs. It can be shown that the optimal filter to minimise (8.18) is given as

$$\mathbf{W}_{\mathrm{opt}} = \mathbf{A}^{-1}\mathbf{C} \tag{8.19}$$

where $\mathbf{A} = E\left\{\mathbf{R}\mathbf{R}^T\right\}$ is the autocorrelation matrix of the reference input and $\mathbf{C} = E\left\{P\mathbf{R}\right\}$ is the crosscorrelation vector of the primary and reference inputs. The minimum can be found iteratively using the LMS algorithm

$$\mathbf{W}_{n+1} = \mathbf{W}_n + \mu\frac{\partial \mathrm{E}}{\partial \mathbf{W}} = \mathbf{W}_n + 2\mu\mathrm{E}_n\mathbf{R}_n \tag{8.20}$$

where the error at the nth iteration is

$$\mathrm{E}_n = \mathrm{P}_n - \mathbf{W}_n^T\mathbf{R}_n \,.$$

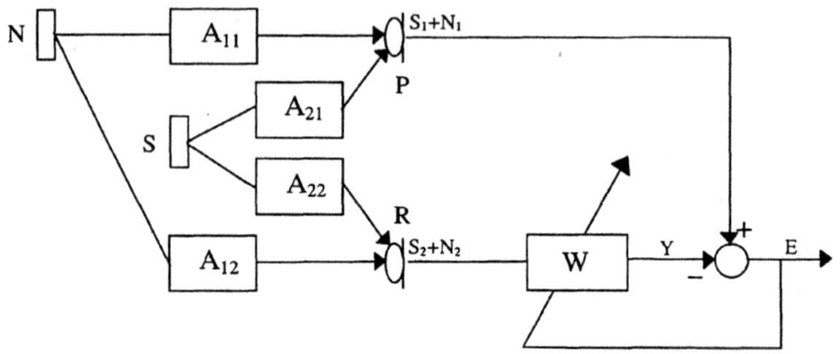

Figure 8.5: The Signal Mixing Model and LMS Adaptive Filter Structure in an Adaptive Noise Cancellation Configuration.

When the LMS algorithm is used for ANC, the configuration of the receivers must be such that the reference input receives only the interfering or noise source N, (Figure 8.5). This then requires that one receiver is positioned close enough to the noise source that leakage of the signal into the reference receiver is avoided. This requirement indicates that the transfer function $\mathbf{A}_{22}$ is insignificant and so the error at the filter output is then

$$E\{E^2\} = E\left\{\left(P - \mathbf{W}^T\mathbf{R}\right)^2\right\}$$

$$= E\left\{\left((\mathbf{A}_{11}N + \mathbf{A}_{21}S) - \mathbf{W}^T\mathbf{A}_{12}N\right)^2\right\}$$

As the noise and the signal are uncorrelated the mean square error is then

$$E\left\{\left(\mathbf{A}_{11}N - \mathbf{W}^T\mathbf{A}_{12}N\right)^2 + (\mathbf{A}_{21}S)^2\right\}$$

The term $E\{(\mathbf{A}_{21}S)^2\}$ does not affect the filter output and so the MSE is minimised when

$$\mathbf{A}_{11} = \mathbf{W}^T\mathbf{A}_{12} \Rightarrow \mathbf{W}^T = \mathbf{A}_{11}\mathbf{A}_{12}^{-1}$$

The filter has then converged to the impulse responses of the differential transfer function of the direct and cross paths of the noise source, which will then give a filter output of

$$\left(\mathbf{A}_{11}\mathrm{N} + \mathbf{A}_{21}\mathrm{S}\right) - \mathbf{W}^{T}\mathbf{A}_{12}\mathrm{N} = \mathbf{A}_{21}\mathrm{S}$$

The filter output is then the source signal with the noise removed. It is possible then to consider applying the classical LMS algorithm and filter structure to the blind separation of sources from their convolutive mixtures. The problem with this type of approach is that, in many practical situations, it is unlikely that the wanted signal will be present in only one channel, i.e. $\mathbf{A}_{22} \neq 0$. One solution is to adapt the filter weights when only noise (or unwanted speech) signals, $\mathbf{N}_1$ and $\mathbf{N}_2$, are present. This could typically occur for a few tenths of a second during a break in conversation. The filter weights at the converged noise cancelling values are frozen when speech is detected, this forms a filter which preferentially suppresses the noise. This then of course requires an additional method of detecting speech and non-speech periods and cannot really be considered as a blind process. A comparative study of LMS-based ANC techniques with the BSS methods developed in Section 8.6 applied to speech enhancement in the presence of noise is found in (Shields, Girolami, Campbell and Fyfe, 1997).

Van Gerven (1996) takes the ANC configuration and extends it to a symmetric structure with an additional filter in the primary channel. The major problem with the direct structure is that the recovered signals can be severely distorted (Van Gerven, 1996; Torkkola, 1996) and so require additional post processing for equalisation. An alternative feedback structure is considered which does not require the additional equalisation. This structure is exactly that given in Figure 8.2c and can be considered as an adaptive filter representation of the temporal anti-Hebbian network considered in Section 8.3. Van Gerven *et al*, (1992) carried out a comparative study of second order and fourth order adaptation update algorithms based on the feedback filter structure (Figure 8.2c) using the following

$$\Delta w_{ij}(k) = -\eta\, y_i(t) y_j(t-k) \quad \forall i \neq j \wedge k = 1 \ldots M$$

and

$$\Delta w_{ij}(k) = -\eta\, (y_i(t))^3\, y_j(t-k) \quad \forall i \neq j \wedge k = 1 \ldots M.$$

They show through extensive simulation that in the case of strictly causal convolutive mixing, second order adaptation provides statistically equivalent separating performance as fourth order weight adaptation which accords with the results reported in Section 8.4.

These results show that no benefit is gained from moving to higher order statistics from simple second order decorrelation. In the instantaneous case higher order statistics are required to ensure independence (Comon, 1994). Platt and Faggin (1992) extend the Jutten and Herrault network to incorporate time delays (Figure 8.2b). They consider explicit minimisation of second and fourth order moments and demonstrate the performance of the network with artificial mixtures of speech and music. Nguyen and Jutten (1995) also extend the original network structure proposed by Jutten and Herrault (1991) to one possessing Finite Impulse Response (FIR) filter weights (Figure 8.2c). They develop algorithms for weight update in attempting to cancel out fourth order cross cumulants at all finite time delays within the filter structure. An alternative algorithm reported in the paper is the use of a decorrelation criterion for all delays and cancellation of fourth-order cross cumulants for zero delay. Weinstein, Feder and Oppenheim (1993), Yellin and Weinstein (1996) consider decorrelation-based algorithms for multi-channel signal separation. Chan, Godsill and Rayner (1996) develop a batch based algorithm based on constrained output decorrelation. They demonstrate the efficacy of their algorithm on recordings of mixture of up to four speakers and excerpts of music. Recordings for the reported simulations are made in an anechoic chamber which exhibits little acoustic dispersion, and so the inverting filters will only be required to identify the cross microphone delays. Principe *et al* (1996) utilise a 'teacher forcing' temporal decorrelation network for separation of artificially convolved mixtures of speech. Empirical comparisons are made between linear and non-linear FIR temporal learning as well as the gamma filter (Principe, de Vries, de Oliveira, 1993).

As with the previous researchers considered, Principe *et al* find no benefit in moving from simple temporal decorrelation to non-linear filtering. A novel use of the network proposed in the paper is to calculate the cross-correlation matrix of a number of signals in an online adaptive manner. Algebraic subspace methods have been proposed by (Gorokhov and Loubaton, 1995) but these methods are slow due to the manipulation of large matrices. Lindgren, Sahlin and Broman (1996) consider source separation using a feedforward structure and a damped Newton algorithm based on a modified Hessian matrix. Their technique relies only on second order statistics, but as the weight adaptation in most second order methods is driven by the level of signal cross-correlation the adaptation speed slows as the signals become less correlated. Lindgren *et al* propose the use of the Newton type update to overcome this problem. Lambert (1996) considers extensions of Bussgang type algorithms for source separation. He develops an FIR algebra which allows computation in the frequency domain giving significant computational advantages, such as convolution in the time domain transforming to simple multiplication in the frequency domain. Lambert reports on separation of speakers in real room environments using the Equivariant (Cardoso and Laheld, 1996) Bussgang type algorithms developed. Cichocki, Amari and Cao (1996) extend their feed-forward and recurrent network algorithms to take into account delays and convolutions. A novel learning rate adaptation algorithm is proposed for signals which may be mixed in time varying environments. The standard cubic non-linearity is used within the reported simulations, which are run on artificial data. The injection of noise into the learning is empirically considered and shown to improve the convergence properties of the algorithm.

As has been discussed, Torkkola (1996) extends the Infomax algorithm (Bell and Sejnowski, 1995) to consider convolved mixtures of sources. A feedback network similar to that proposed by such as Nguyen Thi and Jutten, (1995) and Platt and Faggin (1992) is considered. This removes the problem of the network output being temporally whitened due to temporal redundancies within the signals being removed by the direct filters. Results reported include separation of a mixture of two speakers recorded in a small conference room with cross channel interference reduction of 12dB reported. Lee, Bell and Orglmeister (1997) extend the work of Torkkola and perform source separation of speakers and music recorded in real acoustic environments. Comparisons of separation performance are made based on recognition rates of Automatic Speech Recognition (ASR) systems. For speech recorded with music, increases of 50% in recognition rates are reported after separation processing. Speech corrupted with competing speech yielded a 19% increase in recognition rate after processing. The novel use of filters with acausal extensions is employed which ensures that the separating filters will be stable even if the inverse mixing filters are non-minimum phase (Oppenheim & Shafer, 1989). Very recently Charkani and Deville (1997) and Deville and Charkani (1997) have considered time domain convolutive source separation algorithms. By explicitly considering the minimisation of the asymptotic error variance separating functions are developed which are related to the probability density functions of the underlying sources. In the following section we will observe that the maximum likelihood framework for parameter estimation will naturally asymptotically minimise the parameter estimation error variance.

It is clear from this review that most researchers (from both the signal processing and artificial neural network communities) have found for convolutive mixtures of signals (speech is the most often considered source signal) second order statistics appear to suffice. No benefit has been found by explicit use of either higher order statistics or sigmoidal non-linearities. In the case of the Infomax temporal extensions (Torkkola, 1996; Lee, Bell and Orgmeister, 1997) maximising the information through a hyperbolic tangent is shown analytically to yield independent components, second order temporal anti-Hebbian learning yields substantially similar separation performance (Section 8.4).

Based on the equivalence of mutual information minimisation and maximum likelihood estimation (MLE) for instantaneous BSS we can consider extending the MLE to include temporal context. In the following section we consider the maximum likelihood framework for source separation (Gaeta and Lacoume, 1990; Pham, Garrat and Jutten, 1992; Belouchrani and Cardoso, 1995; Pearlmutter and Parra, 1996; Cardoso, 1997) and apply this to separation of convolutive mixtures. The maximisation of the sum of marginal negentropy would also be a suitable route to take based on Chapter 7. However, the application of MLE to this particular BSS model allows yet another valuable perspective on the problem and as such becomes the subject of the following section.

8.6 Maximum Likelihood Estimation and Source Separation

We shall first consider the link between Maximum Likelihood Estimation (MLE) and blind source separation. Cardoso (1997) has recently shown that the Infomax algorithm (Bell and Sejnowski, 1995) is equivalent to MLE.

Let us consider N independent observations of a random variable vector $\{\mathbf{x}_i\} : i = 1 \ldots N$, which will take values in $\Re^{L \times N}$ where L is the vector dimension. The variable is distributed according to the probability density function $p(\mathbf{x};\theta)$ where $\theta \in \Theta$ is the set of parameters describing the form of the density function. Let $p(\mathbf{x};\hat{\theta}) : \hat{\theta} \in \Theta$ be a parametric estimation of the pdf $p(\mathbf{x};\theta)$ after observing $\{\mathbf{x}_i\} : i = 1 \ldots N$. The likelihood that the observations are drawn from a parametric pdf $p(\mathbf{x};\hat{\theta})$ is given as

$$\prod_{i=1}^{N} p\left(\mathbf{x}_i ; \hat{\theta}\right)$$

with a log-likelihood given as

$$\frac{1}{N} \log \prod_{i=1}^{N} p\left(\mathbf{x}_i ; \hat{\theta}\right) = \frac{1}{N} \sum_{i=1}^{N} \log p\left(\mathbf{x}_i ; \hat{\theta}\right).$$

We wish to parameterise the density estimate such that the likelihood of the observed data being drawn from the parametric density is maximised. The MLE is defined as

$$\hat{\theta}_{ML} = \arg \max \left(\frac{1}{N} \sum_{i=1}^{N} \log p\left(\mathbf{x}_i ; \hat{\theta}\right) \right) \tag{8.18}$$

If the observations of $\{\mathbf{x}_i\} : i = 1 \ldots N$ are independent and identically distributed (iid) as $p(\mathbf{x}; \theta)$ then $\hat{\theta}_{ML} \xrightarrow{P=1} \theta$ as $\mathrm{N} \rightarrow \infty$. So the ML estimate of the pdf parameters tends to the true parameter values with probability one as the number of observations tends to infinity. We must also note that the MLE in the limit will reach the Cramer-Rao bound for densities which are members of the exponential family, which indicates the parameter estimates will be unbiased and the asymptotic error variance

$$\sigma^2 = E\left\{ \left(\hat{\theta} - \theta\right)^2 \right\}$$

will be minimised (Deco and Obradovic, 1996). So we have that the parameter estimation error tends in distribution, to the zero mean normal distribution with covariance equal to the inverse of the Fisher information matrix **M**, $\sqrt{\mathrm{N}}\left(\hat{\theta} - \theta\right) \rightarrow N\left(0, \mathbf{M}^{-1}\right)$ (Ripley, 1996; Deco & Obradovic, 1996; Cover and Thomas, 1991).

Now as we have the following :-

$$N \to \infty \Rightarrow \hat{\theta}_{ML} = \underset{\hat{\theta}}{\arg\max}\left(\int p(\mathbf{x};\theta) \log p(\mathbf{x};\hat{\theta}) d\mathbf{x} \right)$$

$$\equiv \underset{\hat{\theta}}{\arg\max}\left(\int p(\mathbf{x};\theta) \log\left(\frac{p(\mathbf{x};\hat{\theta})}{p(\mathbf{x};\theta)} p(\mathbf{x};\theta) \right) d\mathbf{x} \right)$$

$$\Rightarrow \underset{\hat{\theta}}{\arg\max}\left(\int p(\mathbf{x};\theta) \log\left(\frac{p(\mathbf{x};\hat{\theta})}{p(\mathbf{x};\theta)} \right) d\mathbf{x} + \int p(\mathbf{x};\theta) \log(p(\mathbf{x};\theta)) d\mathbf{x} \right)$$

$$\Rightarrow \underset{\hat{\theta}}{\arg\max}\left(-K_L\left(p(\mathbf{x};\theta) \| p(\mathbf{x};\hat{\theta}) \right) - H(p(\mathbf{x};\theta)) \right) \tag{8.19}$$

where $K_L(a \| b)$ is the Kullback-Leibler divergence between the estimated and the true pdf, (Cover and Thomas, 1991; Ripley, 1996). H(a) is the standard Shannon differential entropy of the given pdf, (Cover and Thomas, 1991). Cardoso (1997) links (8.19) to source separation for instantaneous mixing matrices; we now extend this to mixing filters. As the parametric model is given by the unmixing / deconvolving filters (8.3) and noting that the rightmost term in (8.19) can be neglected as it is not a function of the estimates of the parametric variables, the generic MLE is then

$$\underset{\hat{\theta}}{\arg\max}\left(-K_L\left(p(\mathbf{x};\theta) \| p(\mathbf{x};\hat{\theta}) \right) \right) \tag{8.20}$$

This is equivalent to

$$\underset{\mathbf{W}(z^{-})}{\arg\max}\left(-K_L\left(p(\mathbf{A}(z)\mathbf{s};\mathbf{A}(z)) \| p(\mathbf{W}^{-1}(z)\hat{\mathbf{s}};\mathbf{W}(z)) \right) \right). \tag{8.21}$$

where $p(\mathbf{A}(z)\mathbf{s};\mathbf{A}(z))$ is the true distribution of the observed data $\mathbf{x}$ and $p(\mathbf{W}^{-1}(z)\hat{\mathbf{s}};\mathbf{W}(z))$ is the parametric estimate where the network filter weights are drawn from the parametric set $\hat{\theta} = \mathbf{W}(z) \in \Theta$. As the unobserved source data will have independent components, $p_{\mathbf{s}}(\mathbf{s}) = \prod_{i=1}^{N} p_i(s_i)$, the form of the parametric model to be used $p(\mathbf{W}^{-1}(z)\hat{\mathbf{s}};\mathbf{W}(z))$ must then be factorable. The maximisation of the MLE (8.20) using the parametric models discussed will then minimise the Kullback mismatch between the parametric pdf of the estimated latent generators $\hat{\mathbf{s}}$ and the actual factorable pdf of the independent source variables. We have an asymptotically efficient estimator for the inverting filters in the MLE. In the next section we develop a network model and learning algorithm to separate, in a blind manner, signals which have been convolved together.

8.7. Temporal Anti-Hebbian Learning Based on Maximum Likelihood Estimation

From Figure 8.2b, the output of each node at time t for an $N \times N$ network with memory based synaptic weights of length L is given as (8.6)

$$y_i(t) = x_i(t) + \sum_{j \neq i} \sum_{k=0}^{L} w_{ij}(t-k) y_j(t-k)$$

where the subscripts denote spatial relations between the nodes within the network and the *(t-k)* terms denote delays of *k* samples from time *t*. The MLE is given as

$$\hat{\theta}_{ML} = \arg\max \left(\frac{1}{N} \sum_{i=1}^{N} \log p\left(\mathbf{x}_i;\hat{\theta}\right) \right)$$

whose value is given by the solution of

$$\frac{\partial}{\partial \hat{\theta}} \left(\frac{1}{N} \sum_{i=1}^{N} \log p\left(\mathbf{x}_i;\hat{\theta}\right) \right) = 0.$$

We note that in the situation where the pdf satisfies regularity conditions (Cox and Hinckley, 1974) we have an expectation and we may change the order of operation to

$$E\left\{\frac{\partial}{\partial\hat{\theta}}\log\left(p\left(\mathbf{x}_i;\hat{\theta}\right)\right)\right\} = 0.$$

This can now be solved iteratively using the Robbins-Monro algorithm such that parameter updates will be

$$\hat{\theta}_{n+1} = \hat{\theta}_n + \mu_n \frac{\partial}{\partial\hat{\theta}}\log\left(p\left(\mathbf{x}_{n+1};\hat{\theta}_n\right)\right) \tag{8.22}$$

The parametric form of the transformed observation (8.6) has only one set of parameters in this case, that is

$$w_{ij}(t-k) \;:\; \forall\,(i \neq j \in 1 \dots N) \wedge \forall k \in 1 \dots L.$$

It was noted in Section 8.6, that the parametric model will be required to be factorable, with this constraint we can then write

$$w_{ij}^{n+1}(t-k) = w_{ij}^{n}(t-k) + \mu_n \frac{\partial}{\partial w_{ij}^{n}(t-k)}\log\left(\prod_{l=1}^{N} p_l\left(y_l^{n+1};w_{ij}^{n}(t-k)\right)\right) \tag{8.23}$$

$$w_{ij}^{n+1}(t-k) = w_{ij}^{n}(t-k) + \mu_n \frac{p_i'\left(y_i^{n+1};w_{ij}^{n}(t-k)\right)\prod_{l\neq i} p_l\left(y_l^{n+1};w_{ij}^{n}(t-k)\right)}{\prod_{l=1}^{N} p_l\left(y_l^{n+1};w_{ij}^{n}(t-k)\right)} \frac{\partial y_i}{\partial w_{ij}^{n}(t-k)}$$

$$w_{ij}^{n+1}(t-k) = w_{ij}^{n}(t-k) + \mu_n \frac{p_i'\left(y_i^{n+1}; w_{ij}^{n}(t-k)\right)}{p_i\left(y_i^{n+1}; w_{ij}^{n}(t-k)\right)} y_j(t-k) \tag{8.24}$$

The generic sequential parameter update algorithm of (8.24) has a number of important points. Firstly as the sample size tends to infinity then (8.24) will converge with probability one to an unbiased estimate of the true parameters of the underlying parametric model. This pre-supposes that the parametric model chosen is correct for the underlying latent data. In Section 8.5 we considered the previous work on blind separation of convolved sources; we now use the generic MLE (8.24) to derive the second order, fourth order and Infomax algorithms previously discussed. Let us choose a parametric model for each marginal pdf based on the generalised Gaussian density. For this example we shall consider the generalised zero mean Gaussian form of pdf which, neglecting normalisation constants, is given as

$$p_i(y_i(t)) \propto \exp\left(- \frac{|y_i(t)|^s}{E\left\{|y_i(t)|^s\right\}} \right) \tag{8.25}$$

When the parameter value $s = 2$, then the generalised Gaussian density becomes the standard Gaussian density. We neglect the normalising coefficients as the derivative of the log pdf will be independent of the normalising term. From (8.25) we have the general form of the derivative of the log probability density

$$\frac{p_i'(y_i(t))}{p_i(y_i(t))} = \frac{-|y_i(t)|^{s-1} sign(y_i(t))}{E\left\{|y_i(t)|^s\right\}} \tag{8.26}$$

Using (8.26) in (8.24) we then have the generic form of

$$w_{ij}^{n+1}(t-k) = w_{ij}^{n}(t-k) + \mu_n \frac{-|y_i(t)|^{s-1} sign(y_i(t))}{E\{|y_i(t)|^s\}} y_j(t-k) \tag{8.27}$$

when s = 2, (8.25) is the Gaussian distribution and we then have

$$w_{ij}^{n+1}(t-k) = w_{ij}^{n}(t-k) - \mu_n \frac{y_i(t) y_j(t-k)}{E\{y_i(t)^2\}} \tag{8.28}$$

This is precisely the temporal extension of second order learning (Matsuoka *et al*, 1995; Van Gervan, 1996) proposed in Section 8.3, for temporal anti-Hebbian learning. It is now clear that this weight update rule (8.28) is seeking to fit the received data to a parametric model based on a product of marginal Gaussian distributions. Let us now re-consider the Hyperbolic-Cauchy distribution, which is defined as

$$p_i(y_i(t)) = \frac{1}{2\sqrt{2}} \sec h^2\left(\frac{y_i(t)}{\sqrt{2}}\right) \tag{8.29}$$

The motivation in choosing this particular form of pdf is that the tails of the distribution are thicker than a standard Gaussian distribution. In the case where we are considering speech or noise, which have finite values of kurtosis, the tails of the distribution will then be heavier than the normal distribution. So this may be a more suitable model than the standard Gaussian distribution for signals such as speech.

Utilising (8.29) in (8.24) and collecting all constant coefficients then gives

$$w_{ij}^{n+1}(t-k) = w_{ij}^{n}(t-k) - \mu_n \tanh(y_i(t)) y_j(t-k) \tag{8.30}$$

It is interesting to note that Torkkola (1996) arrives exactly at this update equation for a feedback structure similar to Figure 8.2b, by extending Bell and

Sejnowski's Infomax algorithm derivation, when the hyperbolic tangent activation function is considered for separation of convolved mixtures. The algorithm which Torkkola develops can now be considered from an MLE perspective where the parametric model for data fitting is chosen as a product of marginal Hyperbolic-Cauchy distributions. If we chart the Hyperbolic-Cauchy distribution and compare it with the Gaussian it is possible to draw some important conclusions regarding update equations (8.28) and (8.30). Considering Figure 8.6, it is clear that the Hyperbolic-Cauchy distribution has heavier tails than the Gaussian. However, if we consider a plot of the histogram of one second of natural human speech sampled at 8.0 kHz (Figure 8.7), we can see that the tails are much heavier than that of the Hyperbolic-Cauchy distribution. The sample of speech was chosen from a ten second record in such a manner that the variance of the sample was relatively constant to ensure an approximately stationary sample. McDonald (1966) was able to show that the pdf of stationary human speech could be approximated by the Laplacian density. Indeed if we consider Figure 8.8, it is clear that the Laplacian density fits the heavy tailed distribution of natural speech more fully than either the Gaussian or the Hyperbolic-Cauchy distributions.

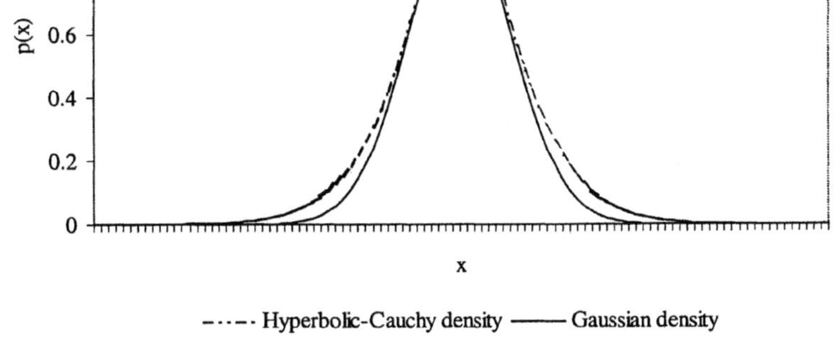

Figure 8.6: Hyperbolic-Cauchy and Gaussian Densities.

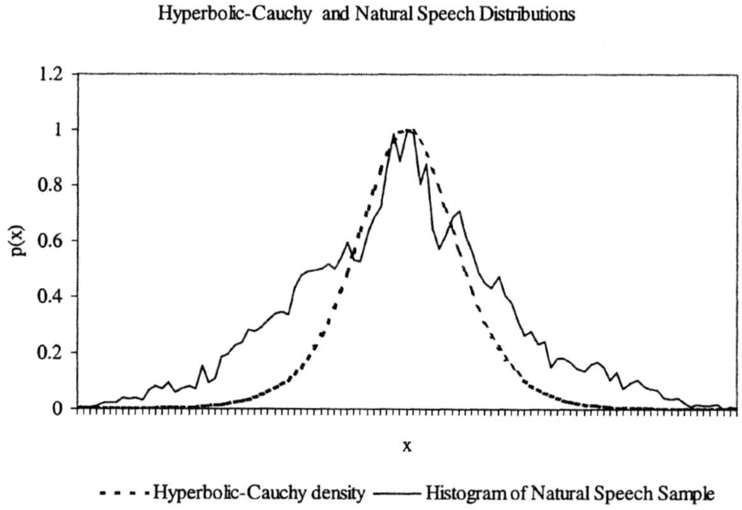

Figure 8.7: Hyperbolic-Cauchy and Natural Speech Densities.

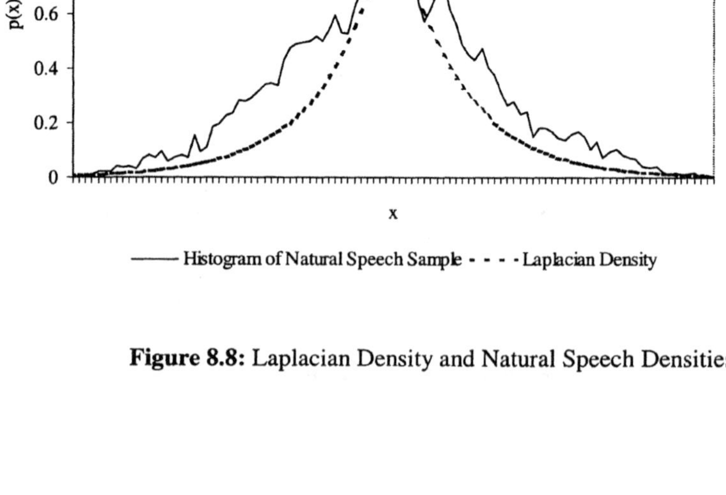

Figure 8.8: Laplacian Density and Natural Speech Densities.

The Laplacian density is a special form of the Generalised Gaussian where s = 1 and in this case it is a simple matter to see that the weight update equation will be given by

$$w_{ij}^{n+1}(t-k) = w_{ij}^{n}(t-k) - \mu_n \frac{sign(y_i(t))y_j(t-k)}{E\{|y_i(t)|\}} \tag{8.31}$$

It should be noted that (8.24) in its general form and the specific cases of (8.28), (8.30) and (8.31) are all forms of anti-Hebbian updates. The empirical findings of Section 8.4 when comparing (8.28) and (8.30) for separating artificially convolved mixtures of speech can now be considered in the light of the maximum likelihood framework developed here. It is clear that for speech the Gaussian and Hyperbolic-Cauchy distributions capture similar amounts of the probability mass at the tails of the distribution. These distributions may then lead to almost similar sub-optimal parametric models, but the form of the Laplacian pdf indicates that it may be an improved estimator when considering data generated by natural speech.

In this section we have developed update algorithms within a maximum likelihood context for separation of convolved mixtures of independent sources. The network architecture is a temporal extension of that proposed by Herrault and Jutten (1986) and Foldiak (1989). This architecture has also been considered in many of the works discussed in Section 8.5. We have shown that the temporal Infomax algorithm developed by Torkkola (1996) can be considered as a specific form of the more general update equation (8.24). Theoretical justifications of the empirical findings of Section 8.4 are given based on the parametric model mis-match of the Gaussian and the Hyperbolic-Cauchy distributions. Similar arguments can be developed when considering updates based on third order moments; these are self apparent when using the form of (8.26) and (8.27) and need not be further developed here. In the following section we report on corroborating simulations carried out in separating speech from speech, and also speech from noise within a realistic acoustic environment.

8.8 Comparative Simulations Using Varying PDF Models

A major problem of recordings made in acoustic environments is the physical phenomenon of what is termed 'multi-path' propagation of signals. A microphone for example will receive a summation of the original transmitted source and delayed reflections. Recordings[1] of natural speech or music in an anechoic chamber will not have the problem of multi-path propagation and so only the delay between the microphones has to be considered. We, however, consider a more realistic acoustic environment in these simulations. A standard living room with soft carpeting and furnishing was used, (dimensions were 8.5m × 6.0m × 2.5m). In this simulation omni-directional microphones were placed 0.4m apart and 0.5m distance from a pair of loudspeakers in a square format. Loudspeakers were chosen for this simulation to ensure physical stationarity of the point sources. If we consider (8.4) and (8.5) clearly the aim of the learning is to identify the differential inverse filters and any movement in the sources will cause a level of non-stationarity in the acoustic transfer functions to be estimated. The level of reverberation within the room is calculated using the standard T_{60} measure (Mackenzie, 1964); an impulse is injected into the room and the time for the impulse response to decay by 60 dB is measured. This was measured to give a value of $T_{60} = 0.34$ seconds which is a typical value for standard domestic accommodation. It should be noted that the simple symmetric structure of sources and sensors reduced the complicating effect of reverberations within the room. To allow quantitative measurements of separation each source was recorded separately on the direct and cross coupled microphones. The simulations reported involve speech corrupted with competing speech and speech corrupted with wideband masking noise. Each signal record was eight seconds long with a sampling rate of 11.025 kHz.

An important point must be highlighted here regarding the nature of natural speech. The MLE framework has the fundamental assumption that the sequences of observations are independent and so there is no dependency between each sample of the data. Natural speech has in some cases strong short-term temporal correlations, which therefore have to be removed for the MLE assumptions to hold true. This can be achieved by a temporal pre-whitening operation where the received mixture of speech has temporal correlation removed. A simple moving average filter can be utilised in the whitening process. We shall consider the case where the signals are temporally pre-whitened initially. The effect that no pre-whitening of the mixtures has on the level and speed of separation will be considered. The signal to noise ratio (SNR) is used as a measure of the separation of the sources which is

[1] M. Girolami is grateful for the support of Mr.D.McLaren (Heriot Watt University, Edinburgh) in providing the environmental set-up and recordings for the reported simulations.

$$SNR = -10 \log \left[\frac{E\left\{ (\hat{y}_i - s_i)^2 \right\}}{E\left\{ s_i^2 \right\}} \right]$$

The original source power is given as $E\{s_i^2\}$ and the residual error power as $E\{(\hat{y}_i - s_i)^2\}$. The first simulation considered the separation of speech and competing speech when the mixtures are initially prewhitened and when no whitening is carried out. The Laplacian density is used as the assumed form of the source pdf such that the weights are updated using (8.31). An autoregressive (AR) filter (Haykin,1991) is used to adaptively whiten each of the mixtures prior to presentation to the separating network. Temporal whitening will remove the short term correlation between successive samples throughout the length of the filter. An independent process such as white noise is characterised by a flat power spectral density (PSD) (Oppenheim and Schaffer, 1991). The driving process methodology (Haykin, 1991) allows coloured signals with high temporal structure to be modelled by an independent white driving process and a colouring filter. By whitening the mixture of speech we are essentially creating a driving process which will then be used in the MLE self-organisation of the network. Note that the power spectral density of a signal is the Fourier transform of the autocorrelation matrix. Consequently, if the signal is white the autocorrelation matrix is an identity with zero correlation at finite lags. This indicates that the energy content is evenly distributed within the dynamic frequency region of the signal. Figure 8.9 shows the PSD of the two original mixtures of speech and the whitened versions, where the flattening of the power spectrum is apparent.

An interesting point should be made here: from a statistical perspective temporal whitening is providing second order temporal independence. For each sample to be fully independent then information theoretic arguments are required. Comparing the PSD of whitened speech using a linear AR filter, one based on the hyperbolic tangent and the signum function show insignificant difference in form. The statistics of the driving process for speech are complex and nonstationary and it appears that gross statistics are insufficient to capture the temporal subtleties of the signal. Nevertheless, second order temporal whitening will be sufficient for our purposes here.

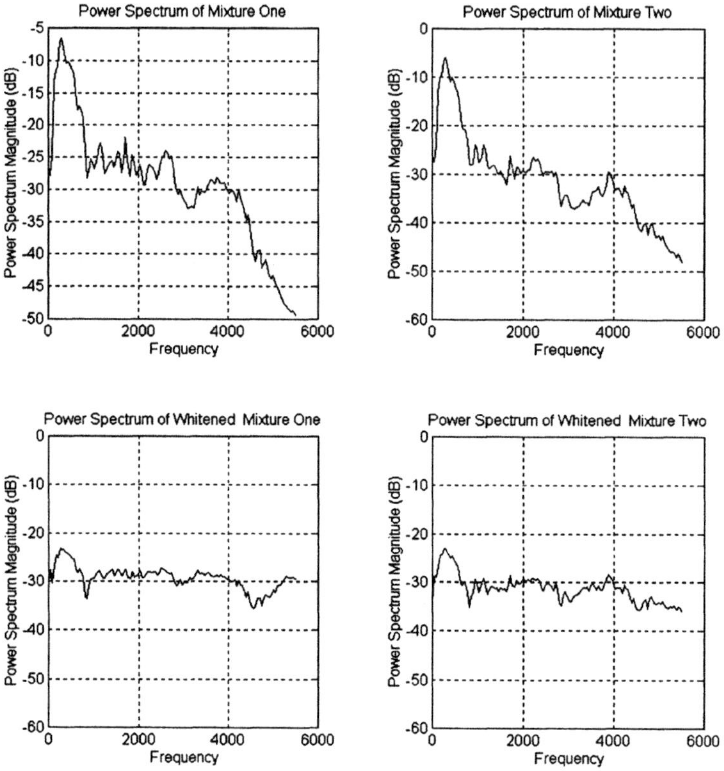

Figure 8.9: Power Spectral Density Plots of the Original and Temporally Whitened Mixtures of Speech.

The results of the simulation are given in Figure 8.10. It is clear that as the number of epochs of self-adaptation increases the separation performance for white and non-white speech is similar. Classical filter theory indicates that whitening will remove the eigenvalue disparity of the autocorrelation matrix and so give faster convergence of the LMS algorithm (Haykin, 1991). The signals under consideration are natural speech propagated in a natural acoustic environment. The complex nature of the signals removes any potential convergence acceleration attributed to temporal whitening. Similar findings are reported in Deville and Charkani (1997).

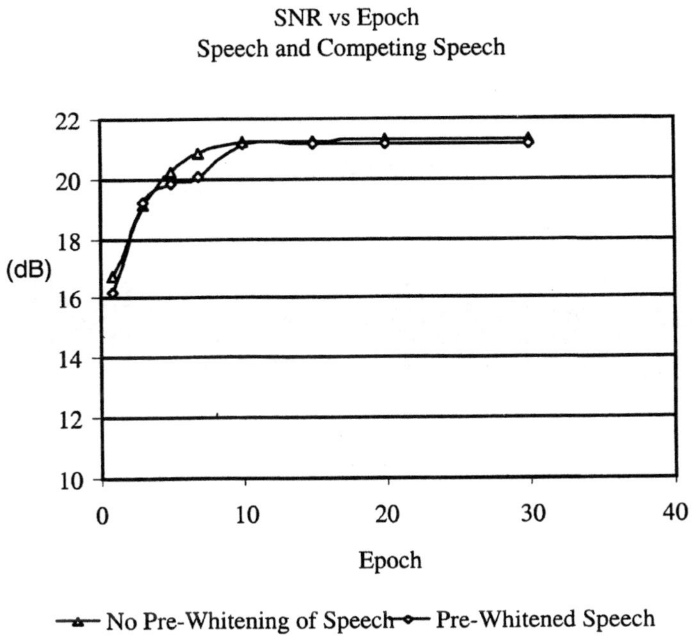

Figure 8.10: Signal to Noise Ratio for Whitened and Non-Whitened Mixtures of Speech.

Figure 8.11 shows the original mixture of speech and the whitened version. It is clear that asymptotically coloured mixtures will achieve the same level of separation as whitened mixtures. The subsequent simulations will not employ whitened mixtures.

Figure 8.12 shows the SNR attainable against the number of passes through the data, sometimes termed the adaptation epochs. The three curves show the performance when the parametric models are based on Gaussian, Hyperbolic-Cauchy and Laplace pdf.

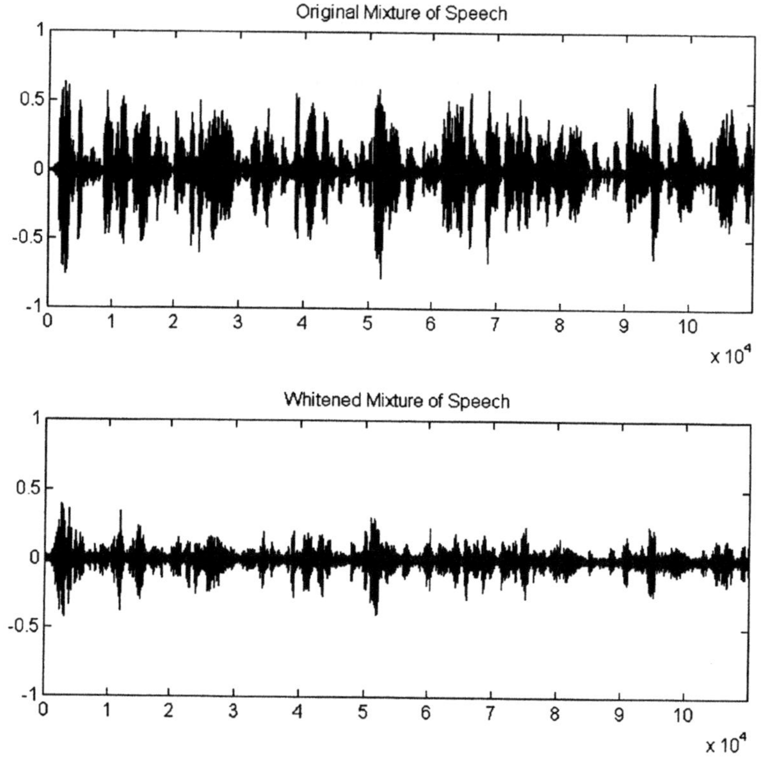

Figure 8.11: Original Mixture Number One and the Pre-Whitened Mixture.

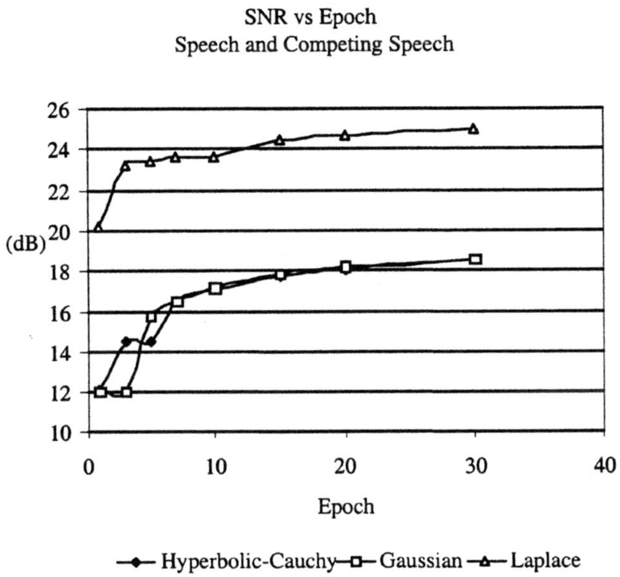

Figure 8.12: Parametric Model Performance Curves: Speech Vs Speech.

It is clear that multiple passes through the data are required indicating that real-time online adaptation is still some way from realisation. We also see, as discussed in Section 8.4, that the Gaussian and Hyperbolic-Cauchy parametric models yield substantially similar performance in both cases. This confirms the findings of Section 8.4 when comparing temporal linear anti-Hebbian learning and temporal Infomax learning. What is significant here is that the better fitting Laplacian pdf model outperforms the other models considered with a 7dB difference in performance for speech vs speech. We should point out that the SNR values reported here are excellent and this is largely due to the simplicity of the recording geometry and the low levels of reverberation. As the levels of reverberation increase the SNR performance drops significantly (Shields, Girolami, Campbell and Fyfe, 1997). Figure 8.13 shows the separation performance when speech is contaminated with speech shaped wideband noise.

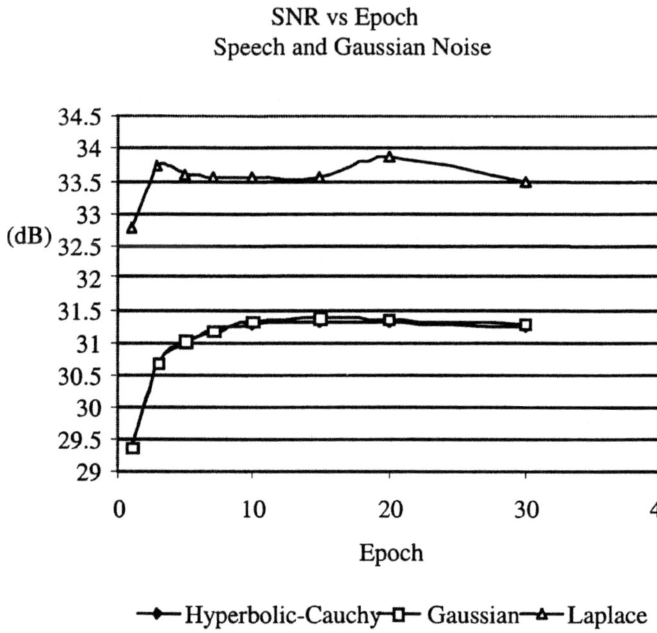

Figure 8.13: Parametric Model Performance Curves: Speech Vs Noise.

The other point to note regarding the SNR performance of the two simulations is that the performance for speech vs speech is typically 10dB less than for speech vs noise. We believe this is largely due to the intermittent characteristics of natural speech. Nguyen Thi and Jutten (1995) and Van Gerven *et al* (1994) propose 'non-permanent' learning to help overcome this problem. The technique consists of tracking the output power of the signals and ceasing weight updates when the output power falls below a certain threshold. This technique has not been implemented in the reported simulations in this chapter. The noise corrupted speech at both microphones is shown in Figure 8.14, and the output of the network after three adaptation epochs is also given, indicating the separation of both signals.

Two simulations have been reported which confirm the theoretic analysis in the previous sections. From an MLE perspective it is clear why simple linear decorrelation and Infomax give similar performance for separation of naturally occurring speech. Prior knowledge of the source signals can be used in choosing the parametric form of the network update algorithm as demonstrated by the use of the Laplace parametric model.

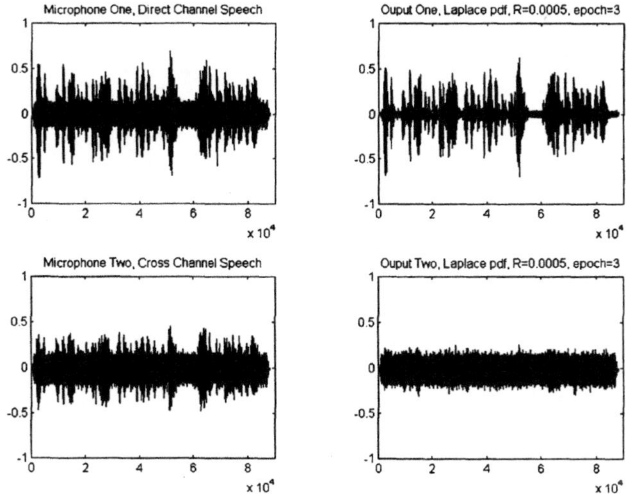

Figure 8.14: Speech vs Noise Simulation, Mixed Signals at Microphones and Separated Signals at Network Output.

8.9 Conclusions

This chapter has considered anti-Hebbian learning with the addition of memory and this has been applied to the 'cocktail party' problem. The self-organisation of a network with feedback has been considered from a maximum likelihood estimation perspective which for source separation is equivalent to mutual information minimisation. This has provided an overall generalisation for many neural and adaptive filter techniques for blind source separation. In the specific case of the 'cocktail party' problem it has been shown that the knowledge of the gross statistical characteristics of speech allows a more efficient algorithm than symmetric adaptive decorrelation or temporal Infomax. The MLE perspective also gives sound statistical reasoning for the ability of simple cross-correlation nulling to provide certain levels of separation of mixtures of speech.

9. *Applications*

9.1 Introduction

There have been a number of applications employing independent component analysis reported in the literature. The most visible, and arguably the one given most attention, has been in speech processing in realistic acoustic environments. However, the results to date are largely disappointing and the problem of dealing with severe but realistic reverberation requires further research focus. One area which has benefited greatly from the development of various ICA algorithms is biomedical signal processing. A number of researchers have successfully exploited linear ICA in processing signals from Electroencephalograph (EEG), Magnetoencephalograph (MEG), and the Electrocardiograph (ECG). There have also been a number of diverse applications in, for example, rotating machine vibration analysis, Nuclear Magnetic Resonance (NMR) spectroscopy, infrared optical source separation, radio-communications and data mining. This chapter will provide a brief review of a small selection of the successful ICA applications that have been reported to date.

9.2 Industrial Applications

This section will review some industrial applications of ICA and BSS. Two applications will be considered – rotating machine vibration analysis (Ypma and Pajunen, 1999) and multi-tag radio-frequency identification system (Deville *et al*, 1999).

9.2.1 Rotating Machine Vibration Analysis

Machine condition monitoring has been a subject of intense research interest within the areas of machine tool design and general mechanical engineering. The tracking of tool wear and the detection of the onset of potentially catastrophic tool or machine failure has been the goal of most machine condition monitoring programmes. The onset of machine failure is often signified by marked changes in the vibration spectrum of the machine. These may be characterised by increased modulatory effects giving rise to increasing harmonics and sidebands. Higher order spectral techniques have been successfully utilised in identifying faults such as bearing failure. It has been proposed in (Ypma and Pajunen, 1999) that due to machine vibration being measured by several sensors placed at different sites on the machine, a suitable combination of the multichannel data may aid in finding robust features for condition monitoring purposes. Indeed multi-variable adaptive noise cancellation techniques have been applied by Hung *et al* (1994) in attempting to improve the discriminating power of a statistical pattern recognition system in tool condition monitoring of a milling machine.

Ypma and Pajunen (1999) propose a second order method of ICA based on the work of (Pajunen, 1999) and apply this to vibration analysis of a submersible pump. The multi-channel measurements from accelerometers sited at various points on the machine are considered as mixtures of sources of vibration. As such these can then be incorporated and projected onto a lower dimensional feature space which, it is conjectured, may lead to more robust classification of faulty operating conditions. The second order ICA method was employed prior to using a five-nearest neighbour classifier to discriminate between the potential modes (classes) of machine operation.

A number of faulty conditions were induced in a submersible pump namely pump imbalance, a loose base foundation and a bearing fault. These three faulty conditions and normal operating conditions gave the four classes that needed to be discriminated. It was found that projections giving features derived from ICA improved the discriminating power of the classifier when compared to other projection methods such as principal component analysis. This machine monitoring application differed somewhat from that reported by (Gelle *et al*, 1999).

In (Gelle *et al*, 1999), the authors employed a temporal source separation approach based on the (Nguyen and Jutten, 1995) approach. In this work the authors were interested in separating the vibration signatures of two rotating machine which were mounted onto the same baseplate so that the original machine signatures could be restored from their mixed and noisy measurements. This technique performed well in the restoration of the spectra of two 300 Watt electric motors rotating at frequencies of 40.5Hz and 64.8Hz. The application of (Gelle *et al*, 1999) is what can be considered as a source separation application of ICA where the mixed wideband signatures of the machines needs to be separated and restored blindly. In contrast Ypma and Pajunen (1999) utilise ICA as a means of robust feature extraction exclusively for pattern classification. It is such an application, which shows the wider potential of ICA for industrial and commercial applications. The next application to be considered was reported by Deville *et al* (1999).

9.2.2 A Multi-Tag Frequency Identification System

The identification of objects on a production line or generic tracking system is commonplace in everyday industrial applications. This may be the identification of a person prior to access to a secure area or the identification of a particular model of manufactured product on an assembly line. There is now a growing trend towards contactless electronic and radio frequency (RF) based security systems. These systems normally take the form of a smart card or tag which will uniquely identify the holder via a digital signature held on an electrically erasable programmable read only memory (EEPROM). This signature is transmitted via a modulated RF sine wave to a base station which can then demodulate the received signal and decode the signature, thus verifying the authenticity of the card holder. Although the contactless nature of such a system is desirable there is one drawback which is encountered when a number of modulated signals are received simultaneously at the base station as could be the case when more than one user is in the vicinity of the base station. In this case the base station receives a mixture of the RF signals and is unable to de-modulate and therefore decode the transmitted signals. In such a situation the application of ICA can disentangle the received signals and allow the decoding of the original sources to continue. This application was developed by Deville *et al* (1999) with the aid of the self-normalised BSS network originally proposed by Cichocki *et al* (1995).

Although the developed system performed satisfactorily there were a number of areas in which further development was required. The number of users in the vicinity of the base-station was restricted to two, and it was considered that loosening this constraint would be advantageous. Also, the distance at which the tags were from the base station had to be controlled; a longer range of operation was seen to be of advantage.

9.3 Biomedical Applications

Without doubt some of the most successful applications of ICA have been those associated with biomedical signal processing. A large number of papers devoted to biomedical signal processing were presented at ICA'99 (Editors Cardoso, J., Jutten, C., Loubaton, P). These ranged from the reconstruction of autonomic cardiac outflow in humans (Vetter *et al*, 1999); evoked fields decomposition via MEG (Vigario *et al*, 1999); development of analysis and visualisation tools for multi-channel single-trial EEG records (Jung *et al*, 1999); cancellation of cardiac artefacts from MEG (Barros and Ohnishi, 1999). Other applications have included the removal of physiological artifacts from EEG (Lee *et al*, 1999), (Vigario *et al*, 1996); producing spatially independent activity patterns from functional magnetic resonance imaging data (McKeown *et al*, 1998). One particular biomedical application, which will now be considered in some detail, is the detection of sleep-spindles in EEG.

9.3.1 Detection of Sleep Spindles in EEG

Recently Rosipal and Dorffner (1998) investigated the possibility of employing the 'Extended Infomax' algorithm (Girolami, 1998) and the 'Fixed-Point' ICA algorithm (Hyvarinen and Oja, 1997) as a way of processing sleep EEG to improve the detection of sleep spindles. Their findings were positive in that the application of ICA did indeed improve the detection of sleep spindles by a trained electroencephalographer.

Sleep spindles are particular EEG patterns which occur during the sleep cycle. They are defined as a group of oscillation's occurring at 11.5 – 15Hz. Sleep spindles are used as a means to classify the stages of sleep. The visual detection of sleep spindles is particularly difficult when multi-channel EEG recordings are used due to inter-channel degradation of the sleep-spindle signatures. It was therefore proposed in (Rosipal and Dorffner, 1998) that the application of ICA could minimise the channel overlap in the transformed EEG thus isolating the independent sleep-spindle patterns. This overlap would then aid the electroencephalographer in identifying the required sleep spindles.

Figure 9.1 shows eight channels of an 18-channel montage of electrodes, which were mounted according to the 10-20 international system. The bottom eight lines in the figure show the marks where the electroencephalographer has identified a sleep spindle in each of the channels. The mismatch between channels illustrates the difficulty of this particular detection problem. The 'extended-infomax' algorithm was applied to the 18-channel data and 12-channels of independent components were identified. It was seen that channels three and five provided the greatest evidence for the existence of sleep-spindles (Figure 9.2). The associated marks identifying the spindles are given in the last channel. The isolation of the sleep spindles into fewer channels has assisted to some degree in the identification of the spindles.

Without doubt some of the most significant applications of ICA have been in the biomedical domain. The next application of ICA to be discussed is as a tool for Data Mining and structure extraction from multivariate data.

9.4 ICA: A Data Mining Tool

An important tool for knowledge discovery in large data sets is unsupervised clustering. Clustering is the term given to the identification of *a priori* unknown classes or groupings in data. There are a large number of approaches, which may be taken to the unsupervised partitioning of data into its associated classes (Devijver and Kittler, 1982). The approach, which is of particular interest to this chapter, is based on maximum likelihood (ML) parameter estimation of a mixture model (MM) which describes the data density. The estimation of the parameters, (using either gradient based or expectation maximization (EM) algorithms) of a generalized mixture of Gaussians (MOG) model provides a tractable means of clustering polychotomous data (Devijver and Kittler, 1982).

The generalized clustering of data can also be achieved by identifying multiple dichotomies within the data. This approach is somewhat appealing as a hierarchic structure can be imposed on the classes. This structure then allows identified classes to be divided further into smaller sub-classes allowing an interactive exploratory sub-division of the data classes. The other significant point worthy of note is that a dichotomy requires only two elements within the mixture model of the data. The dichotomy, as will be shown, can be simply achieved by the application of the 'extended infomax' algorithm. Maximum likelihood estimation (MLE) approaches to data clustering employ mixture models to seek transition regions of high and low density and so identify potential data clusters.

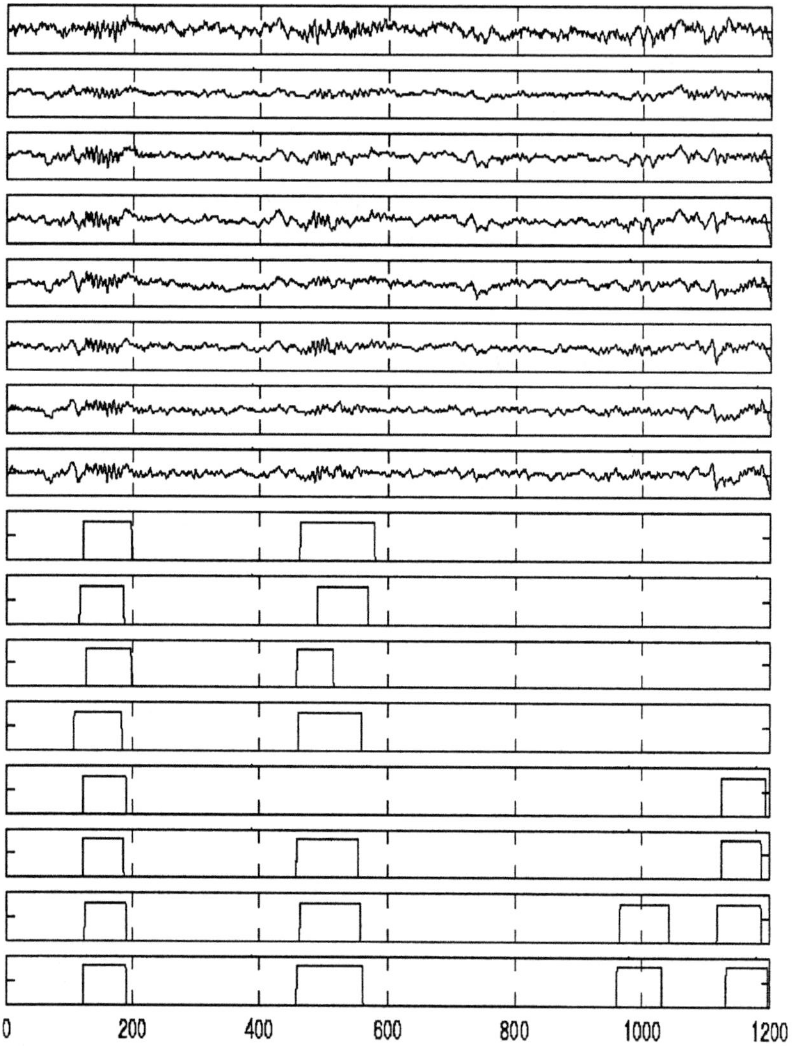

Figure 9.1: 12 Seconds of 8 EEG Channels with the Sleep Spindles Marked by the Electroencephalographer.

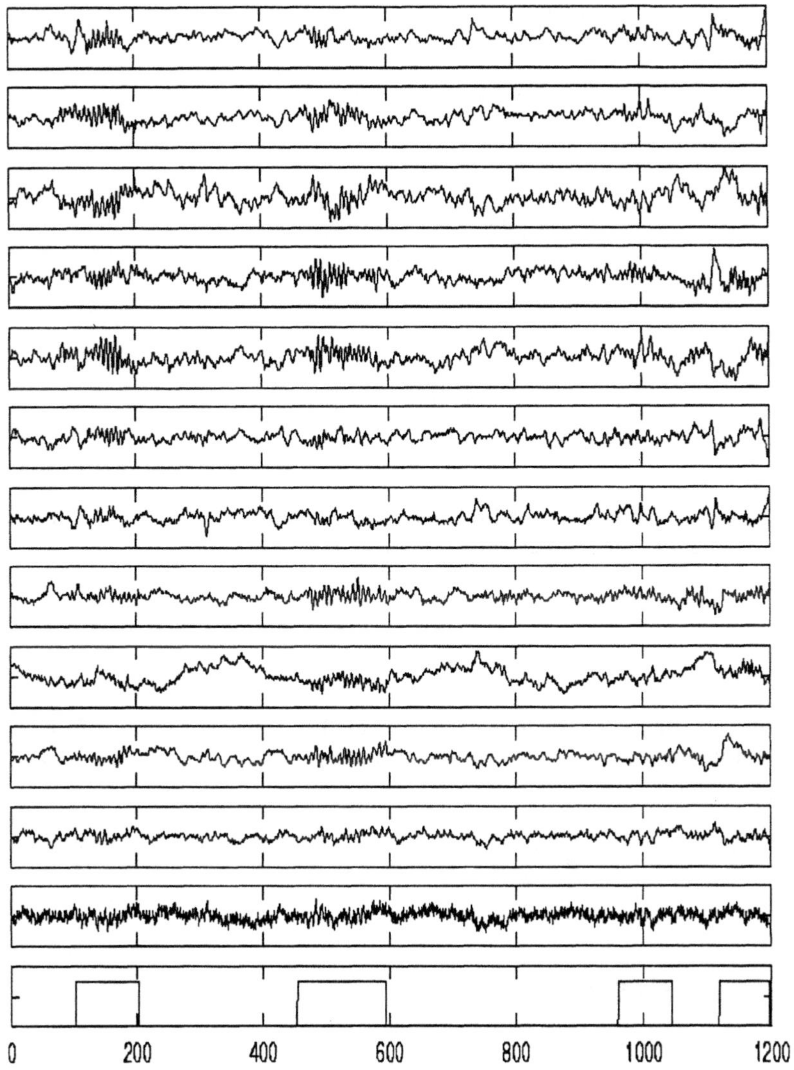

Figure 9.2: 12 Independent Components with the Sleep Spindles Marked by the Electroencephalographer.

The log-likelihood of P observations of an N dimensional variable $\mathbf{x}_j \in \Re^N$, which consists of a mixture of L normal distributions

$$p_i(\mathbf{x}_j) \sim N(\mathbf{m}_i, \Sigma_i),$$

is

$$\hat{p}(C_k \mid \mathbf{x}) = \frac{a_k p_k(\mathbf{x})}{\sum_{i=1}^{L} a_i p_i(\mathbf{x})}$$

The following constraint

$$\sum_{i=1}^{L} a_i = 1$$

is imposed to ensure that the MM integrates to unity. The number of clusters L is given *a priori* for this particular data model. The parameter set

$$\theta = \{a_i, \mathbf{m}_i, \Sigma_i\}$$

can then be estimated in an iterative manner. The simplest form of ML clustering utilizes the dual class hypothesis and so attempts to dichotomize the data. In this case the likelihood is

$$P^{-1} \sum_{j=1}^{P} \ln\left(\pi \, p_1(\mathbf{x}_j) + (1 - \pi) p_2(\mathbf{x}_j)\right)$$

and the reduced parameter set

$$\theta = \{\pi, \mathbf{m}_1, \mathbf{m}_2, \Sigma_1, \Sigma_2\}$$

requires to be identified. Iterative approaches based on gradient ascent or expectation maximization (EM) can be taken in learning the parameter set. If the data consists of multiple classes i.e. a polychotomy, then the identification of multiple dichotomies has been proposed for the partitioning of the data set. This may take a hierarchic approach where each identified cluster is then considered for further dichotomizing. This approach is particularly appealing as will be discussed shortly.

Let us consider an invertible transformation to the observed data $\mathbf{W} \in \Re^{M \times N} : M \leq N$, which reduces the dependency between each of the marginal components of the observation vector $\mathbf{x}_j \in \Re^N$ such that each marginal is approximately independent. For the particular case where $M = N$ and each transformed observation is $\mathbf{y}_j = \mathbf{W}\mathbf{x}_j$, the log likelihood admits

$$P^{-1} \sum_{j=1}^{P} \ln \left| \det(\mathbf{W}) \right| \sum_{i=1}^{L} a_i p_i(\mathbf{y}_j).$$

Consider now the particular case where a dichotomous structure is imposed. As the dependency reducing transformation $\mathbf{W}$ will reduce the mutual information of the output variables then

$$\begin{aligned} p(\mathbf{y}_j) &\equiv \prod_{k=1}^{N} p_k(y_{kj}) \\ &= \prod_{k=1}^{N} \pi_k \, p_{k1}(y_{kj}) + (1 - \pi_k) p_{k2}(y_{kj}) \end{aligned}$$

The density of the transformed observation variable is then a product of a number of univariate Pearson mixture models with individual mean and variance components given as μ_1, μ_2 and σ_1^2, σ_2^2. The case where the individual component parameters are fixed such that $\mu_1 = -\mu_2 = \mu = 2$ and $\sigma_1^2 = \sigma_2^2 = \sigma^2 = 1$ corresponds to the analysis performed in Chapter 7.

It is a well known result (Amari, 1998) that the natural gradient serial parameter update for maximizing the data likelihood is given by

$$\mathbf{W}_{n+1} = \mathbf{W}_n + \eta_n \left(\mathbf{I} + f(\mathbf{W}_n \mathbf{x}_n) \mathbf{x}_n^T \mathbf{W}_n^T \right) \mathbf{W}_n$$

The function $f(\mathbf{W}_n \mathbf{x}_n)$ acts componentwise on the vector $\mathbf{y}_n = \mathbf{W}_n \mathbf{x}_n$ such that each elemental component is the score function. The intention is to seek appropriate dichotomies of the observed data. The simplest mixture model which can be employed in the score function is the symmetric

Pearson model. For the case where π = ½ and the individual component parameters are the score function (7.19) is defined as

$$\frac{-y}{\sigma^2} + \frac{\mu}{\sigma^2}\tanh\left(\mu y / \sigma^2\right)$$

The strictly symmetric case which exhibits two distinct and equiprobable modes has a score function given by $f(y) = -y + 2\tanh(2y)$. Employing this particular function yields

$$\mathbf{W}_{n+1} = \mathbf{W}_n + \mu_n\left(\mathbf{I} + 2\tanh(2\mathbf{y}_n)\mathbf{y}_n^T - \mathbf{y}_n\mathbf{y}_n^T\right)\mathbf{W}_n$$

Consider for a moment the form of this iterative update; from the perspective of ICA this will seek to maximize the likelihood of the data when the hypothesized distributions of the sources is zero-mean, symmetric and negatively kurtotic. As far as clustering is concerned it is clear that this seeks to maximize the likelihood of the data based on a symmetric dichotomy. This ICA algorithm will seek appropriate symmetric dichotomous partitions of the observed data. Hierarchic approaches to the partitioning of data have been applied both in traditional statistics and unsupervised competitive learning. In this approach a top-down clustering of the data which are in the subset partitioned in the previous level takes place. As the application of the above ICA algorithm will seek to identify dichotomies it is clear that subsequent partitioning of the clustered data subsets will eventually lead to an effective partitioning of multi-class data. It should be stressed that this methodology is proposed as an interactive unsupervised data analysis tool. The following section reports on data analysis experiments using two real-world data sets.

9.5 Experimental Results

This section now reports on two experiments using the *Oil Pipeline*[1] and *Swiss Banknote*[2] data sets. The *Swiss Banknote* dataset consists of 200 observations:

[1] http://www.ncrg.aston.ac.uk/GTM/3PhaseData.html
[2] Supplied by Dr Sigbert Klinke, Institute of Statistics, Catholic University of Louvain.

100 genuine and 100 forged banknotes. The data is six dimensional with each dimension corresponding to a particular measurement of the size of the banknotes.

9.5.1 The Oil Pipeline Data

The *Oil Pipeline* data arises from synthetic data modelling of a non-invasive monitoring system which is used to measure the relative quantity of oil within a multi-phase pipeline carrying oil, water and gas. The data consists of twelve dimensions, which correspond to the measurements from six dual powered gamma ray densitometers. The beams are arranged in such a manner that one set of three parallel beams are directed across the pipeline in a horizontal manner with the other set orientated down through the pipeline cross section in a vertical manner, (Bishop *et al*, 1997). There are three particular flow regimes which may occur within the pipeline namely laminar, annular and homogenous. The laminar flow is characterized by the three phases flowing in a linearly stratified manner. Annular flow is similar but the boundaries between the phases are circular. Homogenous flow indicates that there are no geometric discontinuities in the flow regime due to physical partitioning of the phases. It is then apparent that the twelve dimensional measurement data is actually generated from three distinct physical causes and as such there are potentially three distinct classes, which describe the data. The aim of the cluster analysis is to identify the underlying causes of the observations and their structure.

The adaptation proposed rule is used for this simulation. The data is first made zero-mean and then the transformation matrix **W** is sequentially updated until it reaches a steady value. A fixed learning rate of value 0.001 was used in this simulation. To comparatively assess the performance of the proposed ICA based clustering tool on this particular data, the generative topographic mapping (GTM) (Bishop *et al*, 1997) and principal component analysis (PCA) are also employed.

The results of the simulation are detailed in Figure 9.3 The results using the GTM are given in Figure 9.3a and these are very similar to those reported in (Bishop *et al*, 1997). It is clear that the three clusters corresponding to the different phases have been clearly identified and separated. In comparison to principal component analysis (PCA) the results from GTM provide considerably more distinct separation of the clusters corresponding to the three flow regimes. Figure 9.3b shows the results using the proposed adaptation rule. Once the transformation matrix **W** has been learned a visualization scatter plot can be generated by projecting the data onto a two-dimensional subspace whose basis are the first two 'ICA' basis vectors.

A first level dichotomy is generated and it is clear that the points relating to the laminar, annular and homogenous flow regimes have been distinctly clustered together. However, it is interesting to note that there exist two clusters corresponding to the laminar flow. As the proportions of each phase change within the laminar flow over time there will be a change in the physical boundary between the phases which will trigger a step change in the across pipe beams. It is this physical effect which gives rise to the distinct clusters within the laminar flow.

It is also clear that this particular dichotomy provides good separation of the flow classes with low intra-cluster and high inter-cluster variance being exhibited. Figure 9.3c, gives the projection of the data onto the subspace defined by the first two principal components, the PCA transformation, in this case, fails to identify clearly any of the latent structure within the data.

9.5.2 The Swiss Banknote Data

This is a most interesting data set and has been employed in demonstrating the efficacy of various projection pursuit indices. The data has two distinct and equiprobable classes viz forgeries and legal tender. Due to the high variance between the two classes, standard PCA is capable of providing an acceptable level of partitioning into the respective classes. However, the data points describing the forgeries are drawn from two distinct sub-classes, i.e. there are two sets of forgers, which have contributed to the corpus of forgeries.

The ICA based clustering algorithm is applied in an iterative manner and as in the previous experiment the clustering is visualized by projecting onto the first two 'ICA' basis vectors. Figure 9.4a indicates the two distinct classes. Inspection of the cluster of points describing the forgeries shows a high level of intra-cluster variance. This is indicative of potentially further structure within the selected data points. A second level clustering is performed on the two clusters and Figures 9.4 b and c show the results. It is clear that there is dissimilarity in a small number of the data points, which are associated with the forgery class, and these form a smaller cluster. The compact nature of the cluster associated with the legal tender is reflected in the second level cluster and strongly indicates that there are no further valid partitions of the data.

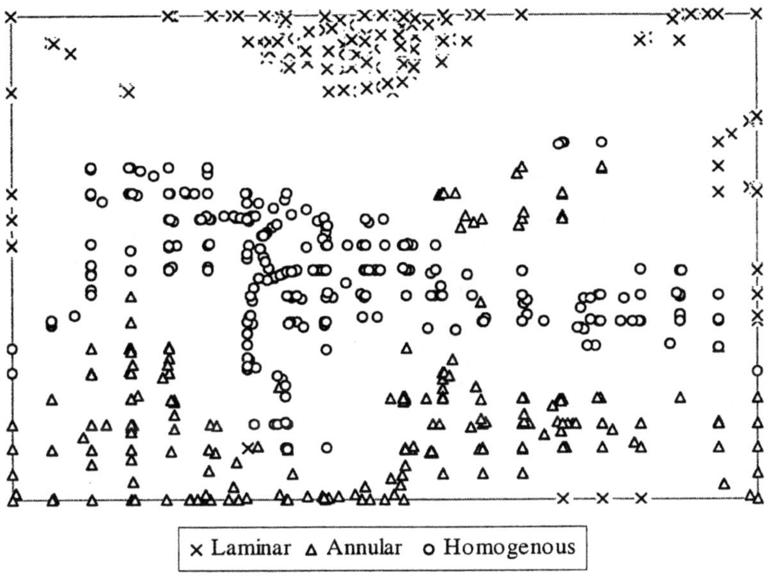

Figure 9.3 a: Plot of the Posterior Mean for each Point in Latent Space using the GTM.

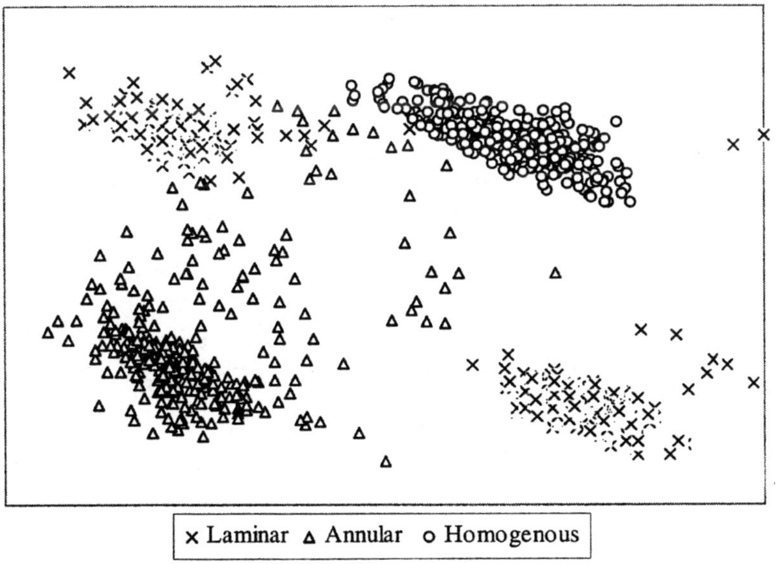

Figure 9.3 b: Plot of the Twelve Dimensional Data Projected onto a Two Dimensional Subspace.

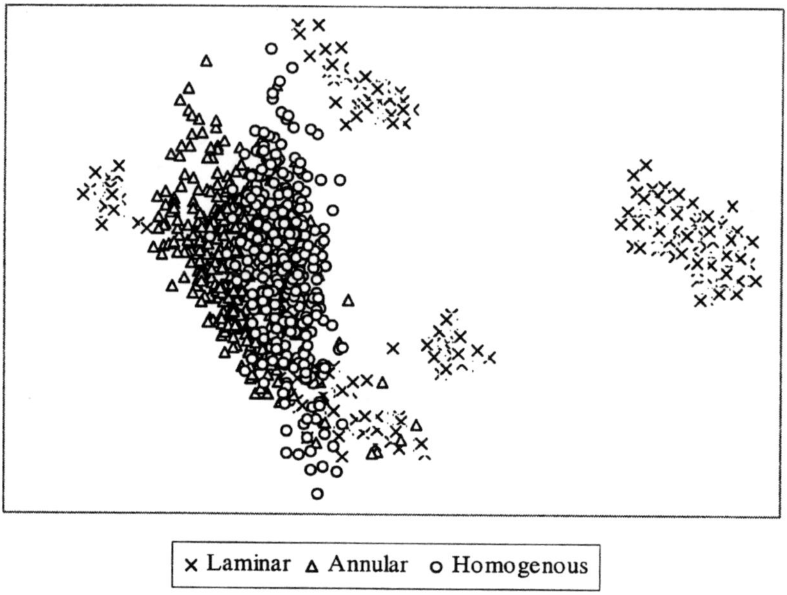

Figure 9.3 c: Plot of the Twelve Dimensional Data Projected onto the Two Dimensional Subspace Whose Basis is the First Two Principal Components.

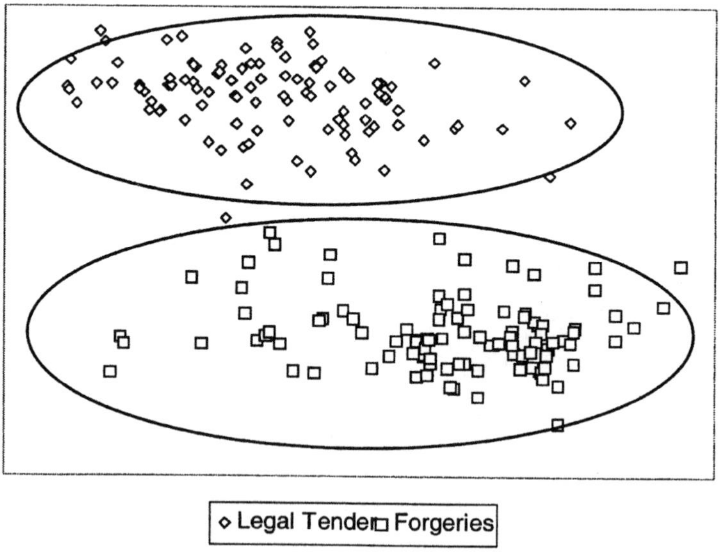

Figure 9.4 a: First Level Dichotomy Indicating the Clustering into the Two Distinct Classes.

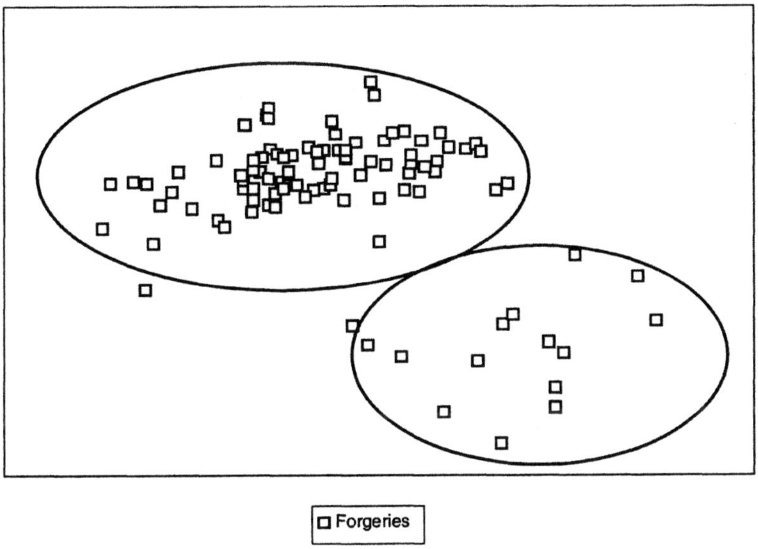

Figure 9.4 b: Second Level Dichotomy for the Forgeries Indicating the Further Clustering into Two Distinct Classes.

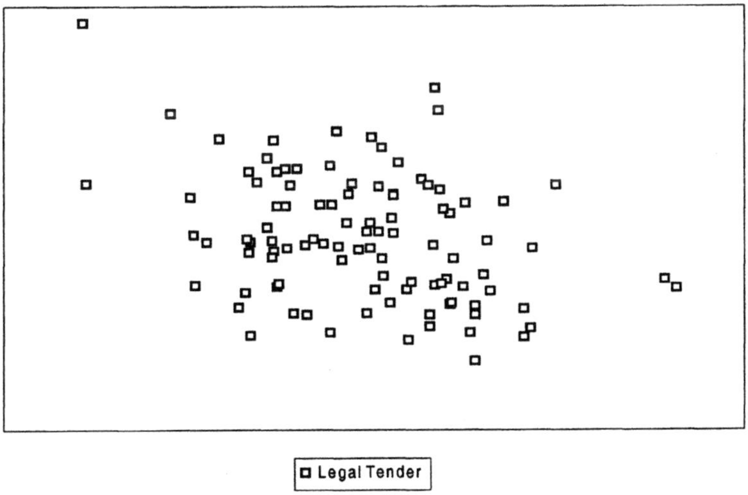

Figure 9.4 c: Second Level Dichotomy for the Legal Tender Indicating That No Further Distinct Classes are in Existance.

9.6 Conclusions

This final chapter has considered a number of successful applications of ICA which extend the range of its utility outwith BSS. The success of the instantaneous ICA model applied to biomedical signal processing has been impressive, but the applicability of the temporal model has yet to be investigated fully. It is still early in the development of the role of ICA within 'real world' applications; however the initial results reported are encouraging and indicative of many further successful applications of this method of signal processing.

References

Amari, S., Cichocki, A, and Yang, H. (1995). A New Learning Algorithm for Blind Signal Separation. *Neural Information Processing*, Vol 8, pp. 757-763. M.I.T Press.

Amari, S. (1967). A Theory of Adaptive Pattern Classifiers. *I.E.E.E Trans. On Electronic Computers*. Vol. EC-16, No.3, 1967, pp. 299-307.

Amari, S. (1997), Natural Gradient Works Efficiently in Learning, *Neural Computation*.**10**, pp.251-276.

Amari, S. (1985), Differential Geometrical Methods of Statistics, Springer Lecture Notes in Statistics, vol. 28,Heidelberg, Springer Verlag.

Amari, S., Chen, T, P., and Cichocki, A.,(1997), Stability Analysis of Learning Algorithms for Blind Source Separation, *Neural Networks,* Vol 10, No 8, pp.1345-1351.

Aris, R., (1962), Vectors, Tensors and the Basic Equations of Fluid Mechanics, Dover Publications, ISBN 0-486-66110-5

Atick, J, J., and Redlich, A, N., (1993). Convergent Algorithm for Sensory Receptive Field Development. *Neural Computation*, 6, pp 45 – 60.

Baldi, P. and Hornick, K., (1988), Neural Networks and Principal Components Analysis : Learning from Examples without Local Minima. *Neural Networks*, **2** : pp 53 – 58.

Barlow, H. B., (1990), A Theory About the Functional Role and Synaptic Mechanism of Visual After-Effects, *Vision: Coding and Efficiency*, C. B. Blakemore (Eds), Cambridge University Press. pp 363 - 375.

Barlow, H, B. (1961), Possible Principles Underlying the Transformation of Sensory Messages. In *Rosenblith W, Sensory Communication*, MIT Press, pp 217.

Barnett, S. (1971), Matrices in Control Theory, Van Nostrand, ISBN : 0-442-00581-4

Barros, A., Ohnishi, N., (1999)., Removal of Quasi-Periodic Sources from Physiological Measurements. *First International Workshop on Independent Component Analysis and Signal Separation*, Ed's Cardoso, J., Jutten, C., Loubaton, P., pp 185-189.

Becker, S., and Hinton, G., (1992). A Self-Organising Neural Network that Discovers Surfaces in Random-Dot Stereograms. *Nature (London)* 355, pp 161 – 163.

Bell, A and Sejnowski, T. (1995, a). An Information Maximisation Approach to Blind Separation and Blind Deconvolution. *Neural Computation* **7**, 1129 - 1159.

Bell, A and Sejnowski, T. (1995, b), Fast blind separation based on information theory. *International symposium on nonlinear theory and applications* **1**. 1, 43 - 47.

Belouchrani, A. and Cardoso, J, F., (1995), Maximum likelihood Source Separation by the Expectation-Maximisation Technique, *Proc. International Symposium on Nonlinear Theoryand its Applications, Nolta'95., Invited Paper, Las Vegas, Nevada.*

Bienenstock, E, L,, Cooper, L, N., and Munro, P, W., (1982), Theory for the Development of Neuron Selectivity: Orientation Specificity and Binocular Interaction in Visual Cortex. *The Journal of Neuroscience*, **2**(1), pp 32 – 48.

Bishop, C., Svensen, M., Williams, C., (1997). GTM: The Generative Topographic Mapping., *Neural Computation*, 10, 1, pp215-234.

Brause, R. (1993). Transform Coding by Lateral Inhibited Neural Nets. *In Proceedings of I.E.E.E Tools with Artificial Intelligence.*

Brilinger, D, R. (1975). Time Series, Data Analysis, Theory. Rinehart, Holt and Winston, New York.

Cardoso, J, F. (1989). Source Separation Using Higher-Order Moments. *Proc I.E.E.E ICASSP*, pp.2109-2112.

Cardoso, J, F. (1990). Eigen-Structure of the Fourth-Order Cumulant Tensor with Applications to the Blind Source Separation Problem. *Proc I.E.E.E ICASSP*, pp. 2655-2658.

Cardoso, J, F. (1991). Super-Symmetric Decomposition of the Fourth-Order Cumulant Tensor, Blind Identification of More Sources than Sensors. *Proc I.E.E.E ICASSP*, pp. 3109 – 3112.

Cardoso, J, F. and Laheld, B, H. (1997), Equivariant Adaptive Source Separation *I.E.E.E Transactions on Signal Processing*, SP-**43**, pp 3017 – 3029.

Cardoso, J, F., (1997), Infomax and Maximum Likelihood for Blind Source Separation, *I.E.E.E Signal Processing Letters*, **4**, pp 109 – 111.

Chan, D, C, B., Godshill, S, J. and Rayner, P, J, W. (1996), Multi-channel Multi-tap Signal Separation By Output Decorrelation, Cambridge University, CUED/F-INFENG/TR 250, ISSN 0951-9211.

Charkani, N., and Deville, Y., (1997), Optimisation of the Asymptotic Performance of Time-Domain Convolutive Source Separation Algorithms., *Proc European Symposium on Artificial Neural Networks*, pp 273 – 278, ISBN 2-9600049-7-3.

Choi, S., and Cichocki, A., (1997a), Blind signal deconvolution by spatio-temporal decorrelation and demixing," *I.E.E.E Workshop on Neural Networks for Signal Processing* .7, pp 426-435.

Choi, S., and Cichocki, A., (1997b), A linear feedforward neural network with lateral feedback connections for blind source separation," in proc *I.E.E.E Signal Processing Workshop on Higher-order Statistics* (Banff, Canada), pp. 349-353.

Cichocki, A., Unbehauen, R. and Rummert, E. (1994). Robust Learning Algorithm for Blind Separation of Signals, *Electronics Letters*, **30**, (17), pp 1386-1387.

Cichocki, A., Thawonmas, R. and Amari S. (1997). Sequential Blind Signal Extraction in Order Specified by Stochastic Properties. *Electronics Letters,* **33**, (1), pp 64 – 65.

Cichocki, A. and Unbehauen, R., (1994). Neural Networks for Optimization and Signal Processing, John Wiley.

Cichocki, A., Kasprzak, W., Amari, S., (1995), Multi-Layer Neural Networks with a Local Adaptive Learning Rule for Blind Separation of Source Signals", *Nolta-95*, **1**, pp. 61-66.

Cichocki, A., Unbehauen, R.,Moszczynski, L., and Rummert, E., (1994), A New On-Line Adaptive Algorithm for Blind Separation of Source Signals", *Int. Symposium on Artificial Neural Networks ISANN-94*, pp. 406-411.

Cichocki, A., Kasprzak, W., Amari, S., (1996), Neural Network Approach to Blind Separation and Enhancement of Images", *Signal Processing VIII. Theories and Applications, EURASIP / LINT Publ.*, **I**, pp. 579-582.

Cichocki, A., Amari, S, I., and Cao, J. (1996), Blind Separation of Delayed and Convolved Signals with Self-Adaptive Learning Rate, *International Symposium on Nonlinear Theory and Applications*, pp. 229-232.

Cichocki A., Amari S.-I. and Thawonmas R., (1996)., Blind Signal Extraction Using Self-Adaptive Non-Linear Hebbian Learning Rule, *International Symposium on Nonlinear Theory and its Applications - NOLTA'96, Proceedings*. Research Society on NTA, IEICE, pp. 377-380.

Comon, P. (1994). Independent component analysis, a new concept ?. *Signal Processing*, **36**, 287 - 314.

Comon, P. (1989). Separation of Sources Using High-Order Cumulants. *SPIE Conference on Advanced Algorithms and Architectures for Signal Processing, Real-Time Signal Processing* Vol. XII. Pp. 170-181.

Comon, P., Jutten, C., and Herrault, J., (1991), Blind Separation of Sources, Part 2, Problems Statement., *Signal Processing*, **24**, pp 11 – 20.

Cover, T. and Thomas, J, A. (1991), Elements of Information Theory, *Wiley Series in Telecommunications*.

Cox, D, R. and Hinkley, D, V., (1974). Theoretical Statistics, *Chapman and Hall.*

Darwin, C. J., McKeown, J. D. and Kirby, D. (1989). "Compensation for transmission channel and speaker effects on vowel quality", *Speech Communication,* **8** (3), 221-234.

Deco, G. and Brauer, W., (1995), Non-linear Higher-Order Statistical Decorrelation by Volume-Conserving Neural Architectures., *Neural Networks*, **8** (4), pp 525 – 535.

Deco G. and Obradovic D. (1996). An Information-Theoretic Approach to Neural Computing. New York: Springer-Verlag, ISBN 0-387-94666-7.

Delfosse, N. and Loubaton, P. (1995). Adaptive Blind Separation of Independent Sources: A Deflation Approach. *Signal Processing*, **45**, pp 59-83.

Devijver, O, A. and Kittler, J, V. (1982). Pattern Recognition. A Statistical Approach. Prentice-Hall, Englewood Cliffs, NJ.

Deville, Y. (1996), Convergence Properties of Cichocki's Extension of the Herrault-Jutten Source Separation Neural Network, *NIPS'96, Workshop on Blind Signal Processing*, Paper Available at

URL. http://www.bip.riken.go.jp/absl/back/nips96ws/nips96ws.html

Deville, Y. and Charkani, N., (1997). Analysis of the Stablity of Time Domain Source Separation Algorithms for Convolutively Mixed Signals. *Proc International Conference on Acoustics, Speech and Signal Processing*, **3**, pp 1835 – 1839.

Deville, Y., Damour, J., Charkani, N. (1999). Improved Multi-Tag Radio-Frequency Identification Systems Based on New Source Separation Neural Networks. *First International Workshop on Independent Component Analysis and Signal Separation*, Ed's Cardoso, J., Jutten, C., Loubaton, P., pp 449-454.

Diaconas, P., and Freedman, D., (1984), Asymptotics of Graphical Projection Pursuit. *Annals of Statistics*, **12**, pp 793 – 815.

Durlach, N.I., Gabriel, K. J., Colbum, H. S., and Trahiotis, C. (1986). "Interaural correlation discrimination: II. Relation to binaural unmasking', J. *Acoust. Soc. Am.* **79** (5), 1548-1557.

Everitt, B, S., (1984), An Introduction to Latent Variable Models, London: Chapman and Hall.

Foldiak, P., (1990). Models of Sensory Coding, PhD Thesis, Physiological Laboratory, University of Cambridge.

Foldiak P. (1989). Adaptive Network for Optimal Linear Feature Extraction. *I.E.E.E/I.N.N.S International joint conference on neural networks.* **1**, pp 401 - 405. Washington, DC: Institute of Electrical and Electronics Engineering, San Diego.

Friedman, J. H., (1987), Exploratory Projection Pursuit. *Journal of the American Statistical Association*, **82** (397) : pp 249-266.

Fyfe, C. (1995). Introducing Asymmetry into Interneuron Learning. *Neural Computation* ,**7** (6), pp 1167-1181.

Fyfe, C and Baddeley, R. (1995). Non-Linear Data Structure Extraction Using Simple Hebbian Networks. *Biological Cybernetics*, **72** (6), pp 533-541.

Fyfe, C., (1997), A Comparative Study of Two Neural Methods of Exploratory Projection Pursuit. *Neural Networks*, **9** (6), pp1-6.

Gaeta, M., and Lacoume, (1990), J, L. Source Separation Without a Priori Knowledge : the Maximum Likelihood Solution, *Signal Processing V: Theory and Applications,* pp. 621-624.

Gelle, G., Colas, M., Delaunay, G., (1999)., Separation of Convolutive Mixtures of Harmonic Signals With A Temporal Approach. Application To Rotating Machine Monitoring. *First International Workshop on Independent Component Analysis and Signal Separation*, Ed's Cardoso, J., Jutten, C., Loubaton, P., pp 109-114.

Girolami, M., and Fyfe, C., (1997a), Stochastic ICA Contrast Maximisation Using Oja's Nonlinear PCA Algorithm. *International Journal of Neural Systems*, Vol 8, No 5 & 6, pp 661 - 678.

Girolami, M and Fyfe, C., (1997b), Extraction of Independent Signal Sources using a Deflationary Exploratory Projection Pursuit Network with Lateral Inhibition. *I.E.E Proceedings on Vision, Image and Signal Processing* , Vol 14, No 5, pp 299 - 306.

Girolami, M and Fyfe, C., (1997c), A Temporal Model of Linear Anti-Hebbian Learning. *Neural Processing Letters* Journal, **4** (3), pp 1-10.

Girolami, M and Fyfe, C., (1997d), An Extended Exploratory Projection Pursuit Network with Linear and Non-linear Anti-Hebbian Connections Applied to the Cocktail Party Problem, *Neural Networks*,Vol. 10, No. 9, pp. 1607-1618.

Girolami, M and Fyfe, C., (1997e), Kurtosis Extrema and Identification of Independent Components : A Neural Network Approach. Proc *ICASSP-97, I.E.E.E Conference on Acoustics, Speech and Signal Processing*, **4**, pp 3329 - 3333.

Girolami, M and Fyfe, C. (1997f) Independence is Far from Normal. Proc *ESANN97, European Symposium on Artificial Neural Networks*, pp 297 – 302.

Girolami, M and Fyfe, C., (1997g), Negentropy and Kurtosis as Projection Pursuit Indices Provide Generalised ICA Algorithms', NIPS'96 Blind Signal Separation Workshop, , Aspen Colorado.

Girolami, M and Fyfe, C., (1997h), Generalised Independent Component Analysis Through Unsupervised Learning With Emergent Bussgang Properties. Proc *I.E.E.E / I.C.N.N, International Conference on Neural Networks, Houston, Texas,* Vol 3, pp 1788 – 179.

Girolami, M and Fyfe, C., (1997i), Fahlman Type Activation Functions Applied to Nonlinear PCA Networks Provide a Generalised Independent Component Analysis. *ICANNGA-97, International Conference on Artificial Neural Networks and Genetic Algorithms*, Springer Verlag Wien, pp 112-115, Norwich, UK.

Girolami, M and Fyfe, C., (1996a), Higher Order Cumulant Maximisation Using Nonlinear Hebbian and Anti-Hebbian Learning for Adaptive Blind Separation of Source Signals. In Proc. *IWSIP-96, IEEE/IEE International Workshop on Signal and Image Processing, Advances in Computational Intelligence*, Elsevier publishing, pp 141 - 144.

Girolami, M and Fyfe, C., (1996b), Multivariate Density Factorisation for Independent Component Analysis : An Unsupervised Artificial Neural Network Approach. Proc *AISTAT-97, 3'rd International Workshop on Artificial Intelligence and Statistics*, pp 223 - 230.

Girolami, M and Fyfe,C., (1996c), Blind Separation Of Sources Using Exploratory Projection Pursuit Networks. In Proc. *Speech and Signal Processing*, *International Conference on the Engineering Applications of Neural Networks*, ISBN 952-90-7517-0, 249 - 252.

Girolami, M, Cichocki. A., and Amari, S, I. (1997). A Common Neural Network Model for Exploratory Data Analysis and Independent Component Analysis, *I.E.E.E Transactions on Neural Networks*, Vol 9, No.6, pp 1495 - 1501.

Girolami, M. An Alternative Perspective on Adaptive Independent Component Analysis Algorithms. *Neural Computation*, Vol 10, No.8, pp 2103 – 2114.

Golub, G, H. and Van Loan, C, F. (1989). Matrix Computations. Second Edition. Baltimore: Johns Hopkins University Press.

Gordon, A, D., (1981), Classification Methods for Exploratory Analysis of Multivariate Data. London : Chapman and Hall.

Gorokhov, A. and Loubaton, P. (1996), Second Order Blind Identification of Convolutive Mixtures with Temporally Correlated Sources: a Subspace Method, *Signal Processing VII, Theories and Applications*, Triest, Italy, Elsevier.

Greenwood, D.,D., (1990), 'A cochlear frequency position-function for several species - 29 years later', *J. Acoust. Soc. of America'*, **86** (6), pp 2592-2605.

Haykin, S. (1991) Adaptive filter theory, 2nd ed., Prentice Hall, Englewood Cliffs, NJ.

Hebb, D. (1949). The Organisation of Behaviour. Wiley.

Herrault J., Jutten C., (1986), Space or Time Adaptive Signal Processing by Neural Network Models, *AIP Conf. Proc.*, Snowbird, UT, pp 206 - 211.

Hertz, J., Krogh, A., and Palmer, R, G. (1992). Introduction to the Theory of Neural Computation. Addison-Wesley Publishing.

Hopfield, J, J., (1991).Olfactory Computation and Object Perception. Proc *National Academy of Sciences*, **88**, pp 6462-6466.

Huber, P, J., (1985), Projection Pursuit (with discussion). *Annals of Statistics*, **13**, pp 435 – 525.

Hung, C, P., Moir, T, J., and Findlay, J., (1994), Multivariable Adaptive Noise Cancellation Applied to a Milling Tool Condition Monitoring System. *Applied Signal Processing*, 1:181 – 187.

Hyvarinen, A and Oja, E. (1996). Simple Neuron Models for Independent Component Analysis. Technical Report A37, Helsinki University of Technology, Laboratory of Computer and Information Science, ISBN 951-22-3257-X.

Intrator, N., and Cooper, L, N., (1992), Objective Function Formulation of thr BCM Theory of Visual Cortical Plasticity: Statistical Connections, Stability Connections. *Neural Networks*, **5** : pp 3 – 17.

Intrator, N., (1992), Feature Extraction Using an Unsupervised Neural Network, *Neural Computation*, **4** (1): pp 98 – 107.

Jollife, I. (1986). Principal Component Analysis. Springer-Verlag.

Jones, M. C. and Sibson, R., (1987), What is Projection Pursuit. *The Royal Statistical Society.*

Jung, T., Makeig, S., Westerfield, M., Townsend, J., Courchesne, E., Sejnowski, T., (1999)., Independent Component Analysis of Single Trial Event Related Potentials. *First International Workshop on Independent Component Analysis and Signal Separation*, Ed's Cardoso, J., Jutten, C., Loubaton, P., pp 173-178.

Jung, T, P., Humphries, C., Lee, T, W., Makeig, S., McKeown, M., Iragui, V., Sejnowski, - T., (1998), Extended ICA Removes Artifacts from Electroencephalographic Recordings, Advances in *Neural Information Processing Systems, 10, pp 894-900.*

Jutten, C Herrault, J., (1991), Blind Separation of Sources, Part 1: An Adaptive Algorithm Based On Neuromimetic Architecture. *Signal Processing* **24**, pp 1- 10.

Karhunen, J Joutensalo, J (1994a), Representation and Separation Of Signals Using Nonlinear PCA Type Learning. *Neural Networks* **7** (1), pp 113-127.

Karhunen, J Joutensalo, J (1995), Generalisations of Principal Components Analysis, Optimisation Problems, and Neural Networks, *Neural Networks* **8** (4), pp 549 – 562.

Karhunen, J and Pajunen, P. (1996), Hierarchic Nonlinear PCA Algorithms for Neural Blind Source Separation. Norsig-96, In *Proc I.E.E.E. Nordic Signal Processing Symposium,* pp 71-74.

Karhunen, J and Pajunen, P. (1997a), Blind Source Separation using Least-Squares Type Adaptive Algorithms, in *Proc I.E.E.E Int. Conf. On Acoustics, Speech, and Signal Processing (ICASSP'97)*, pp 3361 – 3364.

Karhunen, J and Pajunen, P. (1997b), Blind Source Separation and Tracking using Non-Linear PCA Criterion: A Least-Squares Approach, in Proc *Int. Conf. On Neural Networks (ICNN'97)*, pp 2147-2152.

Karhunen, J. (1996), Neural Approaches to Independent Component Analysis and Source Separation. *Proc. ESANN'96,* pp 249 – 266.

Karhunen, J, Wang, L and Joutsensalo, J. (1995). Neural Estimation of Basis Vectors in Independent Component Analysis. *International Conference on Artificial Neural Networks*, **1**, pp 317 - 322.

Karhunen, J., Oja, E., Wang, L., Vigario, R., Joutsensalo J., (1995) A Class of Neural Networks for Independent Component Analysis. *I.E.E.E Transactions on Neural Networks*, **8**, pp 487 – 504.

Karhunen, J Joutensalo, J (1991a), Tracking of Sinusoidal Frequencies by Neural Network Learning Algorithms, *Proc, I.E.E.E, ICASSP'91*, pp 3177 – 3180.

Karhunen, J Joutensalo, J (1991b), Frequency Estimation by a Hebbian Subspace Algorithm. In *T Kohonen, ed., Artificial Neural Networks*, pp 1637 – 1640.

Karhunen, J Joutensalo, J (1992a), Nonlinear Hebbian Algorithms for Sinusiodal Frequency Estimation, In *I. Aleksander and J. Taylor, eds., Artificial Neural Networks*, 1-2, pp 1199 - 1102.

Karhunen, J Joutensalo, J (1992b), Learning of Sinusoidal Frequencies by Nonlinear Hebbian Algorithms, In *S, Y Kung et al (eds) Neural Networks for Signal Processing II, I.E.E.E Press*, pp 39 – 48.

Kopriva, I., Persin, A., (1999). Blind Separation of Optical tracker Responses into Independent Components Discriminates Optical Sources. *First International Workshop on Independent Component Analysis and Signal Separation*, Ed's Cardoso, J., Jutten, C., Loubaton, P., pp31-36.

Lacoume, J, L. and Ruiz, P. (1988). Source Identification: A Solution Based on the Cumulants. *Proc 4th ASSP Workshop on Spectral Estimation and Modeling*, pp. 199-203.

Lambert, R., (1996), Multichannel Blind Deconvolution: FIR Matrix Algebra and Separation of Multipath Mixtures. PhD Thesis, University of Southern California.

Laughlin, S, B. (1981), A Simple Coding Procedure enhances a Neurons Information Capacity. *Z. Naturf.,* C 36, pp 910-2.

Lee, T,W., Bell, A.J., and Orgmeister, R. (1997), Blind Source Separation of Real World Signals. In Proc. *I.E.E.E / I.C.N.N, International Conference on Neural Networks,* Vol 4, pp 2129 - 2134.

Lee, T, W., Girolami, M., and Sejnowski, T. (1999), Independent Component Analysis using an Extended Infomax Algorithm for Mixed Sub-Gaussian and Super-Gaussian Sources. *Neural Computation*, Vol 11, No2, pp 606-633.

Lee, T.W, and Sejnowski, T. (1997), Independent Component Analysis for Sub-Gaussian and Super-Gaussian Mixtures, 4th Joint Symposium on Neural Computation", Volume 7, pp 132-140, Institute for Neural Computation.

Lii, K, S. and Rosenblatt, M. (1982). Deconvolution and Estimation of Transfer Function Phase and Coefficients for Non-Gaussian Linear Processes. *The Annals of Statistics*, **10**, pp. 1195-1208.

Lindgren, U., Sahlin, H., Broman, H., (1996), Source Separation Using Second Order Statistics,*Signal Processing VII, Theories and Applications*, Triest, Italy, Elsevier.

Linsker, R. (1986). From Basic Network Principles to Neural Architecture, *In Proceedings of National Academy of Sciences.*

Linsker, R. (1992). Local Synaptic Learning Rules Suffice to Maximise Mutual Information in a Linear Network. *Neural Computation*, **4**, pp 691-702.

Macchi, O., and Moreau, E. (1994), Self-Adaptive Source Separation, Part 1: Convergence Analysis of a Direct Linear Neural Network Controlled by the Herrault and Jutten Adapation Law, submitted to *I.E.E.E Transactions on Signal Processing*.

Mackay, D., (1996), Maximum Likelihood and Covariant Algorithms for Independent Component Analysis. Draft 3.1, Cavendish Laboratory, University of Cambridge.

Mackenzie, G.W,. (1964) Acoustics, London & New York, Focal Press.

Malouche, Z., and Macchi, O., (1997), A Linear Adaptive Neural Network for Extraction of Independent Components, *ESANN'97, Special ICA Session*, pp 261 – 266.

Malouche, Z., and Macchi, O., (1996), Extended Anti-Hebbian Adaptation for Unsupervised Source Extraction, *Proc I.E.E.E ICASP' 96*, Vol 3, pp 1665 – 1668.

Matsuoka K., Masahiro O., & Kawamoto M. (1995). A Neural Net for Blind Separation of Nonstationary Signals. *Neural Networks* **8**, pp 411-419

McClelland, J., Rumelhart, D, E., and Group, T, P, R. (1986). Parallel Distributed Processing, Volume 1 and 2. MIT Press.

McCulloch, W, S., and Pitts, W., (1943), A Logical Calculus of the Ideas Immanent in Nervous Activity. *Bulletin of Mathematical Biophysics*, 5, pp 115 – 133.

McDonald R. (1966). Signal to noise and idle channel performance of differential pulse code modulation systems- Particular applications to voice signals. *BSTJ*, **45** (1123-1151).

McKeon, M., Jung, T, P., Makeig, S., Brown, G., Kindermann, S., Lee, T, W., Sejnowski., (1997). Transiently Time-locked fMRI Activations Revealed by Independent Component Analysis., *Proceeding of the National Academy of Sciences*, 95: 803-810.

Minorsky, N., (1962). Nonlinear Oscillations. Van Nostrand Reinhold.

Moncur, J.P., Dirks, D., (1967). 'Binaural and Monaural Speech Intelligibility in Reverberation', *J. of Speech and Hearing Research*, **10**, pp 186-195.

Moreau, E., and Machi, O., (1993a), Two Novel Architectures for the Self-Adaptive Separation of Signals, *Proc. I.E.E.E Int. Conf. On Communications*, pp 1154 – 1159.

Moreau, E., and Machi, O., (1993b), New Self-Adaptive Algorithms for Source Separation Based on Contrast Functions. Proc *I.E.E.E Signal Proc. Workshop on Higher Order Statistics*, pp 215 – 219.

Nadal, J, P. and Parga, N. (1994). Non-Linear Neurons in the Low Noise Limit: A Factorial Code Maximises Information Transfer. *Network* **5**, 565-581.

Nguyen Thi H L., Jutten C.,(1995), Blind Source Separation for Convolutive Mixtures, *Signal Processing*, **45** (2), pp 209 - 229.

Nikias, L, C. and Mendel, M, J. (1993). Signal Processing with Higher-Order Spectra. *I.E.E.E Signal Processing Magazine*, 1053-5888/93, pp 10 – 35.

Nikias, L,. C. and Petropulu, P, A. (1993). Higher Order Spectral Analysis, Englewood Cliffs, NJ, Prentice Hall.

Oja, E. (1982). A Simplified Neuron Model as a Principal Component Analyser. *Journal of Mathematical Biology,* 15, pp. 267 – 273, 1982..

Oja, E. (1989). Neural Networks, Principal Components and Subspaces. *International Journal of Neural Systems.* **1**, pp 61 – 68.

Oja, E., Ogawa, H., and Wangviwattana, J., (1991), Learning in Nonlinear Constrained Hebbian Networks, *Artificial Neural Networks (Proc. ICANN – 91)*, pp 385 – 390.

Oja, E. (1997), The Nonlinear PCA Learning Rule and Signal Separation-Mathematical Analysis. *Neurocomputing,* 17: 25 – 45.

Oja, E., and Karhunen, J. (1995), Signal Separation by Nonlinear Hebbian Learning, In *ICNN'95,* pp 83 – 97.

Oja, E., (1983), Subspace Methods of Pattern Recognition. *Letchworth, England: Research Studies Press, and New York,* NY: J Wiley.

Oppenheim, A, V. and Schafer, R, W. (1989), Discrete-Time Signal Processing, Prentice Hall, ISBN : 0-13-216771-9.

Pajunen, P., (1999). Blind Source Separation of Natural Signals Based on Approximate Complexity Minimisation. *First International Workshop on Independent Component Analysis and Signal Separation,* Ed's Cardoso, J., Jutten, C., Loubaton, P., pp 267-270.

Palmieri, F. (1993). Linear Self-Association for Universal Memory and Approximation. *In World Congress on Neural Networks,* pp 339-342.

Palmieri, F., Zhu, J., and Chang, C., (1993). Anti-Hebbian Learning in Topologically Constrained Linear Networks: A Tutorial. *I.E.E.E Transactions on Neural Networks,* **4** (5): pp 748 – 761.

Papoulis, A. (1984). Probability, Random Variables and Stochastic Processes, 2nd ed. McGraw-Hill, New York.

Parsons, T. (1987). Voice and Speech Processing. McGraw-Hill, NJ.

Pearlmutter, B and Parra, L, (1996). A Context Sensitive Generalisation of ICA. *International Conference on Neural Information Processing,* Springer, Vol. 1, pp 151 – 156, 1996.

Pearson, K. (1894), Contributions to the Mathematical Study of Evolution. *Phil. Trans. Roy. Soc.* A 185, 71.

Pham, D, T., Garrat, P., and Jutten, C. (1992), Separation of a Mixture of Independent Sources through a Maximum Likelihood Approach, *Proc. EUSIPCO,* pp. 771-774.

Platt, J, C. and Faggin, F. (1992), Networks for the Separation of Sources that are Superimposed and Delayed, *Neural Information Processing Systems,* **4**. pp. 730-737.

Plomp, R., (1976). Binaural and Monaural Speech Intelligibility of Connected Discourse in Reverberation as a Function of Azimuth of a Single Sound Source (Speech or Noise)., *Acoustica,* **31**, pp 200-211.

Plumbley, M., (1991). On Information Theory and Unsupervised Neural Networks. PhD Thesis, University of Cambridge.

Plumbley, M. and Fallside, F., (1988). An Information-Theoretic Approach to Unsupervised Connectionist Models. *In Proceedings of the 1988 Connectionist Models Summer School.* Morgan Kaufmann, pp 239-245.

Press, W, H., Teukolsky, S, A., Vetterling, W, T., and Flannery, B, P. (1988). Numerical Recipes in C. Cambridge University press.

Principe, J, C., Wang, C., and Wu, H, S. (1996), Temporal Decorrelation using Teacher Forcing Anti-Hebbian Learning and Its Application In Adaptive Blind Source Separation, NIPS'96, Blind Signal Processing Workshop, (Org, A, Cichocki and A, Back). , http://www.bip.riken.go.jp/absl/back/nips96ws/nips96ws.html

Principe, J, C., de Vries, B., de Oliveira, P, G., (1993), The Gamma Filters : A New Class of Adaptive IIR Filters with Restricted Feedback, *I.E.E.E Transactions on Signal Processing*, **41** (2), pp 649-656.

Redlich, A, N., (1993), Redundancy Reduction as a Strategy for Unsupervised Learning. *Neural Computation.*, **5** : pp 289 – 304.

Ripley, B. (1996), Pattern Recognition and Neural Networks, Cambridge University Press, ISBN 0-521-46086-7.

Robbin, H. and Monro, S. (1951)., A Stochastic Approximation Method. *Annals of Mathematical Statistics,* **22**, pp 400-407.

Rosenblatt, M. (1985). Stationary Sequences and Random Fields, Birkhauser, Boston.

Rubner, J. and Tavan, P. (1989). A self-organising network for principal component analysis. *Europhysics Letters*, **10**, 693-698.

Russ, J, C., (1992), The Image Processing Handbook, CRC Press.

Sanger, T., (1990). Analysis of the Two-Dimensional Receptive Fields Learned by The Generalised Hebbian Algorithm in Response to Random Input., *Biological Cybernetics.*

Shannon, C. (1948). A Mathematical Theory of Communication. *Bell System Technical Journal.*

Shields, P.W., Campbell D.R.,' (1997), Multi-Microphone Sub-Band Adaptive Signal Processing For Improvement of Hearing Aid Performance: Preliminary Results Using Normal Hearing Volunteers', Proc. ICASSP-97, *I.E.E.E Conference on Acoustics, Speech and Signal Processing*, **1**, pp 415-418.

Shields, P, W., Girolami, M., Campbell, D, R., and Fyfe, C. (1997), Adaptive Processing Schemes Inspired by Binaural Unmasking for Enhancement of Speech Corrupted with Noise and Reverberation. *Neuromorphic Systems, Engineering Silicon from Neurobiology, Progress in Neural Processing* 10, World Scientific, pp 61 – 74.

Schuster, H, G., (1992), Learning by Maximising the Information Transfer Through Non-linear Noisy Neurons and Noise Breakdown, *Physics Review.*, A**46**, pp 2131 – 2138.

Sorouchyari, E., (1991). Blind Separation of Sources, Part 3., Stability Analysis., *Signal Processing,* **24**, pp 21-29.

Stuart, A and Ord, J, K. (1987). Kendall's Advanced Theory of Statistic, Vol 1, Distribution Theory, John Wiley, New York.

Toner,E., Campbell,D.R., 'Speech Enhancement using Sub-Band intermittent adaptation' (1993), *Speech Communication*, **12**, pp 253-259.

Torkkola, K., (1996), Blind Separation of Convolved Sources Based on Information Maximisation, *I.E.E.E Workshop on Neural Networks for Signal Processing, NNSP'96* , Kyoto, Japan.

Torkkola, K. (1999). Blind Separation for Audio Signals – Are We There Yet?. *First International Workshop on Independent Component Analysis and Signal Separation*, Ed's Cardoso, J., Jutten, C., Loubaton, P., pp 239-244.

Van Gervan S., Van Compernolle D., Nguyen Thi H L., Jutten C., (1994). Blind separation of sources: a comparative study of 2-nd and a 4-th order solution, *Signal Processing VII: Theories and Applications*, Edinburgh, Scotland, pp 1153 - 1156.

Van Gerven, S., (1996), Adaptive Noise Cancellation and Signal Separation with Applications to Speech Enhancement., PhD Thesis, Katholieke Universiteit Leuven, ISBN 90-5682-025-7.

Vetter, T., Vesin, J., Celka, P., Scherrer, U., (1999). Observer of the Autonomic Cardiac Outflow in Humans Using Non-Causal Blind Source Separation. *First International Workshop on Independent Component Analysis and Signal Separation*, Ed's Cardoso, J., Jutten, C., Loubaton, P., pp 161-166.

Vigario, T., Hyvarinen, A., Oja, E., (1996)., ICA Fixed-Point Algorithm in Extraction of Artifacts from EEG. In Proc *IEEE Nordic Signal Processing Symposium*, Espoo, Finland, pp 383-386.

Vigario, R., Sarela, J., Jousmaki, Oja, E., (1999). Independent Component Analysis in Decomposition of Auditory and Somatosensory Evoked Fields. *First International Workshop on Independent Component Analysis and Signal Separation*, Ed's Cardoso, J., Jutten, C., Loubaton, P., pp 167-172.

Wang, L., and Karhunen, (1996), A Unified Neural Bigradient Algorithm for Robust PCA and MCA., *International Journal of Neural Systems*, **7**, (1), pp 53 – 67.

Watanabe, S. (1969). Knowing and Guessing. Wiley, New-York.

Weinstein, E., Feder M., & Oppenheim A. (1993). Multi-Channel Signal Separation by Decorrelation. *IEEE Transactions on Speech and Audio Processing*, **4**, No 1, 405-413.

Widrow, B. and Stearns, S, D. (1985), Adaptive Signal Processing. Prentice Hall.

Widrow, B. (1975), Adaptive Noise Cancelling : Principles and Applications. *Proceedings of the I.E.E.E*, **63** (12), pp 1692 – 1716.

Yellin, D. and Weinstein, E., (1996), Multichannel Signal Separation: Methods and Analysis, *I.E.E.E Transactions on Signal Processing*, **44** (1), pp 106 - 118.

Ypma A., Pajunen, P. (1999). Rotating Machine Vibration Analysis with Second-Order Independent Component Analysis. *First International Workshop on Independent Component Analysis and Signal Separation*, Ed's Cardoso, J., Jutten, C., Loubaton, P., pp 37-42.

Index

GPSR Compliance

The European Union's (EU) General Product Safety Regulation (GPSR) is a set of rules that requires consumer products to be safe and our obligations to ensure this.

If you have any concerns about our products, you can contact us on ProductSafety@springernature.com

In case Publisher is established outside the EU, the EU authorized representative is:

Springer Nature Customer Service Center GmbH
Europaplatz 3
69115 Heidelberg, Germany

Batch number: 10704713

Printed by Printforce, the Netherlands